When Jesus Answers

When Jesus Answers

Returning to the Healing Mercies of God's Presence

Workbook with Music Included

Loren Loving

Book Design & Production
Columbus Publishing Lab
www.ColumbusPublishingLab.com

Copyright © 2018 Loren Loving.
All rights reserved. No part of this book may be used or reproduced by any means, graphic, electronic, or mechanical, including photocopying, recording, taping or by any information storage retrieval system without the written permission of the author except in the case of brief quotations embodied in critical articles and reviews.

All Scripture quotations are taken from the Holy Bible.
Unless otherwise indicated, all Scripture quotations are from the New King James Version, ©1982 by Thomas Nelson, Inc. Used by permission. All rights reserved.
Scripture quotations marked NASB are taken from the New American Standard Bible, ©1960, 1962, 1963, 1968, 1971, 1972, 1973, 1975, 1977, 1995 by The Lockman Foundation. Used by permission. All rights reserved.

Scripture quotations marked NIV are taken from the New International Version, NIV, ©1973, 1978, 1984 by the International Bible Society. Used by permission of Zondervan Publishing House. All rights reserved.

Scripture quotations marked NLT are taken from the New Living Translation, ©1996 by Tyndale House Publishers, Inc. Used by permission. All rights reserved.
All emphasis within Scripture quotations is the author's own emphasis. The author has consistently capitalized all personal pronoun references to God the Father, God the Son, and God the Holy Spirit.

All songs presented in this book are intended solely for the communication of Biblical truth and not as an endorsement of any denominational affiliation of the artist or songwriter.

Because of the dynamic nature of the Internet, any web addresses or links contained in this book may have changed since publication and may no longer be valid. The views expressed in this work are solely those of the author and do not necessarily reflect the views of the publisher, and the publisher hereby disclaims any responsibility for them.

Print ISBN: 978-1-63337-191-0
E-book ISBN: 978-1-63337-192-7
Library of Congress Control Number: 2018931936

Printed in the United States of America
1 3 5 7 9 10 8 6 4 2

CONTENTS

PART II: THE GARDEN PATH—THE KINGDOM WAY

APPENDIX

ACKNOWLEDGMENTS

This book has been both a writing project and a ministry aide for over ten years prior to its publication. The musical allegory, "The Journey Few Have Taken" (Chapter 8), was written first. I shared the allegory in group and individual counseling settings in America when I was practicing law, and then over seas when I was in the mission field for eight years.

Hence, due to the input of so many people, the book has wonderfully evolved over this time to become the resource and encouragement you have in your hands today. I am very grateful for the important contribution and feedback of those who journeyed in this book, and I am especially grateful for their renewed hearts; for the editorial advice of Joette Whims, Karen Oliver, Jemimah Wright, Jeaneen Eckhardt, and the staff at WestBow Press; and I have a very special gratitude in my heart for the encouragement and counsel throughout this project of the one who first shared with me the journey that every heart must take, Ken Unger. Ken, and also Elisabeth Brown, LMHC, who had ministered many years with Ken, contributed invaluable counsel for "The Journey Few Have Taken."

I would also like to thank the many people in my life whose lives have deeply touched and influenced mine. These treasures are mentioned throughout this book. Finally, and most importantly, I want to thank my best Friend, my Savior and my Healer, Jesus Christ whose life and love transformed my heart, and my entire life. His immeasurable and wonder-filled love was the inspiration and the sole reason for the writing of this book.

BEFORE YOU BEGIN THIS BOOK

Dear Reader,

This book is for the faithful and faithless alike. It's for those who know in their hearts there is so much more to life than what they have heard or experienced. For thirty years I went to church religiously, obeying church tenets and traditions. I attended one of the country's most respected Bible universities and after college, for many years, sat under one of the most well-known Bible teachers in America. But despite all that, I never heard about the truly remarkable life for which I was created or—most importantly—how to attain it. Unfortunately, it seems I spent more time listening to people's opinions about God than listening to God Himself tell me about His amazing destiny for me.

When one does not know the real purpose of life, life's roads will lead to discontentment. Many times they lead to despair, even in the midst of personal success. It was in that time of despair that, by God's grace, I finally found what I had been searching for all my life—a very intimate walk with God, lived in the wonder of His Presence. I discovered that God came not only to seek and to save lost saints like me, but that the passionate Pursuer of broken hearts also came to heal me and set me free from the lies hidden deep within my heart. He brought people into my life who radiated His love and shared with me how He heals our brokenness. He also took me to many countries around the world to experience His astonishing, miraculous power—something that religion could never show me.

While this book chronicles my healing journey into the depths of the love of God, I urge you to read it as God's very personal invitation to embark on your own inward journey with Him. If you allow Him to lead you on an expedition into His heart and yours, He will transform and renew your life so that you can live the way you were intended to live. It is a life filled with unshakable peace, love deeper than you have ever experienced, songs of hope, and miraculous awe and wonder. Your life, like mine, can be filled with amazing spiritual encounters with God and His people that you may never have imagined or dreamed possible.

Like a tour guide, I've designed for you a careful itinerary. In Part I of this book, Chapters 1–7 show you how God guided and tenderly held me every step of my journey. The music-animated allegory in Chapter 8, entitled "The Journey Few Have Taken," will help you embark on your own personal path to experience the freedom and tranquility we all long for. Chapters 9–13 show you your wonderful destination, the daily encountering of your heavenly Father's intimate love for you as you listen to Him speak His words of truth and love, and the way you can be "endued" or clothed with God's power in your life. Finally, Part II shows you how to remain continuously in the peace and joy of God's Presence and how you can always be assured that the inner voice you are hearing and following is His.

If some of the stories in this book are difficult to believe, please remember two things. First, the experiences I've recorded are supported not only by Scripture but also by empirical evidence—my direct, firsthand observations and life experiences among diverse cultures and religions around the world. Second, when you read something that is outside your paradigm or theology, please examine all the scriptural evidence before you return to your former thinking, your former way of life. Most importantly, in your heart of hearts, always ask this very simple question: "Jesus, is this Your heart?"

May God bless you on your journey with the intimacy of His Presence. I know He will.

Loren Loving
Rome, Italy
2010

PART 1

The Journey Back to Eden

CHAPTER 1

The Day Hope Died

The Lord is my Shepherd,
Even though I walk through the darkest valley, I will not be afraid,
for You are close beside me. Your rod and Your staff comfort me.
Surely Your goodness and unfailing love will pursue me all the days of my life.
And I will live in the house of the Lord forever.

—*Psalm 23:1, 4, 6 NLT*

In October 2007, while I was living in Italy, I lost a dear Italian friend of mine. She was beautiful and talented, a loving friend and mother, and she was only thirty-six years old. I had already endured the death of a dear child, and the death of my marriage of twenty-nine years. My walk through the shadows of the darkest valleys was a very long journey. When I thought I would never find a way out of that darkness, my Shepherd took my hand and led me to a place I had never been. I had not known it even existed. But when I heard Him speak His words of truth to me, I knew I would never leave that place. Oh, how anxious I was to take my friend's hand and journey along beside her in her valley, for I knew the way out; I knew the path to take.

The day finally arrived when my friend and I commenced our journey together, passionately pursuing life as it was intended to be lived. It seemed like our pilgrimage had just begun when, one day, our winding path brought us to a small gate, a beautiful gate. We stood there together, waiting expectantly, listening for inaudible direction. I will never forget that day. The Shepherd walked up to my friend and smiled radiantly at her! And when He spoke to her, creation paused to listen. He unlatched the gate and opened wide its door. There before us was a narrow garden path. The edges of the path were manicured and unruffled. Few had journeyed here. The garden before us spoke of wondrous beauty, unfathomable love, of being home. As we walked through the gate, my friend paused, and smiled at me when she told me what her Shepherd had said to her! We continued on our journey together, hand in hand, our Shepherd, my friend, and I. My friend's eyes began to glisten. I felt the radiant warmth of peace surround us, of love consume us.

The Way It Was Intended to Be

Day by day, as I prayed for my friend, I was certain—so very certain—that she would be healed of her terminal illness and that she would dance again with her children. However, just a few months later, my friend went to sleep one night, never to awaken again in her home on earth. I struggled terribly with her loss. Confused and heartbroken, I would spend much time each day reflecting upon the tragic circumstances and difficult questions surrounding her death. Many days I would write about my deepest feelings, hoping that putting them down on paper would end their constant domination in my mind. What I discovered on paper and in prayer about this experience became not only the first chapter of this book but also a summation of its theme.

I have learned in my travels of over fifty years, through over a dozen countries, and through the deepest of heartaches, that life is simply a journey back to where we were created to live. When we return to that place, we experience what we were created to experience: peace unshakable and love inexpressible. Truly, everyone's heart has been broken, and many people do understand the need for healing. Unfortunately, however, most understand neither how God heals nor the true destination of the healing journey.

To understand this destination, we have to go back, very briefly, to the beginning—to God's original plan. God created us in His image to be like Him, so that we could live intimately with Him in a perfect environment, a garden. God Himself planted Eden especially for mankind. There we would see our Creator and meet with Him daily. We would walk and talk with Him and hear Him call us by name. We were loved perfectly and unconditionally, and we radiated that love—a love so wondrous and glorious that it enveloped us. It was our only clothing. God designed us, in His image, to be literally clothed in His glory—His perceptible or manifested Presence—so that we could experience the depths of His love and then radiate that love to others. God was not only our Creator, but He was also our heavenly Father—our protector and provider, the perfect parent, and our very best friend. As we listened to His voice, His words of truth and love spoken to us each day would nurture complete confidence, security, and peace in our hearts. We would grow to become just like Him, to think like Him, to love like Him. Our lives were fulfilled and content as our heart beat in unison with our Father's heart.

Tragically, that incomparable and inexpressible intimacy with our Father in Eden was broken when mankind chose to listen to another voice that said God is not good and life would be better apart from Him. That choice stole the light of truth from our hearts and tore us from the peace of our Father's Presence to live in a world of confusion and fear—a world in which we never intended to live.

Now, instead of being molded by God's love, our value and purpose are influenced by the actions, opinions, and judgments of imperfect people. So our once tender, spiritual heart, created to be so sensitive to the sound of our Father's voice and the feelings of the love and peace of His Presence, became imprisoned to the lies of the enemy. Life is no longer lived in a garden but upon the battlefield of lies, where war is waged for the healing of broken hearts, and broken homes.

♫ I would like you to please pause here and take a few minutes to listen on YouTube.com to Misty Edwards' songs "Take My Heart" and "All I Know." Though named as two separate songs, "All I Know" is really the ending of "Take My Heart," so look for the full nine-minute version, and type Take My Heart/All I Know in YouTube's search bar. I don't know of any other song that more powerfully communicates the reason we were created and, accordingly, the resulting, deepest cry of every heart. As with all the songs I share with you throughout this book, the music is as important as the lyrics. And truly, this song cannot be fully appreciated without the musical communication. Whenever you listen to the songs, be sure to close your eyes and picture the words. There is so much more to see, and hear.

The Incomparable Love of God

But God, full of mercy and compassion and unfailing love, would not forsake His original plan for us. Knowing that every heart living outside of Eden would be broken, God, our Father, sent His Son, Jesus, to rescue us—to heal us and set us free from a life of bondage to fear. His Presence would be our refuge.

Fear is the heart's response to separation from our Father's Presence (Genesis 3:8, 10) and the remedy for fear is love, perfect love. *There is no fear in love; but perfect love casts out fear, because fear involves torment. But he who fears has not been made perfect in love* (1 John 4:18). Imagine that. We are the ones who went our own way and turned our backs on God's perfect plan for our lives, and yet perfect love died for us on a horrible cross (Isaiah 53:6)! The beauty and power of God's resurrection plan would be the Spirit of Jesus Christ living inside of us, speaking His words of truth and love into our hearts to set us free from the lies that imprison us. Only the voice of Jesus can do this. Once freed, we can live again in a garden of wonder, a refuge of peace, clothed with His beauty.

I know that my friend entered into the garden and refuge of God's Presence here on earth despite the emotional and physical pain she endured. I know this with absolute certainty because she told me the words of truth Jesus spoke to her in our last prayer together—words that could have come only from the Lover of her soul. That day her Healer gave her a brand-new name, a name that spoke His heart. Truly, my friend discovered the narrow and often hidden path to the refuge found only in His Presence. And this is what I hope you, too, will discover in this book as we travel together on a journey few have taken, to the place of safety and rest, where peace pervades and where perfect love can be seen and felt.

The Short Life of Valchiria

My friend Valchiria and her younger sister Vanessa were born in Rome, Italy. When Valchiria was eight years old, she, Vanessa, and her mother were abandoned by their father. A heartbreaking divorce ensued, followed by years of painful financial and emotional struggles for the broken family. At age fourteen, Valchiria met Piero. Almost ten years later, Valchiria and Piero became husband and wife, and their marriage was blessed with two beautiful children. It seemed that Valchiria's broken life had been healed. But then tragedy returned. In February 2006, Valchiria was diagnosed with stomach cancer. In December 2006, Piero was killed in a motorcycle accident. Valchiria grieved terribly over the loss of her loved one. A little less than a year later, on October 11, 2007, Valchiria died. That day was also Piero's birthday. The children had lost both parents. They were only and nine and five years old. How could this happen? It made no sense.

Many people had earnestly prayed with and for Valchiria. We prayed the Lord would heal her as we also fervently contended for the healing of her children's hearts. I had been in the mission field for four years and had witnessed many miraculous healings prior to the time I began praying for Valchiria. I had no doubts that Valchiria would also be miraculously healed despite her surgeon's prognosis. Isn't God Jehovah Rapha, the almighty Healer?

At the Tomb of Jesus

One of the last times I prayed with Valchiria was shortly before her last birthday. We were talking about one of my favorite passages in the Bible, John 20, the story of Mary Magdalene weeping at the tomb of Jesus. We often talked about the Presence of Jesus—about hearing Jesus speak His words of truth and love to us. That day I told Valchiria I had heard Jesus speak to me for the first time in my life while reading the story about Mary Magdalene. I had been a Christian for more than thirty years but had never known such intimacy with the Lord. As I read John 20, I paused to reflect on the setting and surrounding circumstances. Verse 3 states that Mary was all alone, weeping at the tomb of Jesus. I wondered where the disciples were that early morning and why they weren't at the tomb of Jesus. Then the word "hiding" came into my mind. Verse 19 later revealed that the disciples, afraid of the religious leaders who had Jesus killed, had retreated to their own homes and locked the doors. This raised an even more important question in my mind: Why wasn't Mary Magdalene afraid? What was so special about Mary that she was not afraid and that she was chosen for a personal visit from Jesus Himself that early morning? Several other women had also been to the tomb that day, but they had not seen Him. Mary, however, was the very first person to whom Jesus appeared after His resurrection (Mark 16:9). So what was it about Mary that brought her, unafraid, to the tomb? Why did she remain there alone, weeping at the grave of Jesus?

I told Valchiria that as I sat there that day wondering why—why it was that Mary was there alone and unafraid—a response suddenly came into my mind. The response was not in audible words, but in this thought: "Jesus healed her." I was absolutely surprised! Where did that thought come from? Of what was Mary healed? I researched every passage in the Bible about Mary Magdalene and discovered that she had suffered from emotional torment—probably terrible despair or depression—and that Jesus had mercifully set her free by expelling seven evil spirits from her soul (Mark 16:9). Thereafter, in most of the passages that mentioned Mary, she was always near Jesus, listening to Him, worshiping Him. When I discovered this, I understood why Mary wept at the tomb of Jesus, for I too had experienced His healing touch in my broken heart. Traditional counseling (psychotherapy) never reached the depths of my brokenness and could never heal the emptiness. When Jesus broke the chains that had bound me for so many years—chains formerly unknown to me—He gave me a new heart that became very sensitive to His voice and overflowed with His love. A heart that has been touched with the healing love of Jesus possesses a love that simply cannot be contained. That heart's deepest desire is to be with Jesus, listening to His words of truth and experiencing that truth filling every empty and broken place with peace and love. This desire means that the only unbearable sorrow in life arises when there is no sense of His Presence. That is why Mary sobbed, *"They have taken my Lord away, and I don't know where they have put Him"* (John 20:13 NIV).

The Compassion of Jesus

Valchiria and I talked about the deep compassion of Jesus as revealed in other Scriptures where He personally sought out the brokenhearted—the blind man whom Jesus healed and who was then thrown out of his synagogue by the religious leaders; Peter, after he lied about knowing Jesus; the Samaritan woman at the well (no Jewish man would ever approach her); the widow whose son had died; His followers after His resurrection, etc. We talked about Mary not recognizing Jesus when He came to her (John 20:14). And we discussed the things that keep us from seeing and hearing Him in this broken world. Many times this is due to our ignorance of the fact that He speaks to us and of the way He speaks His truth into our minds—His Spirit speaks to our spirit through thoughts and impressions of truth and love. Jesus said our existence is entirely dependent upon the words that He speaks into our minds as they are *"spirit and they are life"* (John 6:36). (His spoken words will always be consistent with His written words in the Bible.[1]) Very often, we don't hear Jesus simply because we aren't listening. Also, it can be due to the wounds in our souls from the wrongs committed against us and the wrongs we have committed. But the fact remains, He is always there, right beside us. So Jesus, the essence of compassion and mercy, asked Mary why she was weeping (John 20:15). He knew how important it was for her to pour out the pain in her heart. Then Jesus asked her the most important question of life: *"Whom are you seeking?"* That one question reveals the ultimate source of and resolution to all our sorrow—we have not found the love of the One for whom we were created. We have not heard Him speak His words of truth and compassion into our broken, wandering souls, and we have not felt His love in our hearts.

---

1 The Bible became alive to me when I saw Scriptures distinguish between God's written words (*logos**) found in the Bible (Hebrews 4:12), and the words of revelation (*rhēma**) His Spirit speaks into our minds (Matthew 4:4; John 10:3,27,2). Because Jesus is the *logos* Word of God (John 1:1,14) the *rhēma* words we hear His Spirit speak into our hearts will always be consistent with God's written words and will have supernatural power to heal us and set us free (John 6:36, Ephesians 6:17). *Greek – the original language of the New Testament. (Re Old Testament see fn. 5 p. 71)

I asked Valchiria, "What do you think was the most wonderful thing Mary heard in that garden as she knelt there sobbing? What was the most precious thing Jesus spoke to Mary?"

Valchiria paused, looked at the passage again, and said, "Her name; Jesus speaking her name."

I emphatically agreed. *"He calls his own sheep by name and leads them out ... and his sheep follow him for they know his voice"* (John 10:3, 4 NIV). He speaks individually and personally to us. (♫ A wonderful song about Mary's encounter with Jesus at His tomb is "Alive" by Natalie Grant. Look for the original lyric version on YouTube.com.)

Mary had not recognized Jesus until she heard Him call her by name. It could have been the special way He had always pronounced her name or possibly the personal inflection in His voice. But one thing was certain in Mary's heart, His voice was the only life-giving voice and it was unique to Jesus alone. It was His voice that had set her free to be all she was created to be. So I asked Valchiria if she had ever heard Jesus call her by name. She said no.

A Brand-New Name

A few weeks before this day, while I was praying for Valchiria, a question about the meaning of her unusual name came into my mind. Upon investigation, I discovered that a valchiria is a mythological figure that gathers the dead bodies of heroic warriors who have been killed in battle, to take them to a special grave where they wait to fight again for the god Odin. As I pondered that, the Lord brought to my mind Isaiah 62:2–4: *"You shall be called by a new name, which the mouth of the Lord will name. You shall also be a crown of glory in the hand of the Lord, and a royal diadem in the hand of your God. You shall no longer be termed forsaken ... for the Lord delights in you."*

So I read those verses to Valchiria. Then I asked her if she would like to pray and ask the Lord what new name He would give to her. She assented and we invited the Lord into our midst to speak to us. I encouraged her to wait quietly for the response in the form of thoughts or pictures the Holy Spirit would bring to her mind and said, "Whether that wait is a few minutes or a few days, I promise you He will speak, in His perfect timing" (John 10:3).

Both of us paused and listened like Mary "at the feet of Jesus." In only a few minutes or so, Valchiria looked up at me and smiled. "Loren, He called me Hope, Hope of the nations." I was amazed, intrigued, and so very thankful that she had heard Jesus speak, and speak such a powerful name to her! Colossians 1:27 states that Christ's Spirit living in us is our "hope of glory." Only the words of Jesus can speak hope into every situation, as only the words of Jesus can combat the enemy's lies of hopelessness. The name Jesus gave to Valchiria, the name Hope, revealed that she was "a crown of glory" and "a royal diadem" in His hand. Jesus had certainly not forsaken her, and He replaced her doubts of His love for her with His words of delight in her.

Ever since that magnificently wonderful time with Valchiria and Jesus, I always called her Hope, the name Jesus gave her—His name. *"Your words are what sustain me. They bring me great joy and are my heart's delight, for I bear Your name, O Lord God Almighty"* (Jeremiah 15:16 NLT).

Prayer for Hope

The last time I saw Hope was the evening of her thirty-sixth birthday party at her home in Guidonia, just outside Rome. A few days later, I returned to the States to be with my sister, whose only child was having surgery. The Lord answered our many prayers for my little niece, and despite the busyness of that trip home, I never missed one day praying for Hope. During those weeks back in America, I never doubted that Hope would be healed. Every morning as the sun rose, I talked with the Lord as I listened to worship music about Him. ♫ One particular morning, I was singing and praying the words to Hillsong's "Mighty to Save." The first verse talks about our need for compassion, a never-failing love, and mercy found only in our Savior. Then the next line states, "Everyone needs forgiveness, the kindness of a Savior, *the Hope of nations*." The chorus talks about how mighty God is to save us (which also means to heal us) and how He moves formidable mountains in our lives because "Jesus rose and conquered the grave!" (Please listen to this song on YouTube.com.)

As I listened to the words "the Hope of nations," a sense of God's Presence surrounded me so strongly that tears filled my eyes for Hope. Each of us is *fearfully and wonderfully made* (Psalm 139:14), and each one of us feels God's all-consuming love in a particular way. When I sense the intimacy of His Presence, tears will immediately appear in my eyes. So once again I prayed for Hope's healing, knowing that Jesus had just poured His heart into mine.

The Day Hope Died

A few days later, I received a phone call from Stefania, my dear friend and hostess in Rome. She revealed the reason the Lord had sent those tears. We needed to pray harder. Hope had taken a turn for the worse and was suffering from the cancer. I saw in my mind the faces of Hope's children and her mother and sister. I told Stefania we needed to gather the church (people who love God) together so that we could all fast and pray until the Lord healed Hope. I booked a return flight to Rome.

As I walked through the long corridors of the Munich airport, my connecting city, I sensed an unusual emptiness in my heart. It was cold and raining outside, and the skies were very gray that eleventh day of October, 2007. My connection seemed intolerably long. Usually I enjoy reading and writing during the long, quiet hours I travel. But on this trip, I was very anxious to get to Rome and pray with everyone. Concentration escaped me. I wandered through the airport and down the myriad corridors of my mind, pausing at the gates in my own life's journey, an unexpected journey that had brought me to Italy, and to pray for Hope.

Stefania met me at the Fiumicino airport in Rome as she always did to help lighten the last leg of the long transatlantic flight. She greeted me in the wonderfully gracious and Italian way, a kiss upon each cheek. However, Stefania's welcoming hug held a distant emotion. This was not Italian. I looked inquiringly into her eyes, but she glanced down to pick up my bag, and we were off. Once out of the airport traffic, Stefania steered her car a little distance off the road and we stopped. She looked at me and told me words my ears would not hear, words my heart could not accept. "Hope died this morning."

"No," was the only word I could utter; the only word I could cry. My shock and disbelief turned the hour-and-half ride to Hope's home into a dazed silence. I was not at all prepared emotionally to see Hope's family, much less to speak with them. However, it would be my only opportunity to visit with them before the funeral. Because many Italian families do not embalm their loved ones, the funeral service was scheduled for the next day.

When I stepped inside Hope's home, most of the family and friends were at the end of the hall in the kitchen. Vanessa had picked up Hope's children at school and sought refuge for them in the home of a friend. Instead of going back to the kitchen, I tried to think of what I could possibly say to Hope's mother. I found no words. My heart was so broken.

I stood in the hallway, paralyzed and praying for the Lord's help, for His words and strength to face Hope's family. Then I felt Stefania's arm around mine as she said, "Let's first go see Hope." Stefania pointed to my left, to Hope's room, where she was lying peacefully in her bed.

I walked into Hope's bedroom and looked down at her terribly thin body. As I stood in that room, the first thing that came to my mind was that this was the place we last prayed together. I got down on my knees to pray next to Hope. And then it came, the bursting of the floodgates of my broken heart, cascading tears of anguished, painful sorrow. I cried out to Jesus, "Where are You in all this!" My anguish was a very deep disappointment, maybe even anger with Him. But it had to come out. Did I fear He was not true to His word?

The Greatest Healing of All

I don't know how long I knelt there, but I do remember once more asking Jesus where He was. Then, quietly and gently, into my mind came a thought; it flowed into my consciousness as a stream of inaudible words. "I'm right here." I laid my head down on the bed and felt an indescribable rest come upon me. I told Jesus how I was so certain, so very certain, that He was going to heal Hope (my way), just like He did in so many other miraculous healings I had witnessed. I was not expecting a response from Jesus, but into my mind came two words: "I did." Immediately, thoughts of Hope hearing Jesus call her by name filled my mind and flooded my soul!

Those two words, "I did," sealed a conviction I now believe with all my heart. The greatest healing we can experience upon earth takes place when we humbly enter into the Presence of Jesus, pour out the deepest burden we carry in our hearts, and then listen to Him respond with His words of hope—words of truth and love. When Jesus speaks His words of truth, we are set free from the hidden lies that have imprisoned our minds and brought so much pain and emptiness into our lives. And when He speaks His words of love to us, we experience an intimacy with Him that fills us with His peace, which "passes all understanding," and answers every heart that cries,"Why, God?"

And the peace of God, which surpasses all understanding, will guard your hearts and your minds through Christ Jesus (Philippians 4:7). His love is deeper and more freeing than any human love we can ever experience. Only His love sets us free to be everything He created us to be—His child who bears His image and identity, a radiance of great worth and affection. And only His love can set us free to experience everything we were created to experience—His Presence clothing us, filling us, and fulfilling us as His love flows from our hearts in the hearts of others. This is our destiny.

Living Hope

Today my dear friend Hope is alive with Jesus, and for that I am so very thankful. We were consoled and encouraged by this wonderful truth at her memorial service. Often I think of Hope forever looking into the face of Jesus and being overwhelmed by the love in His eyes for her. Oh, how she must be dancing and singing joyfully in the brilliant radiance of His Presence. *In heaven God will wipe away every tear from their eyes, there shall be no more death, nor sorrow, nor crying. There shall be no more pain, for the former things have passed away* (Revelation 21:4).

Many people long for a day like that so much that they actually give up on life here on earth. Physical exhaustion from the battle and deep emotional wounds, both hidden and known, such as the loss of a loved one (as Hope had experienced), can cause people to choose to escape rather than to fight to live. When we choose to live in the garden of God's Presence, we find a place of refuge. (The power to choose is truly a life-and-death power.) It is the only place where every tear—shed for the sorrow of death, the fear of loneliness, the shame of our sin, and the pain of sickness and rejection—is wiped away. It is a place where we can never be shaken by economic, political, and geological disasters, or by wars and terrorism. When Hope and I welcomed the Presence of Jesus and prayed to hear Him call her by name, an amazing, pervading peace came into Hope's room. There was no room for thoughts of cancer or tears of sorrow, just peace and quietness as we listened to His still, small voice speak her name, "Hope."

Our Journey Together

This book is about the journey back to the garden of God's Presence which every heart must take to discover life as it was intended to be lived. In the following chapters, I share my own healing journey into the heart of Jesus. My intent is not to focus on pain but upon a Person—upon the unrelenting faithfulness and unstoppable love of the passionate Pursuer of broken hearts. As you see the many ways the Lord was trying to get my attention, to speak to me, to rescue me, please know that He has been trying to talk with you, too, throughout your life. Every day He stands at the door of your heart, calling out to you. "*Behold, I stand at the door and knock. <u>If anyone hears My voice</u> and opens the door, I will come in to him and dine with him, and he with Me*" (Revelation 3:20). He will never stop pursuing you. *Surely Your goodness and unfailing love will pursue me all the days of my life* (Psalm 23:6 NLT). ♫ One of the most powerful songs I have heard about our passionate Pursuer is called "Unstoppable Love" by Kim Walker-Smith. I hope the love you hear in that songs touches you deeply. Please listen to this song on YouTube.com.

By the time you arrive at Chapter 8, you will have the hiking gear to begin your own personal, life-changing journey. You will travel this road through the eyes and the world of a brokenhearted boy who is still just a child. Jesus says, "*Whoever does not receive the Kingdom of God like a little child will by no means enter it*" (Luke18:17). This child journeys through a small gate and follows the narrow way of the journey few have taken, which is the title of Chapter 8's allegorical and music-directed healing journey. He is lost and alone, and desperately seeking his way home. Indeed, this book has been written for those who have chosen to do whatever it takes to find healing, to find purpose and peace. And you will certainly find it: *"But from there you will seek the Lord your God, and you will find Him if you seek Him with all your heart and with all your soul"* (Deuteronomy 4:29). Truly, it is in our brokenness and through our brokenness that we find our Healer and the Author of our life—life as it was intended to be lived, in a garden.

Hope's Song

Please know that the journey you are on must include music. You will miss the point, purpose, and effectiveness of this book if you do not also follow its musical path. God said we are to enter into His Presence, fight every battle, and communicate to others with songs about Him. We are to speak to, teach, and admonish one another not with lectures and arguments, but with songs, hymns, and spiritual songs (Ephesians 5:19, Colossians 3:16). Note that God Himself "inhabits" the praises of His people. That is why when we worship Him in song, we most powerfully sense His Presence. Hence, His music will open the closed doors of our hearts, doors that prose can only knock upon, so we can enter into the deepest place of His heart. I realize musical tastes vary greatly,[2] but I know that many of the songs, both contemporary and traditional, in this book will speak to you even more personally and profoundly than this book ever could. With songs that are new to you, be sure to listen to the song a couple of times as you close your eyes and picture the words. After the song ends, just sit quietly and wait for thoughts and pictures of truth and love to come to your mind. This is Jesus speaking to you.

♫ I can think of no better song to conclude this particular chapter than a song written by Hope's husband, Piero, shortly before he died. "La Tua Presenza Gloriosa" ("His Glorious Presence") is a very simple song that communicates profoundly a truth you will experience in this journey: God's glorious Presence is a love and a peace that can be felt. Please put this song's title, "La Tua Presenza Gloriosa," in the YouTube search bar. The English translation is provided.

2 As you journey through this book, please go the book's web site, LorenLoving.com, or email additions@LorenLoving.com, to share your own worship songs and Scripture verses that have had the greatest impact upon your life. Thank you!

CHAPTER 2

My Unexpected Journey

You keep track of all my sorrows. You have collected all my tears in Your bottle. You have recorded each one in Your book.

—Psalm 23:1, 4, 6 NLT

My journey into the heart of Jesus was completely unexpected. I had been a Christian for more than thirty years, and yet there were so many things I still did not know about my Savior. It was a journey that I had no idea I needed to take; one I did not even know existed. Let me explain how I arrived in such a barren place.

I grew up in Columbus, Ohio, in a very religious family. The mission of our church was to save the lost, to tell them that Christianity was not a religion but a relationship with Jesus. However, the only relationship message I ever heard in church was the message of salvation—that Jesus was my Savior, which made me a "brand-new creation." I never heard the rest of the salvation message—that of the very intimate relationship with Jesus for which I was created and for which I longed. So I never took that "next step" with Jesus, because I didn't know Him as my Healer or Lover of my soul. There was so much to experience with Jesus, but I just stayed in one very routine and intellectual place.

My parents were extremely strict and prohibited my two brothers, my sister, and me from engaging in anything that was disobedient or disrespectful. I had to be good, and so I sincerely believed I was good. If I wasn't, punishment was swift and severe. My life after becoming a Christian really didn't seem any different. I remained the same good person I thought I always had been. Unfortunately, my goodness was only outward obedience to rules and regulations. I knew nothing about the liberating freedom and amazing love I could experience as a passionate follower of Jesus.

Because I did not realize Jesus died so that I could enter into a very intimate relationship with Him, I had no idea that He had been constantly pursuing me to enter into that refuge of His Presence. But looking back now, I can see so clearly how He was always trying to communicate this need to me and how He never left my side.

Two experiences in my youth were very distinct and remarkable. My earliest recollection is of first grade, sitting on the floor in my school's large meeting room. All the elementary grades had gathered to sing Christmas carols. The youngest children were seated about a dozen feet or so from the piano. We sang many carols that day. However, when we sang "Little Drummer Boy," it seemed as if something all of a sudden drew me into the song. Although I had always wanted to play the drums, it wasn't the drum accompaniment that drew me. As I sang the song, I stood up and, in front of everyone, walked to the piano. I placed my hand on the piano and sang along with my music teacher: "I am a poor boy too, pa rum pum pum pum … I have no gift to bring that's fit to give a king, pa rum pum pum pum … I played my drum for Him … I played my best for Him… *and then He smiled at me*, pa rum pum pum pum … me and my drum!" I saw the baby Jesus smile that day even though no one ever told me that it was possible for me to look into the face of my risen Savior and see Him smiling at me. *O God, You have taught me from my youth; And to this day I declare Your wondrous works* (Psalm 71:17).

The second experience occurred in a church service, but it was unlike anything I had ever seen or experienced at a church or youth group gathering. I was around thirteen years old when my mother took me to hear a minister speak at a tent meeting. We sat on a wooden bench near the front, close to the speaker's podium. I did not understand what happened to my heart that evening, but as this minister spoke, I could sense something very different about this man and something very different in me. Every time he talked about the love of Jesus, tears came to his eyes. I had never seen a grown man cry before, and as he spoke of Jesus' love, something stirred deeply inside me. I thought to myself, *I want that. I want to know the love of Jesus so deeply that it would bring tears to my eyes*. As a little girl, I had always loved stories about Jesus. My favorite pictures were of Jesus surrounded by animals and children. But after that meeting, I desired so much to discover that minister's secret that I began memorizing one Scripture after another. I thought that maybe discipline was what was lacking in my life. Psalm 27:4 became one of my favorite verses, and it remains so to this day: *One thing I have desired of the Lord, that will I seek: that I may dwell in the house of the Lord all the days of my life, to behold the beauty of the Lord, and to inquire in His temple.* (♫ One of the most beautiful violin renditions of this verse is a song titled "One Thing I Ask" by Ruth Fazal on her *Inside Your Heart* CD, on YouTube. Please also listen to the intimate song "My Desire," by Kelly Willard on her *Heaven's Whisper* CD.) Psalm 27:4 communicated my deepest desire, but how to experience it, and live it, still escaped me. I had no idea Jesus was trying to tell me.

Pursuing Success for Significance

For more than thirty years, I never experienced what that minister possessed. Life went on. I attended church, read my Bible, prayed, and tithed—all the good things good Christians do. I also busily pursued what others told me was most important in life—a good education followed by a high-paying job. As I listened to the opinions of others, intense competition entered into every aspect of my life. I had to win at everything, whether that was the honor roll in school, tennis matches or equestrian events, a race for a political office, or even a casual ping-pong game with a friend.

Childhood is a time of reaction, not a time of analysis. So as a female child in a home where boys were highly prized and adored, I reacted by fighting and competing with my older brother, who was one year older than I. I became a tomboy extraordinaire and tried to be better than my brother in all our activities. Consequently, winning titles became the entire measure of my value and worth in life. I considered "winning" the pinnacle of life. But all my efforts to gain the attention and affection my brother was given seemed unnoticed and ineffective.

I attended a well-known Bible university and studied Bible doctrine, theology, hermeneutics, and religions of the world, but I did not learn how to know the love of Jesus so deeply in my heart that tears would appear. At this point, I concluded that it was childish to want to feel such emotions.

Right after college, I married my husband on the first day of June and moved to his hometown of Cleveland, Ohio, where I taught elementary school. A few years later I went to graduate school to specialize in remedial reading. For many years in Cleveland, I sat under the teaching of one of the most well-known Bible teachers in America. Despite marriage, career, and church, contentment escaped me. Then I had our first child, Kristen. It was a wonderful experience! I loved being a mother. ♫ Whenever I cuddled little Kristen, I would always sing to her the only two songs I knew by heart: "In the Garden" and "Turn You Eyes Upon Jesus." Hearing Jesus speak to me ("In the Garden") and seeing Jesus ("Turn Your Eyes Upon Jesus") remained a fascination of mine, but not a reality. I had no idea the Lord was singing those songs to me (Zephaniah 3:17). Despite my overwhelming love for my baby, the constant turmoil in my heart, and the voices of the women's liberation movement in my head (telling me that there was much more to life than motherhood) propelled me toward "more significant" outward achievement. My life was completely misinformed and entirely out of balance.

The desperate need to be successful in the eyes of others drove me to greater heights of competition. One evening, I went out for dinner with my family. Everyone who walked by our table was told the wonderful news that my older brother had been elected president of his class in medical school. Rarely was my presence at the table acknowledged. I sat there feeling invisible. A short time later, I battled against feelings of insignificance by pursuing a law degree. I entered law school when my daughter Kristen was only six months old. After graduation, I chose the most competitive practice of law—litigation. The combative arena of litigation was a natural for me. I considered "injustice" the greatest foe to defeat. As an attorney, I fought passionately against social ills, such as abortion, the removal of our Judeo-Christian values and culture from our schools, and attacks on First Amendment religious speech freedoms. I had no idea that the most formidable foe of all lay hidden and festering in my own heart. Unaware that my inner life was a dismal failure, I pressed on toward greater outward success.

In my law practice, I thought each case I worked on posed a greater abuse of justice than the previous one. In one case, I worked relentlessly for almost four years to vindicate the life of an unborn child who had been negligently killed. I believed Ohio's law was terribly unjust to deny significant monetary damages for the worth of that child simply because she had not been born alive. I also believed the pain of her mother had to be recognized and greatly compensated. She suffered over the loss of her child and over the fact that our system of justice would not recognize the significance and value of her child's life.

I wept for this mother because I, too, had lost a child, but through miscarriage. I, too, felt no one understood my pain because my child had lived for only three months of the pregnancy. But this mother had lost her child at term, and I felt my heart entwine with hers.

It was during this wrongful-death action that I witnessed my first "legal miracle." The Lord stepped into that case and created a new law in my state, and in America, to prove and establish the great worth of His creation, the "preborn." I remember one time praying about this case and asking the Lord how I could vindicate this child's life in a court of law. Into my mind came the thought, *humanize the child.* As I pondered this thought, the idea of pursuing compensation for the child's pain and suffering emerged. Because I did not know the Lord talked to me through thoughts of truth, I thought the idea was my own. For the first time ever, a court of law allowed a new cause of action for an unborn child's pain and suffering while in her mother's womb. Further illustrating God's hand in that case, the court assigned the largest monetary figure ever recorded for the value of the life of an unborn child. It was a wonderful legal—and, of course, personal—success!

Despite the legal victory, I later lamented that I did not know more about the healing of hearts than I did the winning of lawsuits. I had worked very hard to right the wrong through financial resolution, but money did nothing to heal broken and bleeding hearts. I did not realize that the case was as much about establishing my own value as a successful lawyer as it was about helping those grieving parents. I was blind to the spiritual needs of that mother and father—needs that were much more important than any amount of money the court could have awarded them. Even now I am sad, as I recall that their marriage ended in divorce just a few years later. Money did not cure their pain; it only added to it.

From Success to Defeat

At that time, I was very far from the "Kingdom life" that the Lord had planned for me. I had come to sincerely believe that Christ's promise to give me a "peace that passes understanding" (Philippians 5:7) would be possible only when I went to heaven. So I went on looking for my next accomplishment in life and ways to make even more money. I did not realize that the only voice I was listening to at that time was the world's. Nor did I know that unconsolable pain, as that mother and father had experienced, would one day come to my own doorstep.

That day came when I discovered a letter written to my husband from another woman. My heart crashed into a pit of agony. Depression became the first opponent in my life I could not defeat. Nothing could console me. Endless talking with pastors and psychiatrists could not help me. Many told me to read the Bible more and pray more. I was already doing that. I was told everything would be fine if I simply forgave. So I obeyed and forgave my husband, but that did not help.

I was also told that depression was not characteristic of a Christian because I was a "brand-new creation" in Christ, so how could I be depressed? Now I felt even worse. I felt condemned. Nothing was working. I desperately needed to escape the pain, but no one in my life told me *how* Jesus healed broken hearts. So in my desperation I turned to antidepressants. When it seemed they were making me more depressed, I turned to other medications. At the same time, adding to my distress, I discovered I was pregnant.

During my first visit to my obstetrician, I told him all the medication I had been taking. He advised me to abort the pregnancy immediately because one of the drugs I had taken caused birth defects. How could all this be happening to me? I was such a "good" Christian. One of my very strong convictions was that abortion wrongfully terminated the beating of a human heart. Now I was thrust into another world, a world many women face when they feel they have no choice but abortion. I faced the dilemma of whether to follow my conviction to protect unborn life even as I was fighting to save my own life. Believing that my husband was going to leave me, fear consumed my every thought, including the fear of taking care of two children all alone, especially when one would be "deformed."

I obsessed over my obstetrician's directive. Heartache and fear overwhelmed me. I felt so alone. I had no hand to hold and no one to confide in, because I did not tell a single friend what my husband had done or what I was planning to do. So I made the appointment and went alone to the abortion clinic. I did not know I had a merciful and compassionate Companion with me that day. I did not know how to hear Him speak to me; nor did I know how to sense the intimacy of His Presence. I could not feel His hand holding mine.

My heart was in shock. I could not believe what I was about to do. When I was told I needed an ultrasound reading (to determine which abortion procedure would be used), I nodded and started to cry. I undressed and waited on the table for the ultrasound technician, praying for God's help and for His forgiveness. The technician came in and politely greeted me. I forced a smile and turned away from his gaze, so ashamed, afraid, and unable to speak. As he moved the probe back and forth across my abdomen, I looked out the window and continued my remorseful prayer. "God, please forgive me." Then the technician spoke words that women in those clinics never hear. He said, "Oh my goodness, look at this," and pointed to the ultrasound screen. I still could not see my Companion next to me. Tears streamed down my face as I looked at the screen and then at the technician. I could not believe what I saw. My just four-month-old baby looked like a perfect miniature-nine-month-old baby. My ignorance astonished me. Then truth flooded my soul. A hidden strength that was not my own helped me choose not to go forward with the abortion. However, I was still too weak to choose not to fear what might not have been detected in the dark gray ultrasound picture of my baby.

Out of Defeat, Love

Day after day, I anguished and prayed and asked for God's help to be strong. Then one day, as I was reading the Bible, I "happened" to see Isaiah 41:13. The verse jumped off the page and captured me. I did not know that this was yet another way Jesus was speaking to me. I read it again and again. *"I the Lord your God will hold your right hand, saying to you, 'Fear not, I will help you.'"* I finally saw very clearly that it was Jesus who had helped me that day at the clinic, so I believed He would continue to help me as I struggled with my doctor's directive. And He did. He spoke to me again, this time through a little angel, my five-year-old daughter Kristen.

One day Kristen was playing on the floor with her dolls and ponies. I was sitting on the couch in front of her when she looked up at me. She saw a tear fall from my eye. A concerned look came upon her little face, and she asked me what was wrong. I put my hand on my very large abdomen (I was about eight months pregnant at the time) and told her I was thinking about the baby. Kristen immediately put down her toys, put both her hands on her little hips, and said confidently and adamantly, "Mommy, the baby is just fine!" I had never before heard her speak that way. When I asked how she knew this, she responded with the utmost confidence in her voice and certainty in her eyes, "Jesus just told me so," and she then resumed playing with her toys. Her words were astounding and remarkable, and so was the peace that followed them. A month later her sister, Victoria, was born, 100 percent healthy and absolutely beautiful.

My eyes still mist for the love of Jesus as I recall those events from so long ago. How faithfully He has carried me through this journey! We do need to become like children to enter into His Kingdom (Matthew 18:3). Kristen's words revealed this wonderful truth: Little children freely talk about seeing or hearing Jesus in their dreams, as they read Bible stories about Jesus, and as they pray and talk to Him. They haven't the faintest doubt about His love for them or their love for Him, because they are free to listen to Him, unencumbered by opinions and doctrines that would close their ears to His voice and their eyes to His smile. And it is that smile that I share with women who have had abortions. I know the fear they felt, I weep with them for their sorrow, and I take them to the Healer of broken hearts (Chapter 8). As they look into the face of their Savior and Healer and discover the compassion and mercy of the Lover of their soul, they are enveloped in a love that washes away all guilt and shame and makes all things new. (musicforthesoul.org has many resources for specific heartaches. See also "The Inheritance," by Graham Cooke on YouTube.)

Unknown Ignorance

After Victoria's birth, life went on. My husband did not leave our marriage at that time. Although I had forgiven my husband, I still struggled with the pain of his actions, and I did not know what to do with it. Without realizing it, I began working even harder and longer. It was just like the causal drinker—a few drinks one day, a couple more the next, and one day he wakes up an alcoholic. One day—I don't know which day or lawsuit it was—I woke up a workaholic.

The big problem with workaholism is that because it is socially acceptable, even rewarded, people don't realize it is an addiction, evidence of something wrong inside. Hence, I was completely ignorant that I had become an unrelenting work addict. However, the signs were there. I developed migraine headaches that put me to bed, nauseated and in excruciating pain, for almost eight to ten days a month. Bouts with anorexia, which had started in college, worsened. I couldn't even hear the family conversation at our dinner table; I turned all my thoughts to my most important project at work. But isn't this what "successful" people have to do? What went wrong? How did this "brand-new creation" end up in such a terribly broken life?

Psalm 34:18 says the Lord is near to those who have a broken heart and saves those who have a contrite spirit, which includes those who don't know they have a broken heart. They don't know the accompanying anger, bitterness, rage, depression, addictions, etc., are evidences of a person imprisoned to fear and in need of Christ's healing. But Jesus does. So He listens for the desperate cry of the broken heart. It is then that He reveals the incomprehensible depths of His love—a love that not only sent Him to Calvary to become our Savior but also resurrected Him to become our compassionate Healer. This was the relationship with Jesus that was tragically lacking in my life.

The Gospel I Never Knew

I believe there were two reasons I wandered so many years without knowing Jesus as my Healer. First, I did not know I could hear Jesus speak to me. Jesus said in His Word that I could hear His voice and live in the peace of His Presence. However, religious leaders taught me I could only read His words in the Bible and that I must not rely upon "feelings" of peace and love, but upon doctrines. So I never sat quietly with Jesus to listen to Him speak to me—through Scriptures, pictures, music, poetry, memories, ideas, nature, circumstances, conviction, repetition, the peace and love of His Presence, or any other way He would choose. In all these ways the Holy Spirit can bring to our minds Jesus' words of truth of love. And because Jesus is called the Word of God (John 1:1, 2, 14) all these thoughts will always be consistent with His written words in the Bible. For over thirty years as a Christian I only talked to Jesus, not knowing that He died and rose from the dead so that His Holy Spirit could live within me to intimately tell me how much He loved me. Hence, when I needed help in the past, I turned only to friends, priests, and professionals and relied entirely upon their counsel to help me. I did not understand that Scriptures shared through people could greatly comfort and encourage me; but only when Jesus Himself (through the Holy Spirit) spoke His words of truth and love into my mind could my heart be healed. Jesus said, "*The words* [rhēma] *that I speak to you are spirit and they are life*" (John 6:63).

The other reason I did not know Jesus as my Healer was that I did not understand the very important step after one's salvation experience. I knew that at salvation, when I repented of living life for myself and not for the love of God, the Holy Spirit would come to live inside my heart and renew my spirit, which had been deadened to sin/selfishness (Romans 8:11, John 3:5–7). The evidence of that salvation experience would be seen in the fruit of the Spirit (the attributes of my Father in whose image I was created) in my life. *But the fruit of the Spirit is love, joy, peace, longsuffering, kindness, goodness, faithfulness, gentleness, self-control* (Galatians 5:22-23). No more fear, no more selfishness. However, I never realized that the work had just begun. Now, with the power that raised Christ from the dead living inside of me, the Holy Spirit could commence the healing of my soul (one's intellect, emotions, and will) of the destructive effects that sin had had (and has) upon my life so that the fruit of the Spirit could be manifested in my life. The Holy Spirit's operative tool would be the two-edged sword of truth—God's written word (Hebrews 4:12) and His spoken word (Ephesians 6:17). *I said, "Lord, be merciful to me; heal my soul; for I have sinned against You"* (Psalm 41:4).

Jesus communicated His mission very clearly in Isaiah 61:1 and Luke 4:18. He said He was anointed to proclaim good news to the humble, to heal the brokenhearted, and to set the captives free. However religious leaders never told me about the very important healing ministry of Jesus. It would be many years later that the Spirit of truth showed me that the Greek word for "salvation" is *sozo* which means to save, to heal, and to deliver—"to be made whole."[3] Therefore,

---

3 Sozo occurs 118 times in 103 verses in the Greek concordance of the *King James Version*; e.g., as salvation in Romans 10:9, as healing in Matthew 9:22, and as deliverance in Luke 8:36. In the Old Testament, the Hebrew equivalent for *sozo* is *yasha* from which we get Yeshua (Jesus). *They cried out to the Lord in their trouble and He saved* (yasha) *them out of their distresses. He sent His word and healed them, And delivered them from their destructions* (Psalm 107:19-20.)

instead of entering into the new life Christ promised—a life filled with His peace and His love—I unknowingly remained imprisoned to the lies and fears that were hidden in my heart. I sought peace and love in ways that could not satisfy. And I sought my identity and value in things that could not last. What I needed most of all was to find my needs met in the Lord's all-consuming, unfailing, healing love for me. I needed to find out that Jesus saves me by healing me.

The Lord is my shepherd ... He restores my soul (Psalm 23:3). But unfortunately at this intersection of my life, I did not even know of my need for the healing and restoration of my soul, much less how Jesus accomplished that. So my merciful and compassionate Companion took my hand and led me on a journey that no one ever told me I needed to take, that would lead me to places I never knew existed, so that I could experience the love of a Father I had never known.

♫

In closing this chapter, I would like to share a favorite song of mine, "Eden," by Phil Wickham ("This is Amazing Grace, "Heaven Song," etc.) I think often of Eden and the magnificent anticipation it must have been to see the Lord every morning. What joy it is for me to sing about meeting my heavenly Father at the garden gate and hearing Him call my name. And oh, how I long to see Him face-to-face, "where being in His arms is the permanent state." The lyrics of this joy-filled song are wonderful to meditate upon and especially to picture (just close your eyes). I hope the music will give you a vision and an anticipation of this amazing journey. Please listen to the song "Eden," by Phil Wickham, on YouTube.com.

CHAPTER 3

The Dawning of a New Day

The people walking in darkness have seen a great light;
on those living in the land of deep darkness a light has dawned.

—Isaiah 9:2 NIV

It is amazing how the Lord mercifully guides our paths through failures, disappointments, and even times of despair in our lives. These things are the Lord's traffic lights, signaling us to take another direction in life—the direction He always intended. But I never did like red lights or red flags. As a teenager, I wrecked two of my father's cars and his motor boat. Later, I just plowed through whatever was in front of me, relentless in my pursuit of "success." I knew of no other way to find purpose and value in my life. Nor I did know this pursuit was evidence of something wrong inside of me. Red lights were flashing, but I could not see them, and no one pointed them out to me. Even months of marriage counseling did not uncover the deepest problem in my heart or my husband's heart that was ravaging our marriage. So, in His compassion and mercy, Jesus Himself started bringing people and songs into my life to rescue me.

The first person who walked beside me in my "land of deep darkness" opened my eyes to the morning glimmers of God's light. The year was 1990, and as usual, I was passionately and relentlessly pursuing one important cause after another. After spending many years litigating, I began thinking that our social ills could be solved more effectively through the political process, so I entered politics. I also thought that "senator" would be a very important title to add to my name so that I could accomplish much good for my community.

However, I lost that election to the Ohio State Senate (thereafter I always said I came in second), but the greater loss was my need to be significant in the eyes of others. Once again, my world crashed. Back again I went into the hopeless world of medication and endless talking to counselors. So many cries for help fell on deaf ears, which, like my own, had never heard of Christ's ministry to the brokenhearted.

Jesus never condemns us. *A bruised reed He will not break* (Isaiah 42:3). He is a gentle healer, a truly wonderful and perfect Counselor (Isaiah 9:6). He saw my incredible selfishness, my total consumption with myself. But He did not scold me, as other shepherds had done. He knew what was wrong. So He started talking to me about my heart by showing me His heart when He brought me my very first prayer partner. I was forty years old. I had met Natalie during my campaign for the Ohio Senate when she offered to help with the overwhelming task. I did not get to know her well during that time. I was just too busy.

One day after the exhausting and discouraging race was over, Natalie came to my house to see how I was recuperating. After sensing how badly I was doing, she asked if she could pray with me each week. I agreed, and every week we prayed together for our families, shared what we had enjoyed most in our individual times reading the Bible that week, and then recited a Scripture verse we had memorized. I saw Jesus in Natalie. Her compassion and sacrifice for me lifted my eyes upward and turned my heart outward, toward Jesus. Each week, I wanted to give her a special treasure I had found in the Bible. This became my first step outside of myself. A light began to dawn. That partnership multiplied and became a wonderfully supportive five-strand group: Natalie, Jane, Janie, Mary, and myself. I began to understand the importance of ministering to others. But I was on a journey, and it would be a while before I realized that the most important ministry was to my own family.

Yet Another Important Project

After my vocational experiences had clearly shown me that litigation and legislation could not solve social ills, I decided to investigate how the Lord might solve these problems. Because I was starting to see the great influence and impact of prayer partnerships and prayer communities, I concluded that the most effective solution to society's problems would be seeking God's help through prayer. So I began working on another project. I thought it was the most important project of all, so I would have to make it be a very big event.

After the campaign in 1990, I was asked to organize the National Day of Prayer (NDOP) in northern Ohio. This would be Ohio's first official recognition of that day, as instituted by then-governor George Voinovich, with whom I had become acquainted during my campaign. Peter Marshall, Jr. (son of the US Senate chaplain Peter Marshall and author Katherine Marshall), was our guest speaker for our NDOP, and the US Marines provided a dramatic procession and color guard.

I also needed special music for the event. I had been giving my daughter Kristen, who was then twelve years old and passionate about music, Christian music recordings by various artists. One day, she told me that Michele Wagner's music was the first music that actually made her stop and think about the Lord. She especially liked the song "You're Someone Worth Dying For." (You will hear Kristen sing this song during your journey in Chapter 8.) Astonished and thrilled, I asked Michele to be our vocalist for the event. The CBS television network gratuitously made and broadcast a TV advertisement for the event that used Michele's song "I Will Pray for You." CBS sent their ad to NBC and ABC so that every national network in Ohio could communicate the event, which made it the largest first-time NDOP event in America.

I could write a book about so many other miraculous events that took place as part of that event all because of prayer—especially the prayers and help of Natalie, Ella, and Faye. For example, I was told by the largest newspaper in Ohio that they would not cover our NDOP event. (I surmised that this was due to a First Amendment dispute I had engaged in with the paper the previous year.) Devastated that we would not get any print coverage, I called Faye, a precious Afro-American friend. She brought her prayer partners to my home, and for several hours they prayed, listened to Jesus, and then proclaimed out loud the Scripture verses He gave them for this event. Our NDOP made it on the front page of that newspaper—honestly, the front page! Also, all of the northern Ohio mayors, except just one, issued resolutions through their city councils recognizing the importance of this observance in their community, and corporations extended their employees' lunch hour to be able to attend the prayer gathering. One corporation put up beautiful blue-and-silver banners on street lights for block after city block to advertise the event. The banners depicted George Washington kneeling in prayer.

The Lord obviously got my attention concerning the importance and power of prayer for our communities and our country. I believe that with all the partings of the Red Sea I had witnessed, the Lord wanted most of all to communicate to me the most important prayer of all—listening prayer, as I had witnessed with Faye, and then, one day with Ella.

Ella was a volunteer who became my right arm for the NDOP and a very dear friend also. I will never forget when she called me to say she could not attend our meeting because she had to quickly get to her son's elementary school. She said Jesus just told her that her son had missed his ride home from school and was sitting all alone on the school's steps. What did she say? Later, when I discovered her story was true, I thought of Kristen hearing Jesus speak to her very clearly about the health of her unborn sister. Then I wondered, *Why? Why can't I hear God speak this intimately to me about my family?* Although very perplexed, I was just too busy to investigate the matter during the prayer event, and I obviously did not know I could simply ask Jesus this question.

Music Opens Doors

After the NDOP, I represented Michele in her contract negotiations with her recording company in Nashville and became her ministry administrator, and friend. One day Michele showed me a letter she had received from a young woman who had been through an abusive past. This woman had not been able to understand the depths of the Lord's love for her until she heard one of Michele's songs. Pondering the letter, I wondered why she had never heard of His love for her anywhere else. That is when I realized that music could open the doors to a heart that prose could only knock upon. I was amazed to learn that people from all over the country had sent similar letters to Michele. What a wonderful and important ministry it would be for me to help Michele communicate the healing message of this music to all the broken hearts in America! A couple years later, while I was listening to Michele's songs, tears of gratitude fell as I realized the Lord had given those songs to me also, for the healing of my heart. Truly, He was surrounding me with "songs of deliverance" as He promised in His Word (Psalm 32:7).

Now I was on a new path—ministering to others. But I still had the same old problem. Not only did my workaholic tendencies not subside when I started volunteering my time in ministry activities, but they got even worse as well! After all, this work was for the Lord, so it was much more important than litigation and legislation, and political and prayer campaigns. Furthermore, because the message of this work was a matter of life and death, I felt my time away from home was completely justified and necessary. I actually believed the work would not get done without me. During this time, Jesus brought to me the book *Experiencing God* by Henry T. Blackaby. Jesus wanted me to see this one statement: God doesn't care as much about my work for Him as He does about my love for Him. Truly, we were created to commune with God, not perform for God. Although I agreed wholeheartedly with Mr. Blackaby, I was unable to curb my workaholism.

In 1995, the many glimmers of light that had come my way through prayer partners and God's music became a brilliant beacon of truth that flooded my soul. The Lord Himself came down to deliver me—to set me free from my hidden sorrow and deception and open the small gate into the garden and refuge of His Presence. *He reached down from heaven and rescued me; He drew me out of deep waters ... He rescued me because He delighted in me* (2 Samuel 22:17, Psalm 18:19 NLT). No religion or theology or church had ever mentioned the existence of this door to me. A complete stranger showed me both the gate and the latch to the gate that would unlock my heart to the relationship with Jesus that had eluded me my entire life.

The Healing Begins

I had been working with Michele's music ministry for about five years when I was asked to join the board of a newly formed Christian music organization in Cleveland. My motive in joining that board as executive director was to be able to influence the Rock and Roll Hall of Fame and Museum in their gospel music exhibits and activities. The museum had just been built in Cleveland, and because of my work with the record companies in Nashville, I assured the museum's board I was their best contact. However, after hundreds of hours of projects and progress, a man on my board said our organization would be more influential if the director were a male. After he became executive director, the organization later disbanded. However, unbeknownst to me, the Lord had accomplished His motive for my involvement in and departure from the Christian music board; He had crossed my path with His own director, and He had much more important work for me to do. I was learning that life's activities are not about projects but about people—planned relationships with people.

During one board meeting of our Christian music organization, I met Ken Unger, a minister and author with One Life Ministries. Ken was burdened with communicating the Lord's healing ministry to those whose hearts had been broken. He said he was saddened by the way Christian counselors were trying to help people find healing. They spent entirely too much time talking about the symptoms of the problem and not enough time listening to the Holy Spirit reveal the cause of the problem. "Why don't these counselors get down on their knees with the broken individual and ask the Lord Himself to reveal the hidden root of the person's pain? Only the One who created the heart can heal the heart," Ken said.[4]

My first reaction was to think Ken was probably one of those roaming "healers" who proclaimed people were healed as they smacked them on their forehead and then asked for money. Ken did neither. Instead, he gave me a priceless gift—the opportunity to encounter Jesus as my loving Healer.

The opportunity came at one of Ken's One Life Ministries retreats. That weekend offered something I had never experienced in traditional counseling—very little talking. We took time to stop and let the Lord's Spirit plumb the depths of our hearts, time for Him to reveal what was hiding there, and time to feel it. As I listened to music and to my heart's response to various written questions, feelings surfaced that I had never known were inside me. During one discussion, Ken noted the similarity in the damage done to the heart with every kind of addiction. When he noted those similarities in the alcoholic home and in the workaholic home, all of a sudden, the Lord's probing light plunged into the depths of my soul. His light revealed a pain so deep I hadn't even known it existed. The floodgates of my heart burst wide open. This pain astounded me because I had assumed that the agony I had experienced in my marriage was my deepest hurt. The pain Jesus revealed that day, which broke through the walls around my heart, stemmed from a time when I was a young girl and received a severe blow to the right side of my head. After that blow, medical examination of the constant pain and ringing in my right ear showed that several bones in my ear were badly broken and my eardrum was completely ruptured. Nothing could be done for my hearing loss. I remember my great sadness when I discovered, because of the hole in my eardrum, I could no longer play underwater at the pool with my friends.

The discovery of this hidden wound in my soul revealed the very deep hole in my heart filled with feelings of rejection. These feelings were the lenses I wore during my childhood, and into adulthood, through which I viewed and interpreted the circumstances of my life. I didn't fit. I wasn't significant. My workaholic pursuits, which I thought were the traits of successful people, were only ineffective and damaging attempts to escape the pain of those feelings hidden deep inside me.

---

4 Note the bio of Judith MacNutt, M.A., at christianhealingmin.org (under "About CHM"). Judith practiced for many years as a clinical psychologist and found psychology alone was simply inadequate to meet the needs of suffering people. When she began incorporating healing prayer into her practice she saw dramatic, miraculous results. Truly, psychotherapy without God is malpractice. The "whole man" must be addressed as body, soul, and spirit are interrelated. Also, 16 basic human psychological needs are achieved through religion, Steven Reiss, PhD., https://researchnews.osu.edu/archive/religdes.htm

Ken encouraged me to tell Jesus all my feelings surrounding this heartache, allowing my heart to grieve freely and fully. As I sat there, I poured out to Jesus tears of rejection—that I was unloved, worthless; that something was wrong with me—and tears of anger and bitterness that I had held in my heart for the way I had been treated as a defenseless child. Then Jesus showed me my great worth to Him as He revealed the depth of His love and compassion for me that day. He set me free from my prison of bitterness when I forgave the one who had hit me. I will never forget the amazing, pervading peace and comfort that surrounded me when my sobbing finally subsided. Never before in my life had I experienced such peace. It was like an enormous weight had been lifted off my back.

The retreat ended on a Sunday afternoon. The next morning, after Kristen left in her car pool for school, I walked with Victoria to meet her school bus. That afternoon, for the first time in many years, I waited at the bus stop for Victoria's return. Gone was my inability to stop working. I could hardly believe it. Too many times I had tried with all my heart to stop working so hard, but I could not cut even one hour of work from my day. However, from that day on, when the school day ended, my workday ended and enjoyment of my children began. It was truly a miracle. I was finally set free from my prison of bitterness and unforgiveness, which was hidden so deeply inside my heart; I was set free now from having to perform for others in my vain and fruitless attempts to seek significance and worth according to the values and standards of this world.

The Spirit's Light of Truth

God was teaching me that He is true to His word. He gave us the fruit of His Spirit and promised us that peace would pass all human understanding. His peace is our litmus test. If we don't possess that peace, if anger's red lights are flashing addictions and despondency, there is something very wrong inside and we need to go to Jesus for healing. Only His Spirit of truth can reveal the wounds, and their accompanying lies, hidden in the deepest places of the broken heart—in everyone's heart—and only He can heal them. Neither counselors nor psychiatrists can heal us; they can only treat us.

Anyone in counseling work would agree that our healing journey begins when the real or root cause of our emotional and spiritual problems is revealed and *felt*. (We can't heal what we can't feel.) The pain that we are experiencing is not from the infliction of a wound itself, but from the believing the lies that the enemy of our souls planted when we were hurt. I was hit very hard on the side of my head, but the pain I felt throughout my life came from the lies of rejection and unworthiness. Rejection and unworthiness are lies, because Jesus has promised He will never leave us and because He said we are precious in His sight—there is no greater proof of this than the terrible death He endured for us. We were created to live a wonder-filled life in His Presence, listening to Him speak His words of truth and love to us. When we listen to lies (spoken by Satan, others, and the world), we leave the protection and peace of His Presence and fall in a world filled with pain—just as Adam and Eve did.

With this new understanding, I noticed why Eden was lost: Eve tragically chose to listen to the enemy's voice instead of going to God to discern truth. Adam, too, chose not to listen to the words of God and listened instead to Eve. Satan's lies about God tore them from the communion of God's Presence. That's why, on that tragic day in Eden, God was walking in the garden looking for Adam, pursuing Adam, asking, "Adam, Where are you?" Torn also was God's heart when Adam responded with the emotion that encumbers and alienates every heart outside the garden of God's Presence—fear. Because Adam listened to lies, he doubted God's love and acceptance for him. Most unfortunately, Adam did not repent but instead blamed Eve. Adam's choices made fear his god.

When we listen to Jesus' words of truth, we are also set free from Satan's "blame game." When we look at what is wrong in our own heart, instead of focusing on the wrongs of the people who hurt and disappoint us, we are set free from the prisons of deception, condemnation, and unforgiveness that accompany a "victim" mentality. Everyone lives outside Eden; all hearts have been broken, including the hearts of our parents, siblings, relatives, and other trusted people in our past who have hurt us. No one has ever received from another human the perfect, unconditional love for which he or she was created. (That's why I believe the Lord created animals for us, especially dogs and horses. They show us what unconditional love looks like!) Perfect love was found only in Eden, in the garden of God's Presence. When Jesus heals us by shattering painful lies with His words of truth, He sets us free to return with Him to live in a garden and refuge. The healing or restoration of our souls, then, is the restoration of our relationship with our heavenly Father—that very intimate relationship for which we were created. And when our relationship with Him is mended, our relationship with others can mend. Only the Spirit of Jesus Christ living and working within us can help us truly forgive from our heart (not just in our head) those who have hurt us.

Another Healing Miracle

I would like to fast-forward many years from the day my ear was damaged so badly when I was a child. I was in my forties when the Lord healed my broken heart regarding that incident. Then, ten years later, Jesus healed my ear! It was my first instantaneous physical healing, and it was an incredible experience. Here's how it happened.

I had made plans to go on a mission trip to southern Italy and Libya with an American mission organization called Youth With A Mission (YWAM). At the last minute, YWAM's plans changed and the mission work was relocated to France and Spain, which was fine. But what was not fine was that the trip was to be by boat, on YWAM's Next Wave ship. Ugh. I had always become horribly seasick on boats. So, thinking the Lord might be telling me not to go on that particular trip, I e-mailed people who pray for me, asking them to pray for clear direction. Everyone wrote back that I was to go forward with the trip. Ugh again. However, one e-mail was most interesting to me. Milly, my dear friend from the Netherlands, who lives with her husband and daughter and many wonderful animals near Orvietto, Italy, wrote that Jesus told her to share the following with me: "Tell Loren I am going to meet her on the boat!" Really! Her e-mail made me laugh, because that's just how Jesus talks to us—in a wonderfully personal and caring manner. So I went. Soon I was living on a boat with around thirty-five other people more than half my age, in very limited space, in the middle of winter, with no heat, no hot water, undependable toilets, and just a few other inconveniences.

One evening our team went to a pastor's house in Palamos, Spain, for dinner and hot showers. The pastor's wife asked how I was doing on the boat, and I told her I was a little chilly. However, I told her my bigger problem was that I had been very seasick even though the boat had been docked in the harbor the entire time. I told her this had always been a problem for me; never had I been able to sit in the backseat of a car, to ride a merry-go-round, or to even watch a boat rock next to a dock without getting sick. She began to tell me about her daughter, who suffered from motion sickness so terribly that she had sought medical help for her. The doctor diagnosed her daughter with an inner ear problem. When she told me that, all of a sudden the memory of being hit on the side of my head as a little girl came into my mind. Until that evening, I had never connected the horrible motion sickness I experienced with the damage to my right ear.

The next day, as my team and I were standing on the top deck during stationary sailing lessons next to the dock, I told Emily, a YWAMer in her twenties, how seasick I was. Then I told her about my conversation and memory at the pastor's house. She looked at me with the compassion of Jesus and told me how sorry she was to hear what had happened to me. Then she suggested that we should pray for the healing of my ear. I only nodded and smiled.

That evening we had communion on the boat, led by our captain, Lehman. It was a precious time with the Lord, thanking Him for His sacrificial love for us and praying for each other. It was then that Emily prayed for the healing of my ear. After she prayed, I politely thanked her and went to my cabin. To be honest, I did not have much faith that I would be healed. Although I had witnessed many physical healings, I personally had never experienced one. (In part II, I describe one of the most amazing healings I have ever witnessed. It took place on a mission base in Jericho.)

Later that evening, I joined some of my team for a movie in the galley. As I was sitting there eating popcorn, I suddenly heard a very loud swooshing sound in my right ear. I opened my jaw, and my ear made more strange, loud sounds. It's hard to describe. It was like "the sound of rushing waters." It seemed my ear had suddenly filled with liquid. The loud rushing and sloshing sound would not stop. I had absolutely no idea what was happening, so I prayed the Lord would protect me from the enemy, who had tried many times to stop me from going on this mission trip. Fear gripped me as thoughts of a terrible ear infection filled my mind. After ten or fifteen minutes, the noise in my ear subsided. I went to bed deeply concerned.

The next morning, the sounds were gone, thank goodness. However, I wondered, *What in the world was that about last night?* As I began my daily morning Bible reading in my bunk bed in my little windowless cabin, the memory of Milly's e-mail came to my mind. When I contemplated those wonderful words of encouragement, I could only ask, "Oh my goodness, Jesus, did you heal my ear last night?"

I did not have to wait long to find out, for that very afternoon we took the ship out to sea for our team's first sail. When the waves started to roll, I felt no motion sickness at all. Incredulous, I went below deck, where in the past my stomach had always become even more upset. Nothing. Then I decided to take the ultimate test: I drank lots of water. (Liquids are taboo if one gets very seasick.) Nothing. *Oh my goodness!* As we were just returning into the harbor, I ran up the stairs to the deck. I found Emily and my cabin mate, Joy (what a great name), and told them the wonderful and miraculous news. Then we danced together around the ship's deck! Jesus heals—physically, mentally, emotionally, spiritually—in every way, in His perfect timing.

♫ I would like to close this chapter with one of the most poignant songs the Lord used in the healing my heart. To this day, every time I listen to it, the Lord touches me deeply. It is called "My Father's Chair" and was written by David Meece. Please go to YouTube and type in the search bar "David Meece My Father's Chair." The song is about three different fathers sitting in three different chairs in three very different rooms. The powerful music will carry you into an amazing encounter in the third room. Through this song I was able to see God as my loving Father for the first time in my life. How my heart cried to see the smile of love and adoration on my Father's face and feel the safety and security of His arms around me. I hope this song will help you, too, see God's Father-heart for you.

My Father's Chair

Sometimes at night I'd lie awake / Longing inside for my father's embrace
Sometimes at night I'd wander downstairs
And pray he'd returned, but no one was there
Oh, how I'd cry, a child all alone / Waiting for him to come home

My father's chair sat in an empty room
My father's chair, covered with sheets of gloom
My father's chair through all the years / And all the tears I cried in vain
No one was there in my father's chair

Sometimes at night I sit all alone / Drifting asleep in a chair of my own
When sweet sleepy eyes peer down from the hall
Frightened by dreams they cannot recall
I hold them close, calming their fears / Praying they always will say

My father's chair sits in a loving room / My father's chair, no matter what I do
My father's chair, through all the years / And all the tears I need not fear
Love's always there in my father's chair

(*The music builds here so powerfully, and so majestically!*)

Sometimes at night I dream of a throne / Of my loving God, calling me home
And as I appear, He rises and smiles /And reaches with love to welcome His child
Never to cry, never to fear / In His arms, safe and secure

My Father's chair sits in a royal room
My Father's chair holds glory beyond the tomb
My Father's chair, my God is there / And I am His eternal heir
Someday, I'll share my Father's chair

By David Meece / Dwight W. Liles, ©1993 Word Music, LLC / Ariose Music Co., (ASCAP) (adm. at CapitolCMGPublishing.com) All rights reserved. Used by permission.

CHAPTER 4

Once I Was Blind

Jesus said… "Blessed are the eyes which see the things you see."

— Luke 10:23 NASB

Once Jesus touches us with His healing love, the walls around our hearts start crumbling, and the boulders from those walls become stepping stones into deeper intimacy with Him. A river of new life flows freely from the wellspring that had been restrained behind walls of anger and unforgiveness. It flows with an amazing sensitivity to God's Spirit inside us and then overflows naturally, sometimes desperately, with His love for others. That is where God took me next. I was absolutely surprised by this new awareness of His Spirit, by this wonder of His manifested Presence. For the first time in my life, I started to "see" Jesus.

Pictures of Jesus

Not very long after the One Life Ministries retreat, I was sitting in my bed and reading my Bible one early Sunday morning. My husband and children were asleep, so it was a wonderful time to be alone with the Lord. While I was reading, a picture came into my mind. This image had curiously and repeatedly come to my mind throughout my life. It pertained to an experience I had when I was about seven years old. In this picture, I was looking down at my all school supplies, which I had dropped on the ground near my home. My scissors, glue, pencils, and crayons had fallen out of the cigar box that I had kept in my desk at school. Workbooks were scattered. School had ended, and I was not able to carry everything home alone.

Whenever that memory came to mind, I wondered why I kept seeing it. Of all the things that had happened in my life, why did this seemingly insignificant event keep coming back to me? That morning, I put down my Bible and asked Jesus, "Why do I always keep seeing that picture, that day, that setting?"

Instantly, I saw myself as an adult in that picture. I was standing next to and looking down at little Loren. Then, for the first time, I saw little Loren look up, and she had tears in her eyes. Oh, how this mother's heart broke! So I knelt down beside her, picked her up, and held her tightly as I gently rocked her back and forth, trying to comfort her. I kept saying to her, "Oh, don't worry. You'll be all right. It's okay; don't cry!"

Then Jesus suddenly walked up to us. I could not see the distinct features of His face, but He was dressed in white and there was a brilliant light around Him. Even though I had never before seen any picture of Jesus like this, I knew it was Jesus. Peace began to surround me. Then Jesus put His arms around both of us, and His love enveloped us. When He did this, I looked into little Loren's eyes and said, "See, you'll never be lonely again."

As I said those words, tears cascaded from my eyes. Then it came back to me how lonely I had felt as a child. I had buried that loneliness far from all memory. But Jesus remembered, and in that moment, He healed me and strengthened me with the truth that I will never experience loneliness in His Presence. As I sat there, truth after truth and promise after promise from God's Word about His faithfulness and love flooded my mind.

After that day, the picture of me as a little girl looking down at her school supplies came to my mind only one more time, when I attended a Prayer Ventures retreat in Minnesota. During communion, as I was contemplating all that Jesus had suffered for me at Calvary, I suddenly saw Jesus, from His waist to His crown of thorns, on the cross with tears in His eyes. His eyes were amazing and piercing. Then, instead of having the perspective of one looking up at the cross, the scene changed so that now I was seeing what He saw as He looked down from the cross: little Loren standing by her scattered school supplies. As His tears began to fall, I closed my eyes with extreme pathos of soul and deep, deep gratefulness of heart, and I thanked Jesus over and over again for dying to heal my broken heart. And I have not stopped thanking Him. I saw vividly that He didn't die just to pay for my sins so I could go to heaven. No, He also died to heal my heart so I could see Him, hear Him speak words of love for me, and feel His love for me.

♫ Please listen on YouTube.com to "Arms Wide Open" by Misty Edwards. To me, no other song communicates more deeply and more powerfully the experience with Jesus I just described for you. And no other song more poignantly communicates the communion experience I now have with Jesus, and the communion experience you can have with Him each day of your life.

The Healing Presence

After my life-changing healing encounters with Jesus, I wanted to learn everything I could about His ministry to the brokenhearted—especially how He healed people in the Bible. The first thing I did was read and reread all the healing miracles of Jesus in Matthew, Mark, Luke, and John. I thought it was my idea, but as you know, Jesus spoke the idea into my mind. I began to see the heart of Jesus as never before—His immense compassion for and merciful pursuit of those whose hearts were breaking. And most importantly, I began to think His words.

I saw that Jesus' greatest desire was to heal people so that they could be loved, and love, as He had always planned. His ministry reconciles relationships—first our relationship with our heavenly Father, and then with others. And I saw how Jesus healed people's hearts—through His spoken words and by His touch. *He sent His word and healed them* (Psalm 107:20). I saw Jesus touching broken people, and I saw them reaching out to touch Him. *And the whole multitude sought to touch Him, for power went out from Him and healed them all* (Luke 16:9). Healing, then, for us too, is intimacy with Jesus—hearing His words of truth and then sensing His Spirit touch us with His peace and love.

At this point of my pilgrimage, I did not understand the touch of Jesus—how His Spirit touches me or how I touch Him. Understanding this is one of those "incomparable riches," a treasure that was waiting to be discovered as I journeyed even deeper into His heart. But I did understand that all healing is related to the Presence of Jesus. In her book *The Healing Presence,* Leanne Payne states that the heart cannot be healed and cannot stay healed until the person has learned to "practice the Presence of Jesus." That truth resounded very deeply in my spirit. If the pursuit of healing is not founded upon intimacy with Jesus, then the troubled soul becomes imprisoned to psychology and religion.

It is in the Lord's Presence, through the deep working of His Spirit, that the hidden wounds are uncovered as we talk to Jesus about our deepest burden. *He will bring to light what is hidden in darkness and will expose the motives of the heart* (1 Corinthians 4:5b NIV). Just as physical wounds need to be cleaned out before healing can commence, so do emotional wounds. It's like a doctor cleansing a wound of debris before putting an antiseptic on it. We clean out the wounds by telling Jesus how we felt when we were wronged (e.g., unworthy, unwanted, ugly, abandoned, lonely, etc). As we listen to Jesus respond with His words of truth, we realize our wounds were infected with lies.

Our hearts are cleansed when we repent and ask Jesus to forgive us for our anger and bitterness toward the one who hurt us and for believing the lies of the enemy. Jesus' forgiveness heals our hearts by replacing our lies with His truth, our bitterness with His peace. That healing restores our souls to our originally intended relationship with our heavenly Father—to live in His intimate Presence to once again hear His words, think His thoughts, and dream His dreams.

Both our salvation (*sozo*) and our healing (*sozo)* are matters of faith. By faith we believe that Jesus' death on Calvary saves us from our sins. *But He was pierced through for our transgression, He was crushed for our iniquities* (Isaiah 53:5 NASB). By faith we believe that the tortuous scourging He endured heals us of our "dis-eases." *The chastisement for our peace was upon Him, And by His stripes we are healed* (Isaiah 53:5 *and* Matthew 8:16, 17).[5]

I could not contain the love for Jesus that came when He healed my brokenness. I had to share with other broken hearts the power of His healing Presence. I started praying with everyone and anyone who wanted to pray for the Lord to heal her heart. Often at the end of our prayer time, I would ask the person to picture Jesus close to her, and then have her wait until Jesus did something. Many times Jesus will do something related to what the person heard Him say during the prayer time. I did not learn this in a book or a sermon or a seminar but from experience, through my wonderful encounters in His Presence.

Debbie's Tears

The very first time I saw Jesus do something at the close of a prayer was when I was praying for a woman who was in prison in Cleveland. I had been asked to represent her in an attempt to obtain her pardon. I was told this woman was a Christian who had been wrongfully incarcerated. At that point, Debbie (I have changed her name to protect her privacy) had served seven years of a twenty-year sentence. I began meeting with her every week to pray for her and tell her how her case was progressing. We also prayed that the Lord would help me find another lawyer who specialized in criminal law to help, because I was a civil lawyer. The Lord did not provide that expert, so I prayed every day for supernatural wisdom to handle the case. Jesus Himself became my co-counsel—the best I ever had.

One day, I was sitting in the visiting room waiting for Debbie to be brought to me. The room seemed colder than usual. Around the room, angry, icy eyes glared at me, and hearts frozen with pain avoided me. When Debbie came into

5 *But He was pierced for our rebellion, crushed for our sins. He was beaten so we could be whole. He was whipped so we could be healed* (Isaiah 53:5 NLT).

the room, a cloud of sorrow surrounded her. Her eyes and nose were red from crying. She told me that her past week had been one of the worst she had ever experienced in prison. A month or so before I started meeting with Debbie, her mother had died. On top of that sorrow was Debbie's grief for her son, who had been killed in an auto accident a few years after she was incarcerated. She told me that all her heartache had burst out uncontrollably that week. Denial was no longer her friend.

My heart broke for her. I couldn't imagine bearing all that pain in such a horrible place. I silently prayed for the words to speak to Debbie. I realized that we had spent so much time on the legalities of her case and praying for help for her physical release that we really had not prayed about her spiritual prison. Together we read the account of the death of Lazarus in John 11 and saw how Jesus cried for the hearts of Lazarus's sisters, Mary and Martha. I could not fathom the depth of sorrow in Debbie's heart, but Jesus did, and through that chapter, she saw how His heart grieved for her in her bereavement.

We were sitting next to each other, so I took her hand, and together we invited the Presence of Jesus into our hearts and into the room. After we welcomed Him, I encouraged Debbie to tell Jesus all her feelings about losing her son and her mother while she was in such a terrible place. Like a good Christian, she responded, "It hurts so much, Jesus, but I know that all things are working together for good."

I stopped her and said, "No, Debbie, tell Jesus how you *really* feel. It is so important that we grieve with Jesus over disappointments and pains in life. Tell Him how awful it was to lose your child and your mother while all alone in this awful place. Tell Him everything you have cried over during this injustice. Ask Him if He even knows you are still imprisoned here."

She looked at me with wide, incredulous eyes. "Do you talk to Jesus like that?"

"Yes, Jesus is my best friend," I said. "I talk to Him very honestly and frankly. He wants me to talk this way to Him." I shared with her Psalm 145:18: *The Lord is near to all who call upon Him, To all who call upon Him in truth.*

Then Debbie prayed, perhaps more truthfully than she had ever prayed in her life. The pain was so deep. When she finished, I encouraged her to wait and listen for Jesus to respond to the cries of her heart as He spoke His words of truth into her mind.

I wish I had recorded every word and promise that Jesus spoke to her! It was amazing—as if she were listening to Jesus read every verse in the Bible to her about His promise to protect her, to guide her, to love her, to provide for her, to never leave her, etc. An amazing peace surrounded us as Jesus spoke to Debbie. When she finished telling me His words, Debbie slumped in her chair, exhausted from crying tears of sorrow and tears of joy for the words Jesus had spoken, and also, I believe, for the weight of the love of Jesus that had come upon us both.

I was silent as Debbie rested, waiting for her to look up or say something. Suddenly a picture came into my mind. It's as lucid today as it was in 1997. I saw Jesus and Debbie standing together in front of a grave. Jesus had His arm around Debbie. The gravesite was located on what seemed to be a little knoll, and to the side, on their left, was a fairly large tree. It was a beautiful day. Spring flowers bloomed, warm sunlight radiated, and a gentle breeze blew through the leaves and through Debbie's hair. Peace and love were everywhere! I saw Jesus push Debbie's hair away from her eyes. Then He took her hand and led her away from the grave, down the other side of that little knoll, and next to a small brook. He knelt, put His hand in the stream, and stood up to wash away the tears from Debbie's eyes. It was such an amazing picture that I asked Debbie if I could share it with her. When I did, tears streamed from her wonder-filled eyes.

She said to me, "Loren, you just described exactly where my mother is buried! Right before my trial, my mother became ill, so she asked me to help her select the family grave site. The setting is exactly like the picture you described!"

I was astounded. I told her to be sure to write down everything Jesus had said said to her during our prayers and also everything He did beside the grave and brook. "If the enemy of your soul ever attempts to make you feel sad again about your mother," I said, "read the words of truth and love that Jesus spoke to you, meditate upon His similar words found in the Bible, and listen to songs about Him. Picture yourself with Him by the little brook. Adore Him with songs about His love and faithfulness, and let Him love you again, and again."

Reality Checks

I left the prison that day with my heart filled with wonder for the love of Jesus. He was touching other broken hearts with His love as He had touched mine. I believe the prayer time with Debbie was as much for me as it was for her. Until that day, I did not realize Jesus would put pictures in my mind to communicate His healing love for another. I was amazed by all the ways Jesus was communicating the reality and power of His healing ministry.

I was also learning more about the reality of the spiritual warfare that takes place to "set the prisoner free," both spiritually and physically. The next time I met with Debbie, the prison's warden confiscated my Bible. "Lawyers," he said, "don't need Bibles in their work." I had to meet with the Ohio State Attorney General's Office to remedy this situation, but that did not stop the onslaught of vindictive treatment and multiple obstacles to follow. The enemy came in like a flood (Isaiah 59:19) and burst open every floodgate as the battle for Debbie's freedom from her physical prison commenced. That battle put Debbie's faith, and mine, to the ultimate test.

♫ In closing, I would like to share with you the song "When You Speak to Me," by Twila Paris. You will find it on YouTube. It reminds me so much of the joy in Debbie's face when she heard Jesus speak to her. The lyrics are a beautiful communication of the amazing power of Jesus' words to answer our every question and fulfill our every need. "When You Speak to Me" could be the theme song of this book. I hope the song will become the prayer of your heart—your earnest expectation and hope. Close your eyes as you listen; there are things Jesus wants you to see. Open your ears to His voice; there is something He wants to say to you about His love for you.

CHAPTER 5

He Sets the Prisoner Free

Therefore, if the Son shall make you free, you shall be free indeed.

— *John 8:36*

Debbie had been a spiritual prisoner to incapacitating heartache, and Jesus set her free to start living in the liberty of His Presence. It's amazing how a person can be freed in her spirit while facing years of physical imprisonment. But that was the next challenge facing Debbie and me—her physical prison. The lawyer with the attorney general's office had told me in our meeting that, according to Ohio law, it would be impossible for Debbie to be pardoned. However, after that prayer with Debbie, I believed with all my heart that the Lord was working to open her literal prison doors. The Lord had created new law in a case dealing with the wrongful death of an unborn child. Now I had no doubts whatsoever that He could change the law here, too. However, He did not change it. He worked above it.

From the beginning of this case, Debbie and I were faithfully supported by the prayers of a small group of women in Chardon, Ohio. Their loyalty and dedication were amazing. With the Lord beside me and these women behind me, I prepared a legal argument that was the most thorough and persuasive I could possibly write and present. But my work was all in vain. I remember the day I had to tell those women that the most exhaustive legal presentation that had ever been made to the parole board (according to a parole board member) for the release of an inmate had been flatly denied. No appeal was possible to this administrative (verses judicial) body. After all my work and time, tremendous expense, and hours and hours of prayer, the board unanimously denied Debbie's parole. I felt terrible and responsible for Debbie's continued incarceration.

Tracy and Peggy, women in this prayer support group, told me that what we needed to do now was fast and pray. This is what the Lord would have us do, they said. They obviously did not understand or appreciate the law and the finality of the board's decision as I did. (And I obviously did not know Jesus like they did.) But they had so faithfully stood by Debbie and me that I conceded simply to show my gratitude to them. I was certain that their prayers could not make any difference at all in the board's decision. After all, *I* was the lawyer.

Praying for the "Impossible"

I will never forget the day the parole board called me. We had been fasting and praying for about a week. From out of nowhere (the place where impossibilities live), the board called me and told me they had reconsidered their decision. They said that I was to present the case again to a full board hearing in three weeks. And they also said that I would be the only one arguing the case. I could not believe my ears. According to Ohio law, whenever there is a hearing for the parole or release of an inmate, the judge and prosecutor in the case and the victim's family must be represented. How could I be the only lawyer there?

I said, "Thank you," and hung up the phone. I sat there, incredulous. This was impossible and not really "legal."

I felt as though I were living in the book of Acts, chapter 12. Peter, one of Jesus' disciples, had been imprisoned as persecution against Christians escalated under King Herod. Herod had Peter bound with chains, and he ordered four squads of soldiers (sixteen men) to stand guard. And because Herod had just executed James, the brother of John, Peter's friends went into hiding. There seemed no possible way for Peter to escape or to be released. All Peter's friends could do was to pray for Peter.

God heard and miraculously answered their prayers. He sent an angel to rescue Peter. While the guards slept unaware, the chains fell off Peter's legs and the iron gate opened for Peter to simply walk out of that prison! Peter went straight to the house where his friends were praying. And when a servant girl told Peter's friends that he was at the door, they said, "You're out of your mind!"

That had been my exact attitude: "We're praying, but nothing can change this impossible situation." I was in a prison myself. Bars over my faith kept me from believing Jesus was the one making the parole board's decisions. Even though I had witnessed a freedom miracle in Debbie's heart, I had not applied that to my prayers for her physical release. Once again I had to experience firsthand the Lord's faithfulness and the depths of His love to set the prisoners free (Psalm 146:7).

This time when I appeared before the parole board, the women in my prayer group who had been praying faithfully for Debbie and me accompanied me to the hearing. They left their homes very early that morning and spent most of the day driving to and from the hearing to pray as I reargued Debbie's case before the board. Several women prayed outside in the parking lot, another woman prayed in the lobby of the building, and the third was allowed to go inside the hearing room with me. As I sat at the table reserved for the attorneys arguing the case, I glanced incredulously at the empty seat reserved for the State of Ohio's attorney.

There was an amazing peace and an unusual stillness in the room that day as I once again presented all the reasons Debbie should be paroled. Instead of glares and eyes turning from contact with me, as I had experienced at the first hearing, there seemed to be a glimmer of compassion in their eyes. Was I imagining all this? Unlike at the previous hearing, the board members' voices were no longer strident and accusatory as they questioned some of my arguments. At the end of the presentation, each board member was given the opportunity to voice his or her opinion regarding this second request for release. At the previous hearing, the most adversarial, antagonistic board member, who had attacked my "audacity" in requesting an early release, was to be the first to share her opinion. When I realized who she was, my heart sank. She stood up, looked at me, looked around at her fellow board members, said, "Thank you, no comment," very politely, and quietly sat down. Around the room it went, with every board member saying "Thank you, no comment." I was stunned! There was no further discussion, and I was excused. The parole board was to call me with their decision. I left the hearing and prayed in the parking lot with those wonderful women who had come to the hearing with me. We thanked the Lord for the decision that He would render in Debbie's release, and I thanked them profusely for their help and support.

Three days later, I received a phone call from the parole board. The board said their decision was unanimous. They ordered Debbie to be set free! It was unbelievable! I immediately called all the women who had gone to the hearing with me and told them this miraculous news. The day Debbie was released these faithful—or should I say full-of-faith—women were all present at the prison's gates to celebrate what the Lord had done and to celebrate His faithfulness to His word. I framed the release document granting Debbie's parole and hung it in the center of my office wall. That document states the release was granted pursuant to Ohio Revised Code regulation with all representatives of the State present. We had seen and participated in another miracle!

Reflections upon a Miracle

The day the parole board called me, my phone buzzed with calls of celebration. I simply could not sit still at my desk as I made call after call to exuberant friends and incredulous, sometimes skeptical, attorneys. I paced around my office with my phone like a child with the biggest and most beautiful birthday present she had ever received.

Finally I sat down and turned my chair to the window and my thoughts to the making of a miracle. Overwhelmed with gratitude, I thanked the Lord for setting Debbie free. I thanked Him for being true to His promises to heal the broken heart and to open prison doors. And I thanked Him for the priceless gift and opportunity to watch Him do those things. I had done so little. What was done through legal procedure cannot even compare to what was done through prayer. I thanked Him for having those faithful women come along beside me. What precious friends! They reminded me of the story in Luke 5 of the friends of a paralyzed man who took a roof apart to lower their friend into Jesus' Presence. Jesus healed him and set him free from the prison of his bed. The Bible says it was *their* faith that healed their friend. These women in my prayer group were like those friends. It was their faith that enabled the impossible. *Jesus looked at them and said, "With men it is impossible, but not with God; for with God all things are possible"* (Mark 10:27).

I was so humbled by the actions and faith of my friends that tears filled my eyes and I lay prostrate on my office floor. I asked the Lord to forgive me for my lack of faith. I asked Him to forgive me for my pride for thinking my friends were ignorant of the legal process and therefore "foolish" in their desire and conviction to fast and pray. I pleaded, "Lord, I want to be like those women, simple in faith, mighty in their love for You, and mighty in their knowledge of the ways You speak and work. I want people to know me not by some legal or political title, but as a woman who loves Jesus with all her heart and who communicates that love in every aspect of her life. Please, Lord. Forgive me for not believing Your promise that incredible miracles, miracles like Peter's release, can happen today. *Please set me free from my prison bars of pride.*"

She Gave Her All

Not too long after the parole board's decision, my dear songwriter friend, Michele, and I were reading about the humble, loving woman in Mark 14 who poured expensive perfume on the head of Jesus. Some of the disciples—men who had more of a head-knowledge than heart-knowledge of Jesus—criticized her sharply. Jesus reprimanded them and said that she had done a beautiful thing and that what she had done would be told of her around the world. The passage touched me very deeply. I told Michele, "You know, it really doesn't matter how many lawsuits I win or how many songs you write. The only thing that matters, the most important thing of all, is that we are remembered for our love for Jesus." She agreed.

♫ Just a day or so later, Michele brought me a song she had written based on that Mark 14 story; it was titled "She Gave Her All." It's one of my favorites now. I don't know of any other song that communicates more passionately the depths of my love for Jesus. And if I move to heaven before the Lord returns, I have asked Michele to sing it at my funeral. I dedicate this song to those beautiful, faithful women whose prayers set Debbie free and set me on my journey deeper into the heart of Jesus. Please listen to "She Gave Her All" on Michele's website: michelewagnermusic.com.

CHAPTER 6

Piercing the Darkness

He reveals deep and hidden things; He knows what lies in darkness, and light dwells with Him.

— Daniel 2:22 NIV

As I continued to pray on my office floor that day, my mind was filled with the miraculous events surrounding Debbie's release and the awesomeness of God doing the impossible. He did not care about legal procedures; He cared about the heart of one lonely, broken woman, discarded by society, doomed to the fate of an impersonal bureaucracy, reduced from a name to a number. So He reached down into her prison, lifted her up, drew her out, and set her free. What immense love! Absolutely nothing could stop His hand from drawing Debbie into His heart.

As I was meditating upon the amazing power and depths of God's love, suddenly, the word "holy" came into my mind. I was surprised, and somewhat perplexed, because all my thoughts at that moment were of God's love and power. So where did "holy" come from? I had always tried to live a "separated" life, which meant to me not participating in things that would displease God. My church had given me a very long list of things not to do. So was God saying my list should even be longer? Again "holy" repeated in my mind. I pondered the word and asked Jesus why He kept bringing "holy" to my mind. He replied with Psalm 27:4. That verse had been my constant prayer: *One thing I have desired of the Lord, that will I seek: that I may dwell in the house of the Lord all the days of my life, to behold the beauty of the Lord, and to inquire in His temple.* I wanted so much to dwell with the Lord, to live in His Presence, and to behold the beauty of

His love. But I had never thought about Psalm 27:4 in terms of holiness. What did the word "holy" mean, anyway? I asked the Lord to show me.

♫ A song that is a good illustration of my thoughts that day is called "What Do I Know of Holy?" by Addison Road. The lyrics describe my state of mind at that time—completely ignorant of the meaning and application of this word, "holy," in my life. As stated in the song, I thought I knew God from what I had read in the Bible. But the stories of Him "were only empty words on a page." You can listen to this song on YouTube and contemplate your own understanding and experience of holiness.

Several years later, Jesus answered my question and showed me things I had never heard or encountered. I discovered that understanding the word "holy" is not only an important part of our healing journey, but that it is also a very important key to unlocking the treasure chest of the wonderful mysteries of God's Kingdom, those incomparable and inexpressible riches that are revealed as we walk deeper and deeper into the garden of His Presence. *Without holiness no one will see the Lord* (Hebrews 12:14).

Ministry, Music, and Marriage

God began to prepare my heart to understand what *He* meant by "holiness." Because of Debbie's case, I set up a charitable organization to provide legal help for indigent and abused women. This ministry also provided help for their bigger problem—their broken hearts. Elisabeth Brown, a young woman who was a licensed counselor, became our faithful advisor. This charity later became known as the Only One Music Group (OOMG). As time went on in my work with OOMG, I did less and less legal work and more and more prayer and worship ministry. In that ministry, I saw clearly that my legal help was merely a bandage, but prayer for broken hearts changed lives forever.

Everything seemed to be going well, now that my focus was less on myself and more on the hearts of others, including my family. I loved watching my daughters grow and excel in the areas that I too loved—music and horses. My older daughter, Kristen, was in every musical play she could find, and my younger daughter, Victoria, discovered her greatest joy was in riding and training horses. My husband preferred riding and building horses made of steel—motorcycles. I was especially blessed when my daughters helped me feed the homeless with the Salvation Army's canteen truck, and assist with Michele's music ministry at churches and conferences. By this time, I was devoting most of my days to helping communicate the Lord's message of hope and healing through music. For the first time, my work was fun! I loved music and I loved ministry, so music ministry was a dream to me. (The dream became even bigger when the Lord recently added horses to the ministry. Today I minister to broken hearts through equine assisted learning/listening activities, or EAP/EAL). Everything seemed to be going well. Even my relationship with my husband seemed better.

And then one day an unknown simmering volcano erupted my life. My husband and I found ourselves back in marriage counseling *again*. I could not believe we were talking about the same subject as we had fifteen years earlier. Back then he had promised me that the heartache was over; that it was only a single incident. I had gone through this before; I could not go through it again. Worse, I could not turn my angry eyes from my husband and look into the merciful eyes of the Lord.

As I look back on that time, I see that the word truly was "could" not. I was unable to get over my anger, not because I would not, but because I could not. I was reeling in pain with the realization that I had been lied to for most of my twenty-eight years of marriage. My trust was shattered; now rage ruled. Devastating thoughts consumed my days, and nightmares devoured my nights. Images of my husband's untold secrets would wake me in the middle of the night, and I would sit alone in the darkness, gasping for breath, feeling my heart beating needles of pain.

No relationship can survive deep wounding unless both people can take their eyes off the other person and look instead at the problems in their own heart. This, I discovered, was one of the most important and difficult points in healing a broken relationship. The issue is not what the other person has done to hurt us; *it is how we respond.* And how we respond depends entirely upon our relationship with our heavenly Father. But the dilemma is that the wounded heart is unable to look inside without the supernatural and compassionate help of the Holy Spirit. There is so much anger and so much hiding there—so many walls, so many lies. Yes, Jesus can heal us instantaneously. But our wonderful Counselor and gentle Healer often takes us on a journey, healing us one layer at a time. And this takes time, because what is most important to Jesus is the time we spend alone with Him, listening to Him speak His words of truth and love to us (Luke 10:39-42).

I had first encountered the healing love of Jesus a few years before this devastating heartache. I knew enough about healing to know that I desperately needed to get rid of the pain. So I poured out my pain to Jesus, but I still could not get over my anger. It was so deep, as deep as had been my love for my husband. He had been a part of my life for more than thirty-two years, but despite the healing I had been through, I was unable to look at him the way Jesus looked at him. Why couldn't I? What was happening? What was wrong?

The Monument

A few months later, another unbearable tragedy occurred. My best friend's daughter, Katie, was killed in a tragic accident in Chile during her study-abroad program in college. Katie and my daughter Kristen had become friends when they were just toddlers. Kristen loved Katie, and so did I. She was a most unusual child, always smiling, always so happy, such a joy to have in our home. Through the years, no matter how far apart life's roads led Katie and Kristen, whenever Katie came into our presence again, she radiated that eternal smile of hers and exuded her endearing sweetness. Katie was only twenty years old when she died, and it was the final blow to my heart.

During the school year, I met weekly in a Moms in Touch International group near Victoria's school to pray for our children, their school, and our families. Our meeting place was not far from Cleveland's beautiful 285-acre Lakeview Cemetery, which is also known as Cleveland's outdoor museum. Lakeview is the burial place of many historic figures including James A. Garfield, the twentieth president of the United States; John D. Rockefeller, founder of the Standard Oil Company; and Eliot Ness, mobster Al Capone's nemesis. It is also the site of the Wade Chapel, a beautiful building listed on the National Register of Historic Places. The interior of the chapel, designed by Louis Tiffany, is magnificent. It contains Tiffany's famous glass window, "The Flight of Souls." The chapel's west and east walls are made entirely of beautiful glass mosaics depicting the history of the Old and New Testaments. But most significant to me is that Lakeview Cemetery is where Katie is buried.

After my early morning mothers' prayer meetings, I would drive to the cemetery and pray for the hearts of Katie's family and for Kristen's heart. To me, there is no more sobering, introspective place on earth than a cemetery. It is a living monument to the brevity of our lives and our desperate need to understand life's true meaning and purpose. And it is also a place where the loneliness of grief can find comfort in the loving arms and surrounding Presence of one's Healer.

Week after week, I sat by Katie's grave and prayed. But my prayers had become one-way discourses, like the agony of Job. I was unable to hear the Lord speak one word to me. I could not get beyond my grief over Katie's death or the anger regarding my marriage. I wondered how my prayers could possibly help Katie's family or Kristen. How could I help anyone? So one day, I asked the Lord to reach His hand into my own tomb and touch my heart with His healing love.

It was a cold day, and the skies were a gloomy Cleveland gray. I began to pray while sitting with my back against Katie's family monument, which was next to her grave. I poured out every emotion I had ever felt over Katie's death. I told the Lord I could not see or hear Him anymore. I actually told Him He was not true to His word to me because He had promised me He would never allow anything into my life that was more than I could bear. I could not bear any longer the loss of a marriage and the loss of a child. So I begged Him to bow the heavens and come down—to please open my heart once again to Him. I waited and waited. The Lord did not put one thought or one picture into my mind. I put my head back against the monument, looked up into the sky, and told the Lord I truly needed to see Him that day.

Often in my past, I would look at the sky and imagine angelic cloud formations moving with the majesty of Jesus, gathering to announce in spectacular display His Presence or coming return. However, on that day I could not see one thing in the sky that communicated the wonder of God's creation. I looked around, hoping to see the trees clap their hands or hear the rocks cry out, responding to the entrance of their Creator. Many times, when I had immersed myself in God's creation along a wooded trail with my horse, or on a sunlit or starlit mountaintop, or on a glimmering, wave-pounded beach, I would feel the grandeur and the power of His Presence. But that day there was only silence and stillness and emptiness. I continued to wait. Suddenly, a figure appeared. I saw a silhouette of what seemed to be a person wearing a long cape standing approximately thirty yards directly across from me. I waited for this person to move, but nothing happened. I had not seen anyone else in the cemetery that day, so I got to my feet and walked in the direction of this apparition.

When I arrived at my destination, I saw a sight I had never seen before: a depiction of one of my favorite chapters in the Bible. It was incredible! It was the setting of my very last prayer with my friend Hope in Italy—John chapter 20. Hope and I talked much about that chapter and the story of Mary Magdalene crying at the tomb of Jesus. And now, standing in front of me was a caped, five-foot stone figure of Mary Magdalene with a jar of oil in her hands. The inscription near the bottom of her statue told of her journey to Christ's tomb to anoint the body of Jesus. About twenty feet away, another sculpted image of Mary showed her kneeling, her head in her arms, crying upon a rock. That was when Jesus came to her and compassionately spoke His words of hope and healing, "Whom are you seeking?"

The Bible describes how the healing of Mary Magdalene's heart filled her a love that could not be contained and that caused her to seek Jesus despite the scorn and fears surrounding His death. I was astonished. Why had the family of this grave site chosen to illustrate that story from John 20 here? I walked the perimeter to gather clues. Nothing. Then, as I crossed the middle of the family's plot, I found four small and simple grave markers. They were identical, flat, and rectangular, made of ordinary gray stone. I read each stone. Only the name and the year each family member was born and died were inscribed. First was the father's grave, and then the mother's, and then their two children's graves. I read their years of death again. Then I saw it. Both children had predeceased their parents. Tears filled my eyes. Could there be any other pain on earth greater than the death of one's child? Is there any way a parent could truly live again without a miraculous healing? I knew only one person who could miraculously heal a broken heart. His name is Jesus, and this family knew Him, too. In the deepest part of their pain, that family—like Mary—had heard Jesus say, "Whom are you seeking?" And they found the one their hearts so desperately needed. Like Mary, they too found the healing love of Jesus more powerful than the agony of death.

So many times in my lonely wanderings around Lakeview Cemetery, I had walked in every direction from Katie's grave, but I had never noticed this burial site. I had never seen Mary's figure in the distance, directly across from me until that day when I cried out to Jesus to please speak. As I stood there, I thanked Jesus profusely for showing me His faithfulness once again. He *is* faithful and true to His promise to never leave me nor forsake me. Though I could not feel His Presence, He showed me He was there, as He always had been.

As I look back on that day, I see clearly now what I could not see then. He was there, knocking on the door to my heart, trying to direct me away from my hopeless path. He was trying to get me to turn my eyes away from my husband's actions and back to His love and faithfulness; from my husband's lack of remorse back to His mercy and compassion. He was trying to turn my thoughts away from my pain and to His Presence; from my circumstances to His unchanging character. But Jesus' words, "Whom are you seeking?" fell on deaf ears that day, preventing those words from bringing their healing power into my mind and piercing the darkness in my heart. A gravestone was hidden in my heart.

In the years following that day in Lakeview, I have walked through other dark valleys that hid from my view what the Lord was doing in my life. I could only see myself and my crumbling circumstances. During those dark times, I have learned that it is critical to *remember* all that the Lord has done for me in my life. I need to stop and meditate on His past faithfulness and goodness—how He has pursued me, provided for me, and protected me all the days of my life. Many times Israel, God's children, turned back in the day of battle and experienced a life of defeat and discouragement because they forgot His works and the wonders of His power He had shown them (Psalm 78). When I remember God's faithfulness, when I reflect on His goodness to me, I am able to stop the thunderous tumult in my ears so that I can hear the Lord's still, small voice speaking the only words that can help me see Him—words of truth. Remembering fuels the miraculous power of thankfulness in my life. Truth pierces the darkest valley (Psalm 23:4) and brings light to the most despondent soul (Hebrew 4:12).

The Devouring Darkness

The death of a marriage and the death of a beloved child brought on the most difficult and painful days of my life. I did not reflect on God's faithfulness. I found no solace in reading my Bible. The Scriptures actually discouraged me because I could not see any of God's promises evident in my life. Peace, joy, and hope had become foreign and faint. Faint, too, seemed Jesus' response to my prayers, and I told Him so. I love the honesty of the psalmist:

O Lord, the God who saves me, day and night I cry out before You.
May my prayer come before You; turn Your ear to my cry.
For my soul is full of trouble and my life draws near the grave.
I am counted among those who go down to the pit;
I am like a man without strength.
I am set apart with the dead, like the slain who lie in the grave,
whom You remember no more, who are cut off from Your care.
You have put me in the lowest pit, in the darkest depths.
Your wrath lies heavily upon me;
You have overwhelmed me with all Your waves.
You have taken from me my closest friends and have made me
repulsive to them. I am confined and cannot escape;
my eyes are dim with grief. I call to You, O Lord, every day;
I spread out my hands to You ...
But I cry to You for help, O Lord;
in the morning my prayer comes before You.
Why, O Lord, do you reject me and hide Your face from me ...
You have taken my companions and loved ones from me;
the darkness is my closest friend. (Psalm 88 NIV)

♫ Once again the Lord came to me in my night with a song. One evening I sought refuge in an unfamiliar church where I could sit alone, safe in my anonymity, safe from familiar faces' grimacing condemning stares. I don't remember the sermon that evening, but I took home a CD written and recorded by a woman who sang a poignant song during the service. The song broke through the gravestone in my heart, allowing Jesus to finally speak to me that evening. I had worked so hard tying to find help, trying to find God, and all I had to do was lie down and let Him minister to me—let His Spirit minister to my spirit. (This is very important.) The song was titled "Trust in Me" and was written by Gail Mangeri, a mother of eight homeschooled children from Cleveland, Ohio. In the first two verses of the song, the troubled soul cries out to Jesus to take away the storm that is raging and blinding her eyes, so that her soul can see His truth and love. In the third verse, Jesus answers and redirects the broken soul to look not at the storm, but at His pierced hands, His side, and His bleeding brow. He tells her that for her love He lives, for her sin He died, and that she is a treasure in His sight—words that heal every heart. (If you like more contemporary songs, "I Will Trust You," by Lauren Daigle is also a good song about our need to trust God.)

The lyrics struck a note in my heart: I could trust Him. I desperately needed to know that. But I didn't hear any words about the problem hidden in my heart. After all, I did good things for my community. I went to church. I paid my tithes. There was nothing wrong with *me*. For months, I slept with that song (and also Gail's song "Come Unto Me") playing on repeat next to my bed. When I would awaken, feeling my heart beating with anxiety, the songs would sing me back to sleep. Helpful too were the instrumental recordings of old hymns that I had sung as a girl. His music consoled my soul and kept me from the greatest darkness. Jesus became my hiding place, surrounding me with songs of deliverance (Psalm 32:7).

What had happened to everything I knew about healing broken hearts? Why did my heart remain so empty, so lifeless? I had initially struggled with saying "I forgive you" to my husband. Just before our divorce, I believed I finally could say it. I remember sobbing at the entrance to the courtroom moments before our final hearing on Valentine's Day, 2002. Tears streamed down my face as I thought of God's command to forgive my husband, even though he had not asked for my forgiveness. I struggled terribly over the fact that he had never even said he was sorry about what he had done. That had fueled the fires of fear in my heart and the nightmares in my mind. So, with much trepidation, I asked my husband—one more time—if he would agree to stop the divorce and go back to marriage counseling. "If you won't do it for me, please do it for the sake of our daughters," I pleaded as I stood there crying. I did not want to bring even more pain into their lives. I did not want them to have to tell people their parents were divorced, to have to cope with separate households, to be thrust into the middle of brokenness they had nothing to do with. I did not want this to shatter their faith in God.

But my husband did not respond with even one word to me. He glared at me and walked into the courtroom.

I felt I had died a thousand deaths. I was utterly and completely broken—more than I had ever been broken in my life. The pieces of my heart lay scattered and open for the deepest healing work of all to begin. The darkest cavern in my soul was now accessible. The Miner plunged to the bottom to illuminate the most entangling "root" to be discovered in my healing journey. At the bottom of the mine lay the most deceptive sin of all, which consumes the heart of every person who believes in her own goodness: self–righteousness. But I did not understand my problem. I believed I was very moral and good, and I thought everyone who did not rise to my standards of morality and goodness was, well, wrong.

A self-righteous pride is the most difficult sin to expose and admit. That is why it usually takes a "thousand deaths" or much brokenness to expose it. I was blind to the fact I had been listening to the voice of the deceiver and living his lies. But there is no darkness too dark for the light of truth.

Late one night, I was all alone in my home in Cleveland when Jesus exposed the darkest stone in my heart. Our beautiful home of sixteen years had just been sold, and I was very tired from packing. Michele had just left after helping me pack all day and—in her unique and eccentric way—trying to make me laugh. I was especially exhausted from fighting back the tears that came with the memories of raising our children in this home—of the birthday parties, Bible studies, music parties, Christmas teas and celebrations, slumber parties, and untold hours of beauty and blessing watching the sunrise from our front porch and eating dinners there together after the sun had set. So many memories. Then Jesus highlighted a very important and timely one.

One day I was praying for protection for my daughters' hearts on the front porch in the early morning. Our white-pillared porch expanded the length of the front side of our home. I was seated at our wicker glass-top table with my head resting on my arms upon the table. After pouring my heart out for Kristen and Victoria, I heard a rustling sound. I looked up. Standing there next to the porch, radiant in the morning mist, was a mother deer and her two fawns. I sat amazed by the sight, filled with love for my Creator for blessing me with this beautiful picture of His creation and His knowledge of my love for my two daughters, and with wonderful evidence that He was there, watching me. The doe stood there looking at me in the spotlight of the morning sun. It was shining through the trees encircling the three of them. The doe raised her head higher, and with eyes and ears alert for possible danger, she slowly yet gracefully walked down the hill to our white horse fence by the road. Her daughters glanced at my curious presence and then playfully followed. Standing next to the road, the doe looked up and down, watching and listening. Then, from a standstill, she leaped up and over the fence. Frantically trying to find a way around the barricade, her little ones ran up and down the length of the fence. Unsuccessful in their attempts, the two fawns ran back to the place where their mother had gone over the fence, and with much difficulty and less grace, they squeezed through it. The way was very hard for them, but they were safe. I will never forget how Jesus spoke to me that morning. I hold His picture and His promise so very close to my heart. There were so many wonderful experiences with God and His creation on our front porch that I had always wanted to put a sign reading "Eden" above our porch door.

Plunging Even Deeper

Now the porch furniture and most of our house furniture was gone. It was dark and I was alone in bed, listening to the nearby creek and the crickets singing their music of the night, when Jesus walked into my room. The bookshelf next to my bed now held only two or three books that had not yet been packed. They were like late-night houseguests waiting to fill my empty, lonely room and sleepless hours. The book I selected that evening was Francis Frangipane's *The Power of One Christ-Like Life*. Though I was no longer a workaholic, I still struggled with having to achieve the "biggest and the best." This title said to me that I could do it all! However, the book should be subtitled *Mercy Triumphs over Judgment*. The Lord had other plans that evening. He came down with the sharpest two-edged sword that ever pierced my soul. I never got beyond chapter 4, "From Indignation to Intercession." In the section "Is Anger Justified?" on page 53, it stated, "Judas changed from an apostle into a person he never intended to become; he became a traitor. Our anger, left unattended, will do the same to us. It causes us to degenerate into something we never planned on becoming: 'Christian Pharisees.' By allowing self-righteousness and a judgmental spirit to grow in the soil of unrepentant anger, we become worse in God's eyes than the evil that offended us."

The sword of truth plunged into the depths of my heart. For the first time in my 40 years as a Christian, I discovered the seriousness of my sin, and the remorse and sorrow of years of self-righteous living came crashing down upon me. There are no words to describe how I felt. Because of my deep love for the Lord and my desire to be like Him, I sorrowed greatly as I contemplated this gulf between us. Knowing Jesus as the essence of humility and meekness caused me to cringe as I looked on my pride. It was worse than any other sin that I had committed, and worse than any sin that had been committed against me. Proverbs 6:16–17 states that the number-one sin is pride. Of all the people from whom I sought approval, Jesus was the most important. Even when others seemed displeased with me, I felt Jesus was truly pleased because He knew my heart. But it was because He knew of the sin hidden in my heart that He had allowed this terrible suffering in my life. He wanted to free me to experience His love more deeply than I had ever known before, to receive love and to give love. Only heartache could break open the stone-encased door to my heart and allow the light of His truth to expose the most entangling root of all, my self-righteousness. Pride had robbed me of the peace and contentment He brings to those who are humble, merciful, and forgiving.

Jesus set me free that day. He showed me how to stop condemning others when they fall short and sin, because I saw the depth of my own sin. "But for the grace of God, so go I." This taught me how to be merciful. I finally walked away from the greatest battlefield in my life—the war with the pride of my own heart. I laid down the artillery of control, and I picked up the keys to His Kingdom—repentance and forgiveness—which unleashed His power to set *this* prisoner free, at last.

How ironic it was that I always encouraged people I was praying with to ask Jesus if there was any hidden unforgiveness in their hearts—to reveal this unknown sin. It seemed to be the biggest cause of pain in peoples' lives and the greatest obstacle to healing. If any unforgiveness was revealed, I encouraged them to ask for His forgiveness and then ask for His help to forgive the person who had hurt them. That night, Jesus showed me that it was my self-righteousness that kept me from looking at my husband the way Jesus looked at him. I asked the Lord to forgive me and help me go to my husband, his family, and our daughters to seek forgiveness for how I condemned and judged my husband, which He did. Thereafter, I frequently wrote to my husband requesting that we return to counseling and try again, just one more time. He never responded.

Going On with the Journey

My confession changed so many things. I saw my former husband in a brand-new light. I saw him through God's eyes and for the first time felt God's compassion for him. I then found in my heart a deep compassion for others who were broken that I sorrowed for them. I wanted to help them more than I wanted to pursue material things for myself. And I discovered in my heart an even deeper love for Jesus. I became passionate in my desire to know and radiate the love of the One who had set me free.

Jesus had been waiting for me to come to this place, and He waits for you, too. With this passion, He takes us into the inexpressible depths of His heart.

It is a most holy place. To go there and experience the amazing things we were created to see and do, we too must be holy. We need to get rid of every hidden hindrance in our hearts that hides Him. *Blessed are the pure in heart, for they shall see God* (Matthew 5:8).

Jesus faithfully and patiently waits for the cries of the broken heart. That's when the healing begins.The shell of selfishness and pride is shattered amid suffering, allowing the love of God to mend and to mold. The healing process is a purifying process. The dross in our lives is burned away, and we come forth as radiant gold—precious treasures in God's sight, bearing the scars of priceless, passionate love. This discovery in my healing journey was to take me to my wondrous destiny, which had been planned for me since the beginning of time.

♫ The song "Healing Begins," a contemporary song by Tenth Avenue North, notes, "This is where the healing starts, when you come to where you're broken within, the Light meets the dark." And in the compassionate "Hiding Place," Sarah Groves sings of how Jesus, who is our hiding place, fills our broken hearts with His songs of deliverance. He sings to us songs of how the weak are made strong. Did you ever know that Jesus truly sings to you? (See Zephaniah 3:17.)

I discovered in my journey that the Lord has three primary objectives, or desires, as He leads us to our destiny: to purify us, to impassion us, and to empower us. Thus far I had experienced the cleansing and purifying process of the wounds and wrongs in my life. Next I was to experience the depths of Jesus' passion for me, which would result in an empowered, miraculous love overflowing from my heart into the heart of others.

CHAPTER 7

Gethsemane's Mingled Tears

Trust in Him at all times, you people; Pour out your heart before Him; God is a refuge for us. Selah.

— Psalm 62:8

Jesus is the Supreme Creator. He knows how many stars shine in the heavens; He knows the number of hairs on our heads. He calms the oceans with His word, and His voice brings peace into our turbulent lives. The psalmist understood this when he wrote, *He sent His Word and healed them, and delivered them from their destructions* (Psalm 107:20). Like a protective father, Jesus carries us close to His heart. When our journey is very painful, He knows when, where, and how to draw us into His strong and healing arms. My older daughter, Kristen, was doing her graduate work at a music conservatory in California, and my younger daughter, Victoria, was leaving for Colorado to commence her college education. For the first time in my life, I would be alone, and I did not want to face that. So I told Jesus that I could not face this loneliness. I just wasn't strong enough. Once again, I needed those strong and healing arms.

Loneliness is a gift that most people avoid like the plague. But sometimes it is only through the brokenness of loneliness that we can learn how to find true contentment alone with Jesus. That is when Jesus draws closest to our hearts. *The Lord is near to those who have a broken heart, and saves such as have a contrite spirit* (Psalm 34:18). It is the time the heart cries desperately to feel the touch that heals. *His left hand is under my head and His right hand embraces me* (Song of Songs 2:6). It is during our alone times with Jesus, listening to His words of truth and plumbing deeper into His love for us, that we see He is all we need. Please listen on YouTube.com to a most powerful song by Kari Jobe entitled, "I Am Not Alone." Also a book suggestion for your consideration is *The Path of Loneliness*, by Elisabeth Elliot.

While spending time listening to Jesus one morning, I was reminded of a Scripture verse that missionary, author, and friend Elisabeth Elliot gave me many years ago about taking "the next step" after a tragedy. She shared this verse with me when I asked her how she went on in life after her husband Jim was killed in Ecuador. Elisabeth and her husband, and several other missionary couples, prayed and prepared for several years to minister to the never-before-reached Auca Indians. Then during their very first contact with the Auca tribe, Jim and the other male missionaries were murdered (*Through Gates of Splendor*, by Elisabet Elliot). "Elisabeth, How did you take that next step?" I asked.

Elisabeth responded to me that after Jim's death, the Lord spoke to her through Isaiah 58:10: *If you spend yourselves in behalf of the hungry and satisfy the needs of the oppressed, then your light will rise in the darkness, and your night will become like the noonday* (NIV).

"Yes, I grieved," she said. "But because of the Lord's mercy, I was not consumed by my grief. Others were suffering. Children were dying because they did not have medicine. An airfield had to be built to bring in the necessary supplies. Jesus' words and His work of ministering to the sufferings of others were my healing."

Elisabeth challenged me to obey the Lord in spite of any cost, no matter how great the risk. She told me to keep my eyes on the character of God, never on my circumstances. She challenged me to go through God's Word and see how God brought everyone to a place where he or she had to choose whether or not to follow Him despite the great risk of harm to reputation or welfare. I did that, and I saw that when we choose God, He always rescues us. But the rescue isn't always immediate. Many times it is part of the journey into the deeper places of His heart. And I saw that the journey always leads down a path where we have to come to the end of self. It is the way of brokenness.

So I began asking the Lord to open my eyes to the suffering of others and to show me where He wanted me to help the "hungry and the oppressed" (Isaiah 58:10). While I prayed about this next step, our ministry's counseling advisor, Elisabeth Brown, called me. (There are no coincidences in the Kingdom.) I told her about Elisabeth Elliot's words to me and that I had decided to visit my cousin Liz in London to hopefully comfort and encourage her during her time of bereavement over the tragic loss of her sister; she had already lost both of her parents. "After my visit with Liz, I would like to go to Italy. Of all the countries in the world, I desire to see Italy most of all because of my love for music, art, history, and architecture," I said to her.

She responded, "I know you, Loren. I know you will want to do much more than just sightsee!" She suggested that I contact Franco Foti, an Italian-American missionary living in Cleveland. His Harvest International Ministries had been taking people on mission trips to Italy for many years.

That sounded like good advice to me, because it was consistent with what I had been hearing in my times alone with Jesus. So I made an appointment to meet with Franco. After I met and prayed with Franco and his wife, Pearl, he invited me on his next trip, which was planned for the same month that I was going to go to London! After visiting Liz, I would meet him in Catania, Sicily.

I have learned that Jesus always repeats Himself when He speaks to us, including when we seek His direction. Both Elisabeths and Isaiah 58:10 told me to go and share the Lord's love with Liz, and then with others on a mission trip. And I know that Jesus told me to go into the world and show His love, specifically in Italy. How do I know that? He gives us the desires of His heart. His Word states in Psalm 37:4, *Delight yourself in the Lord, and He will give you the desires of your heart.* It has all been planned since the beginning of time. *"I know the plans I have for you," says the Lord. "They are plans for good and not for disaster, to give you a future and a hope"* (Jeremiah 29:11 NLT).

The Discovery of a New Kingdom

Jesus is faithful! He knows how much we can bear, and He provides a way of escape for us—and it is always within His heart, in the midst of His Presence. So Jesus led me away, not only to Italy (Rome became my mission home base for eight years) but also to other lands to see and experience things about His heart and about my heart. In almost a dozen countries, including many countries of Africa, India, Egypt, Israel, and various countries of Eastern and Western Europe, I gained an understanding, an appreciation, and a love for life in God's Kingdom that I had never before known. I discovered that the real Kingdom life is unlike anything I had ever imagined. I thought I had a great deal of faith until I met people who lived entirely by faith. I saw Jesus meeting every single need of those who lived for and depended upon Him alone. There I found joy in simplicity. Simple people who lived simple lives were simply happy. Materialism was an irrelevant foreign language, but family was spoken fluently. I had never seen so much appreciation for my love for Jesus and for my desire to see broken hearts set free. It was as though Jesus was loving me back through the wonderful people and incredible experiences everywhere He sent me.

The "Why" of Love

After my mission trip to India in February 2005, I planned to return to the States in March for a family visit. However, when I stopped in Rome to pack things for my return, I sensed that old foe, discouragement, beginning to creep back into my heart. When I am living and ministering in the mission field, my heart is so free. We dance. We take time to listen to Jesus. But when I return to the States, I face so many people and places that are not "freedom friendly" and my heart and my spirit feel restrained and sad. Most weighty of all were my thoughts about the forthcoming wedding of my former husband in March. I knew this trip home was going to be especially difficult. I felt my feet beginning to slip and my heart beginning to ache. Once again, "why" questions assailed my heart. The most painful "why" of all I asked Jesus was, "You died to bring healing and reconciliation to our brokenness, so why didn't this happen in my broken family? Why?" I did not believe I was strong enough to face the reality of my husband's remarriage. So I told the Lord I needed Him more than ever before, as I had told Him so many times in the past. And He responded, as He always did, with arms wide open.

Ever since my marriage had ended and my heart and family had broken into a thousand pieces, I had thought many times about the garden of Gethsemane. I had said so often, "If I ever get to go to Israel, I want most of all to go to Gethsemane. I want to lie down there and cry with Jesus. Only He can understand the pain of abandonment and rejection, because He, too, experienced it."

So at the end of my trip to India, instead of returning to the States, I went to the garden of Gethsemane in Jerusalem. There I experienced profound healing. I use the word "profound" because the healing I experienced in Gethsemane revealed one of the deepest truths about the healing ministry of Jesus I had never before contemplated.

On to Jerusalem

When I arrived in Jerusalem, I stayed in a monastery of French-speaking nuns. Their beautiful vespers sang me to sleep each night and gently awakened me in the morning. On the day of my husband's wedding, I took my Bible and walked outside the large stone wall encircling the convent and down to the historic and majestic walls of Old Jerusalem. To avoid getting lost in the city's narrow and winding streets, I followed the wall outside the Old City. As I walked toward Gethsemane, I contemplated the foreboding gold dome of the mosque on the Temple Mount and sensed the tears falling at the Wailing Wall.

When I arrived at Gethsemane, I was a little early, so as I waited for the gate to open I walked around behind the garden. I noticed a bronze plaque on the back stone wall. On it was inscribed the words of Matthew 26:39: *He went a little farther and fell on His face,and prayed, "O My Father, if it is possible, let this cup pass from Me; nevertheless, not as I will, but as You will."* The next sentence on the plaque cut to my heart. "Jesus was able to face His darkest hour when, after much suffering, He surrendered to the will of His Father." I knew the Lord had shown me that plaque so that I would carry its piercingly relevant words with me into the garden.

Once inside, I sat down with my back to the stone wall, facing the ageless olive trees, and read all God's words about Gethsemane in the Gospels (Matthew 26; Mark 14; Luke 22). As I began to pray for the hearts of my children, Kristen and Victoria, a grief came over me that was so strong that I could only lie down and cry. I begged for the Lord's help to heal and guard their hearts and heal the hearts of our family. "Lord, please help me accept 'this cup,' to accept Your perfect will, and to believe Your promise that You will give me a future and a hope" (Jeremiah 29:11).

As I prayed, the Lord's Spirit brought to mind everything Jesus suffered in Gethsemane. But this time I found myself focusing on how *He* felt in that place—His deep distress, His soul being *"crushed with grief, to the point of death"* (Matthew 26:38 NLT). What agony! And then I meditated on His feelings of abandonment, rejection, and loneliness.

Have you ever poured out your heart to a friend, only to have her say, "I understand how you feel?" Did you think to yourself that there was no way she could ever understand the depths of your pain unless she experienced every detail of it? That thought is true. But when we meditate on Jesus' experience in Gethsemane, described in Matthew 26, we find a friend who truly has experienced all our sorrow. I had read Matthew 26 many times before, but this time, I saw that Jesus had experienced deeper sorrow and pain than I had ever known or would ever know. I saw the rejection Jesus experienced by those He trusted and loved. I saw His abandonment by those who said they would never leave Him. I saw the betrayal by one who walked with Him, dined at His table, and kissed Him. I saw those He trusted lie about Him. I saw Him denied by one who vowed faithfulness until death. Jesus had experienced deeper sorrow and pain than I had ever known. It was then that I realized that Jesus truly knew my sorrows. As I sat in Gethsemane crying for myself, I came face to face with the reality that Jesus cried in that place, for me. And because of that, He was the only one who could intimately understand and care for me—the only one whose arms could comfort me. I could trust Him with my heart.

My tears that day began to flow from another well source. For the first time in my life, I grieved for Jesus. My heart broke as Jesus spoke this truth into my mind: "My suffering in Gethsemane was for you, Loren, so that you would not have to live in the Gethsemane of your soul." Then I thought of the passion of Christ for me in Isaiah 53:3–5 (NLT): *He was despised and rejected— a Man of sorrows, acquainted with deepest grief ... Yet it was our weaknesses He carried: it was our sorrows that weighed Him down ... He was beaten so we could be whole. He was whipped so we could be healed.* I no longer had to suffer alone; nor would I have to suffer for endless years. With resurrection power, Jesus set me free from my suffering just as He had set me free from my sinfulness—my selfishness.

My Faithful Husband

After contemplating all that Jesus had suffered for me, I sat quietly and listened. For each pain I had cried about, Jesus responded faithfully and lovingly by placing His words of truth into my mind. He reminded me that He would never leave me nor forsake me (Hebrews 13:5) and that His Presence would go with me and give me rest (Matthew 11:28). He said that He loved me with an everlasting love (1 John 3:1), and that I was precious to Him (Psalm 116:15). And He said He would be my faithful Husband, loving me unconditionally, providing for my every need, and carrying my every burden (Isaiah 54). I had heard a few of these comforting Scriptures before from the lips of dear friends, but this time, when Jesus Himself put those truths into my mind, my heart was comforted with a healing I would never forget and that would last forever.

For the first time in my life, I began to understand the meaning and importance of "the fellowship of His sufferings." Philippians 3:10 states, *That I may know Him and the power of His resurrection, and the fellowship of His sufferings, being conformed to His death.* To know Jesus truly, I had to enter into the secret place of His sufferings and, as He did, die to self. In that place, our tears mingle together as I pour out the pain of my broken heart while resting against His comforting chest (Deuteronomy 33:12). In that secure embrace, I can hear His heartbeat, and I realize that the bitter tears I weep for myself cannot heal. But the tears that flow from Jesus' eyes and onto my cheek can heal me because they flow from the pain He endured to save me. *From now on let no one trouble me, for I bear in my body the marks of the Lord Jesus* (Galatians 6:17).

It's so incredible to realize Jesus thought about me and you in His most painful moments. When I think of this, I—like Mary at the tomb of Jesus—weep for His love for me. Then I can hear my risen Savior calling me by name. ♫ Please listen to "I Will Rise" by Chris Tomlin.

Focus On Jesus the Person, Not the Pain

A few days later, I was walking down the streets of Jerusalem when I saw a shop selling Scripture rings with raised-letter Hebrew words on them. One caught my attention. I purchased a gold ring with Songs of Songs 2:16 written on it: "I am my beloved's, and my beloved is mine." Song of Songs is a wedding song from the bridegroom to his bride. The words in that verse went straight to my heart. That day, Jesus became my Husband for the first time in my life. Isaiah 54:5–6 (NIV) sealed that truth in my heart and mind: *"For my Maker is my husband—the Lord Almighty is His name—the Holy One of Israel is my Redeemer; He is called the God of all the earth. The Lord will call me back as if I were a wife deserted and distressed in spirit—a wife who married young, only to be rejected," says my God* (NIV, personalized).

My experience in Gethsemane and my experiences praying for the broken hearts of others have shown me how important it is to focus on the heart of Jesus, His Presence, and His words of truth during our healing journey. Without that focus on the Person who heals, we will get stuck in the healing process if we focus on the pain that kills. As I experienced in Gethsemane, something very powerful happens inside when we come out of ourselves and our pain, and encounter the passion, and compassion of our Healer. As we encounter His tenderness while listening to His words of truth, we experience the love that sent Him to Calvary—a love so much deeper than any human love we have ever experienced or ever will experience. It will truly take a lifetime to apprehend what Jesus endured to set us free, and to understand everything that He accomplished for us on Calvary.

♫ As I end this chapter, I think of two songs that would be wonderful to include here: "He Knows," by Michele Wagner and Mark Hauth, and "Communion Song" by Laura Kaczor. "He Knows" describes so well the anguish I shared with you in this chapter. "Communion Song" communicates so powerfully all that Jesus endured to send His Holy Spirit into our hearts so that we no longer have to live within the Gethsemane of our souls. You will listen to "He Knows" in the beginning of the next chapter. So for now, please go to YouTube and prayerfully listen to "Communion Song." My favorite line presents the dilemma and discord within our rational minds—our ability to picture the soldiers guarding Jesus' tomb that resurrection morning, contrasted against our inability to even imagine the "blinding glory of our risen Lord." Listen carefully as Jesus sings the chorus to you. Meditate on the words in the chorus, noting especially the power and joy found in "the cup of forgiveness."

Please know the next chapter, Chapter 8, was written to help you begin the most important journey of your life—your journey into the garden of God's Presence. The journey will help reveal anything hidden in your heart that inhibits you from living the life God had planned for you since the beginning of time. When Jesus tears down the wall around our hearts, He sets us free to experience a life of intimacy with Him that few people have ever imagined or thought possible. This is the destination of our healing journey. It is the desire of His heart; It is the reason He died for you. So let Him take your hand and take you home—to the place He always intended for you to live. *Nevertheless I am continually with You; You hold me by my right hand. You will guide me with Your counsel, And afterward receive me to glory* (Psalm 73:23–24).

CHAPTER 8

The Journey Few Have Taken

Every valley shall be exalted and every mountain and hill brought low;
the crooked places shall be made straight
and the rough places smooth.

— *Isaiah 40:4*

Jesus taught His disciples saying ... For the gate is small
and the way is narrow that leads to life,
and there are few who find it."

—*Matthew 7:14 (NASB)*

Preparing for Your Journey—Very Important

"The Journey Few Have Taken" is an allegorical and music-directed pilgrimage that contains eight short journeys filled with songs, Scriptures, and prayers. The journey is the story about boy, still just a child inwardly, whose heart has been broken. The child is desperate to find his way home—to a place that is truly safe, where he always feels welcome, wanted, and deeply loved. Although the child's journey was at times long and hard, the home he found was more wonderful than he could have ever imagined or even dreamed. He discovers this home, this refuge, in a garden valley, inside a world filled with wonder.

"The Journey Few Have Taken" will lead you on the narrow road to freedom. Most people only travel the broad road, imprisoned by the voices and opinions of others. Both roads in life lead to a destination. The road we choose determines whether we live a life of peace and contentment or a life of uncertainty, fear, and pain. Therefore, this choice is the most important choice we will ever make. Traveling this road will affect our lives, forever.

But from there you will seek the Lord your God, and you will find Him if you seek Him with all your heart and with all your soul (Deuteronomy 4:29). When we choose to travel the narrow road and seek God, the success of our pursuit is directly related to the desire of our heart. We persevere on this journey when we desire above all else a peace this world cannot provide, and a love and joy that are greater than any we have experienced or ever will experience in another person. The choice, then, to find Jesus as your Healer and to come to know Him as the Lover of your soul, is yours. The reward is a priceless treasure—the riches and wonders of life lived in His Presence. But all treasures have a cost; this one cost Jesus His life. Will you also lay down everything for the priceless gifts He has for you? Before you seek His "pearls of great price," you will need to know the following about the journey you will take:

1) You are not alone on this journey. Jesus Himself will guide you and carry you each step of the way. *The Lord is near to those who have a broken heart, and saves such as have a contrite spirit* (Psalm 34:18). So each day, invite the intimacy of the Lord's Presence as you begin the journey. Ask Jesus to open your ears and your eyes to see hear and see what He wants to reveal to you. *Draw near to God and He will draw near to you* (James 4:8). Jesus speaks to us through His Spirit by highlighting Scriptures and by bringing thoughts and pictures of truth and love to our mind. These thoughts and pictures will always be consistent with His written word (*logos*)—the Bible. Our very lives are dependent upon hearing Jesus speak to us. *But He answered and said, "It is written, 'Man shall not live by bread alone, but by every word* [rhēma] *that proceeds from the mouth of God'"* (Matthew 4:4, Deuteronomy 8:3). Jesus said His *rhēma* words *"are spirit and they are life"* (John 6:63). When Jesus' Spirit speaks His words of truth and love to us, we become alive to live the life He created us to live. Please know, because Jesus is the Word of God, the words He speaks to us will always be consistent with who He is and therefore possess the power to do what He has spoken.

We cannot conjure up or depend upon our rational minds to "figure out" the words Jesus wants to speak to us. We must simply sit still and let His Spirit bring the thoughts and pictures into our minds. This is why the Bible says not to lean on our own understanding but in everything to seek Jesus intimately

(Proverbs 3:5–6). Many times I encourage people to step out of their rational world and into the spiritual world by asking them to think about what Jesus would say to them regarding the question or matter. Remember that the enemy is on a mission to speak lies to us. So whenever a thought of truth and love enters your mind, Jesus won that battle and He is speaking to you.

If you have never read about Jesus in the Bible, it is important you read one of the Gospels— Matthew, Mark, Luke, or John—along with your journey so that you can become more sensitive to the Lord's voice. Each Gospel presents a specific aspect of Jesus' character. Matthew was written to the Jews and presents Jesus the Son of David—the promised Messiah, and Immanuel who is the God who is always with us. Mark presents Jesus as the sacrificial, powerful Servant whose suffering gives hope and meaning to our sufferings. Luke presents Jesus as the Savior of the whole world—all people and all nations, the rich and the poor, the powerful and the downcast, and the outcast (especially women). John presents Jesus as the Son of God, the eternal God, the great and glorious "I am" who, through faith in Him, gives us life, abundantly. Note the very words of Jesus and listen to His heart as you read—the more truth you read, the more truth you will hear Jesus speak to you. Romans 10:17 says that faith comes from hearing Jesus speak to us and we hear Him because we have listened to His words of truth in the Bible: *So faith comes by hearing, and hearing by the word* [rhēma] *of Christ* (Romans 10:17 NASB). Write down any of Jesus' promises that jump off the page or interest you; that is Jesus speaking to you.

<u>Also, a prayer partner or two would be a wonderful and most effective help in this journey, and in your life</u> (Part 2, Section VI). Note that Jesus had 3 prayer partners: Peter, James, and John. I highly encourage you to invite a friend who loves Jesus to journey with you. A friend who loves Jesus is an excellent listener, and a most faithful encourager. That friend will also bring the very necessary component of accountability into your life - something we *all* greatly need!.

2) Although the eight journeys are short, they require much time for worshiping, meditating, listening, and journaling. I recommend working on one per week. Don't give up after a couple of journeys. Persevere to the end to be able to understand and *experience* the entire journey.

3) Start each day of your journey, and the rest of your life, with worship music. (I find it amazing that very few books and classes on healing even mention the subject of worship music.) It is a most powerful way to enter His Presence. God's Word says we pass through His gates when we sing songs of thanksgiving, and we enter into His courts when we sing songs of praise (Psalm 100:2–4).

Constantly singing about God and to God is a vitally important discipline. We were created to worship our God; it's our spiritual DNA—Our Father designed us in His image to worship Him in spirit and in truth (John 4:24). When we are in God's Presence, worshiping Him, we are enveloped in His healing love and the more we are with Him the more we become like Him.

God is put back on the throne of our life and everything is brought back into His perspective when we worship Him. During worship, God manifests His glory (His perceptible Presence): truth is seen and heard; peace and hope return to rule and reign as He speaks to our hearts; worry, doubt, fear, despair, loneliness, and pain and their enveloping lies are dethroned. The enemy is defeated simply by His Presence—*nothing* can compete with His position of preeminence. His Spirit can be felt as it surrounds us; then all our dreams and desires are realigned and refined. Worship in song every day. Don't leave your time with the Lord each day until your spirit has sensed the closeness of His Presence! ♫ A really wonderful song about our important need to wait on the Lord's Presence each day is "Waiting Here for You," by Christy Nockles.

Note that the list of suggested worship songs at the beginning of each journey provides a variety of styles for varied musical tastes. Always select worship songs that communicate with *your* heart, either from this list or other sources, such as worship music websites, recommendations in the iTunes Store, and YouTube's suggestions for similar artists and songs. So important is this subject that I would encourage you to go to Part 2, "Look into the Light of His Face with Songs," where I share more thoroughly how to effectively worship in song. As this entire book presents, listening to Jesus is paramount. Always close your eyes during worship; there is so much to see when you personalize the song and turn the words into a prayer. After each song has played, listen to some quiet instrumental music, or just sit quietly and write down what pictures came to your mind and what Jesus said during the song or during your time of meditation after the song.

4) *Journal.* Be sure to write down the thoughts and pictures that come to your mind as you worship, as you read the allegory and listen to its accompanying song, as you meditate on the Scriptures, and as you listen to your heart answer the questions in each journey. Writing things down is more than a recording; it is also an important process of revelation. Also, *ask Jesus questions.* He is always speaking to us, so we need to listen. When we ask Him questions, our spirit becomes alert as we listen for His response, and aware when He responds. When Jesus responds with thoughts of truth and love, go to a good Bible concordance or topical index and look up the word or topic that He brought to mind; then meditate on the related Scriptures. Cross-reference these Scriptures. He wants to

have a conversation with you. The best concordance I have found is *The Treasury of Scripture Knowledge*, which is available online at sites like blueletterbible.org, biblehub.com, and biblestudytools.com. Also, you can ask Google "where in the Bible does it say, etc." Always include the word "Bible" with your questions in Google's search bar.

I used to wonder if the thoughts that came into my mind when I asked questions (and when I said to myself, "What would Jesus say to me?") were my thoughts or His. I learned several things:

a. Every thought of truth or love that enters my mind was put there, victoriously, by Jesus.

b. Jesus faithfully repeats Himself to assure me that He is the one speaking; I never have to guess or worry. Sometimes I simply ask, "Jesus, is this You speaking?"

c. If I don't get an immediate response to the above question, I need to wait and listen, because Jesus always answers. ("Jesus Answers," by Michele Wagner, is a wonderful song to remind us of this truth.) Sometimes the answer will come a few days later as I listen to worship music or a sermon, as I read the Bible or a book about Him, as I talk to others who love Him, or, especially, as I simply sit quietly in His Presence. Because Jesus died to heal the brokenhearted, I assure you He *will* speak to you; this is how He heals us. You will never have a more faithful and compassionate friend than Jesus. His words alone breathe new life into your soul (John 6:63). Friends' sharing of Bible verses can comfort us, but only the words Jesus speaks to us can heal us. *"Come to Me with your ears wide open. Listen, for the life of our soul is at stake"* (Isaiah 55:3a NLT). It is so vitally important that we listen *more* to Jesus Himself than to man's opinions, spoken or written, about Jesus. Man is fallible. Jesus is infallible. (See "You Are Created to Hear God's Voice and Understand the Bible" in Appendix A.)

5) There is a special song for you after each allegory story. (Please finish each journey before you listen to the next journey's song!) You will find each song on this book's website: LorenLoving.com. Because music plumbs to the depths of the soul and opens doors to the heart that prose can only knock upon, *expect* the Lord to open your heart to things you do not know concerning your heart and His. The songs will also help open your heart to what the Lord wants to reveal through the questions that follow the song. (All the songs were written by Michele Wagner Jacobsen, who graciously gifted my daughter, Kristen Vail Connell, the opportunity to record six of the eight songs.)

6) Each journey presents a variety of Scripture verses. To allow them to permeate your life, approach them this way:

a. First, understand that God's words possess His supernatural, miraculous power to accomplish what He has promised (Isaiah 55:11; Jeremiah 23:29; Romans 1:16; 2 Corinthians 1:20; 1 Peter 1:23; John 6:51; John 1:1, 14). According to Ephesians 1:19–20, the power that raised Christ from the dead is available to you. Hebrews 4:12 states, *For the word of God is alive and powerful. It is sharper than the sharpest two-edged sword, cutting between soul and spirit, between joint and marrow. It exposes our innermost thoughts and desires* (NLT). What makes God's Word so alive and so very powerful? It is a two edged sword—the Word is both *logos* and *rhēma*. When the truth of God's written word (*logos*) is spoken or revealed (*rhēma*) into our souls through Christ's Holy Spirt, the hidden lies that have bound us are broken and we are healed and set free to live as we were intended to live—in the intimacy of His Presence. *He sent forth His word*[6] *and healed them* (Psalm 107:20).

b. Second, memorize those verses that mean the most to you—that is Jesus speaking to you. These verses will have the most powerful impact upon your life. Turn these verses into a prayer to Jesus. Personalize them (insert "I, me, mine"). Meditate on that verse until it fills your soul. Be sure to always speak the verses out loud. Proverbs 18:2 states, *Death and life are in the power of the tongue.* There is a powerful difference between thinking about one of God's promises and speaking that promise out loud. The Genesis account of creation did not simply list everything God made. It shows us that God spoke everything into existence. God's words alone have the power to create, sustain, and give new life. When we speak His words aloud, they will remove the mountains of doubt and fear and shatter the lies that blind and bind us. Hence, speak out loud, into every problem, those Scriptures God's Spirit has impressed upon your spirit. Jesus said, *"Assuredly, I say to you, whoever says to this mountain, 'Be removed and be cast into the sea,' and does not doubt in his heart, but believes that those things he says will be done, he will have whatever he says"* (Mark 11:23).

c. Third, when one of the verses jumps out at you (which is Jesus speaking to you) look up related verses (the cross-references) in a reference Bible (e.g., a Thompson *Chain Reference Bible*) or go to the suggested websites to use the *The Treasury of Scripture Knowledge*. Meditating on several verses about a subject will give you the whole picture. Every part of the Bible needs to be interpreted in light of the whole Bible.

---

6 *Dabar:* The Hebrew equivalent in the Old Testament for the Greek words *logos* and *rhēma* in the New Testament is *dabar*—just one word. Not until the Spirt that raised Christ from the dead was sent to dwell in the bodies of believers would all believers in Christ be able to hear Jesus speak His revelatory *rhēma* words of truth and love into their minds.

A word of encouragement as you commence your journey: If you have never heard Jesus speak to you before, I assure you that you will hear Him clearly at some point in this journey as you patiently wait, seek, and listen. He died to restore you to an intimate relationship with Him. This can only come about through talking honestly with Him. Don't be afraid of the pain that erupts on this journey. That's Jesus cleansing the wound filled with lies. Healing requires feeling, so be sure to grieve freely and fully with Jesus on this journey. Psalm 56:8 states, *You have collected all my tears in your bottle. You have recorded each one in your book* (NLT). Listening to Jesus respond to our pain with His words of comfort and truth shatters the lies. Jesus will always be right by your side. Think about how He brought you to this book. And think of all the other ways He has been "knocking" on the door of your heart throughout your life, pursuing you, wanting so much to sit alone with you and talk to you. Jesus said, *"Behold, I stand at the door and knock. If anyone hears My voice and opens the door, I will come in to him and dine with him, and he with Me"* (Revelation 3:20).

And please also remember this final point: Jesus can heal your heart any way, anywhere, and at any time He wants. There is no formula or precise process. The Holy Spirit will not conform to a program, a meeting, a method, a denomination, or any person's book. He cannot and will not be put into a box. Where the Spirit of the Lord is, there is freedom, because the truth sets us free. And when the Son sets us free, we are free indeed. When Jesus speaks His words of truth and love personally and individually to us, we are healed, set free from the lies that have imprisoned us, set free to soar to heights we have never before imagined or dreamed … free to live again, in a garden of wonder.

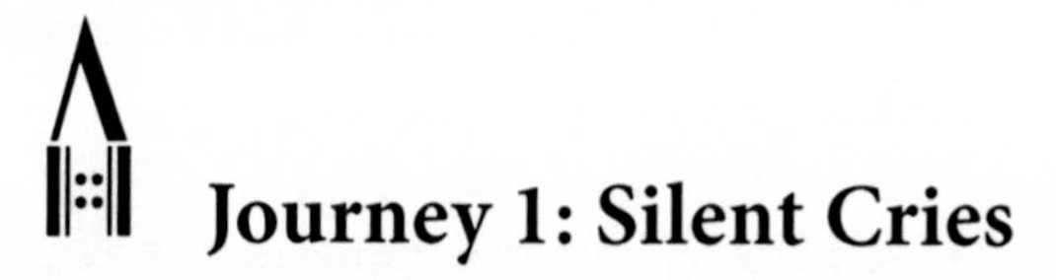

Journey 1: Silent Cries

Pray to Invite the Intimacy of the Presence of Jesus

Ask Jesus to open your ears to hear Him and your eyes to see Him. *Draw near to God and He will draw near to you* (James 4:8). Also, ask Jesus to show you things in the story that are you.

Worship Him

Suggestions: "Yet I Will Praise" and "Ever So Gently," by Vineyard Music; "When You Speak to Me," by Twila Paris; "The More I Seek You," by Gateway Worship; "This Heart of Mine," by Sheri Carr; "After All," by Shelia Walsh; "Come to Me," by Ruth Fazal; "Be Still," by Kari Jobe; "There is None Like You," by Hillsong; "God of My Everything," by Bebo Norman; "Even When It Hurts," by Hillsong United; "Be Still My Soul;" "I Love Your Presence," by Vineyard Music; and "You're Not Alone," by Meredith Andrews.

Could you picture Jesus in any of the worship songs as you closed your eyes and contemplated the words? What was He doing? Did He use a song to draw out feelings you have never before felt? If so, be sure to always talk to Him about these feelings.

Please do not forget to worship in song every day of the week as you work through this journey.

Experience the Story

Daylight fades. The night stalks a slender and drooping figure, wandering deeper and deeper into the valley. The silhouette of a child, bending under an invisible burden, stumbles along an uncertain path. Black clouds gather, blanketing the ominous mountains. The weary child's eyes reflect a hollow emptiness, a despairing loneliness. His journey homeward has been hard, more painful than his tender heart can bear.

With each bend in the path, the child seeks shelter, a warm and welcome smile, or at least a safe place to rest and hide. Longings and doubts lay buried deep within his heart. He wonders, "Can anyone understand the way I feel … Does anyone even care?"

Lightning explodes from the angry clouds as giant raindrops mingle with the child's tears, hiding his sorrow from all who would pass by. Fearful and weary from his seemingly endless journey, the child crawls under the cleft of an overhanging rock to sleep, hoping that some magical fantasy or magnificent dream might offer a welcome escape from his emptiness and sorrow. The child has never felt more alone. Troubled thoughts make him toss and turn. Feelings of abandonment and rejection caused by those he trusted and those he loved have taken their terrible toll.

Indeed, that night the child dreams a dream unlike any other. The rock formation enclosing the child transfigures into arms—arms stronger than those of a protective father and more comforting than the caressing cuddle of a loving mother. As he lies nestled in that secure embrace, beautiful music begins to play. A gentle and compassionate voice softly and melodically begins to sing. And within the lyrics of love, the child hears his name. The warmth and peace that surround him radiate more passionately than flames dancing in a campfire. When the child awakens, a genuine sense of hope still lingers. *Maybe this wasn't a dream*, he thinks.

♫ Listen to the Music

He Knows

The child in you is hurting all alone / No one to talk to, no one seems to know
The weight you are carrying / Is too much for you to bear
You pretend that nobody cares / Well, God is well acquainted with your ways
All your thoughts and how you fill your days /So why are you avoiding
The One who knows you best? / Jesus longs to give you rest!

Chorus:
He knows all the struggles you are going through
He knows the pain you're feeling
He hears the silent cries you hold within your heart
And He wants so much to show you, that He knows

Remember that our God became a man
To feel the way we feel and now He understands
When life brings you heartache, let Him comfort you
Believing that He's been there too

Vocals by Kristen Vail. Written by Michele Wagner & Mark Hauth ©1987 Meadowgreen Music Company (ASCAP) (adm. at CapitolCMGPublishing.com). All rights reserved. Used by permission.

Meditate upon Truth

- *Then Jesus came with them to a place called Gethsemane, and said to the disciples … "My soul is exceedingly sorrowful, even to death. Stay here and watch with Me." … Then all the disciples deserted Him and fled.* (Matthew 26:36–56)

- Jesus weeps for us when we lose a loved one (John 11:17–36). *You care about the anguish of my soul.* (Psalm 31:7b NLT)
- *He is despised and rejected by men, a Man of sorrows and acquainted with grief … Surely He has borne our griefs* [sicknesses] *and carried our sorrows* [pains]. (Isaiah 53:3-4)
- *"Can a mother forget the baby at her breast and have no compassion on the child she has borne? Though she may forget, I will not forget you. See, I have engraved you on the palms of My hands; your walls are ever before Me."* (Isaiah 49:15-16 NIV)
- *You are the helper of the fatherless.* (Psalm 10:14)
- *When my father and mother forsake me, then the Lord will take care of me.* (Psalm 27:10)
- *"So it shall be, while My glory passes by, that I will put you in the cleft of the rock, and will cover you with My hand while I pass by."* (Exodus 33:22)
- *The Lord your God in your midst, the Mighty One, will save; He will rejoice over you with gladness, He will quiet you with His love, He will rejoice over you with singing.* (Zephaniah 3:17)

(See also Hebrews 4:15-16; Psalm 103:13-14; Matthew 27:26-46; John 14:18; 1 Peter 5:7.)

Life Principle:

Journey 1 is realizing the *truth* that Jesus, unlike any other, understands our pain because He has experienced it.

Seek Truth:

1. Did any worship songs remind you of a verse of Scripture? If so, Jesus wants to talk about it. What thoughts or pictures came to mind as you read the allegory and as you listened to the accompanying song? What truths do you think Jesus wants to communicate to you?

2. What Scripture verse meant the most to you in this journey? Why? This is Jesus speaking to you. Cross-reference the verse to have a conversation with Jesus and seal its truth in your heart and mind. Make the verse a prayer and meditate on the verse frequently. How can you apply the verse to your life? Remember to always personalize and constantly say aloud verses that touch your heart, e.g.:

"The Lord my God is by my side, the Mighty One will save me; He will rejoice over me with gladness, He will quiet me with His love, He will rejoice over me with singing!" (Zephaniah 3:17)

3. What major heartaches have you experienced in life? List three in order of difficulty. As you reflect on these experiences (or as you reflect on the song or allegory), does your heart begin to ache? If so, be sure to grieve freely and fully with Jesus. Describe to Him in detail how the painful event made you feel about yourself. Then sit quietly and let Jesus bring His words of comfort and truth to your mind. Please do this whenever and where ever in the journey your heart begins to ache.

4. How had you dealt with each of these pains in the past? What effect have they had on you—what cost did they incur in your life?

5. Do you feel fatherless in any way? If so, how? Is it really true that there is no one to be a father to you? Describe what an ideal father looks like to you. Whom does this resemble? What would you like your heavenly Father to give you that your earthly father hasn't given you? Ask Him. Please write down His response.

Healing comes as we pour out our heart to Jesus, the Creator of our heart, the only One who can truly understand our heartache and heal our brokenness. Always talk to Jesus about pain that you feel. Because He personally experienced injustice, rejection, abuse, shame, loneliness, fear, powerlessness, and terrible physical pain, you can ask Him if He ever experienced pain similar to yours (Isaiah 53:3–4). Wait patiently and listen carefully as Jesus speaks to you in the form of thoughts (and pictures) of truth and love that He places in your mind. When thoughts of Christ's suffering arise, and that suffering is similar to yours, that's Jesus speaking to you. As you reflect on Christ's sufferings, please remember that the reason He suffered and was "tested in every way" was to assure you that He understands and sympathizes with your pain and that you can come to His throne of grace with confidence. There you will always receive His comforting mercy and hear His healing words in your time of need (Hebrews 4:15–16).

6. With what suffering of Jesus do you most identify? What has Jesus said to you about this particular suffering? Can you sense a fellowship or intimate connection with Jesus in this shared heartache?

From now on let no one trouble me,
for I bear in my body the marks of the Lord Jesus.

(Galatians 6:17)

Journey 2: Miracle of Hope

Pray to Invite the Intimacy of the Presence of Jesus

Also, ask Jesus to give you pictures of hope.

Worship Him

Suggestions: "The More I Seek You," by Kari Jobe; "Light of the World," by Lauren Daigle; "It is Well (Live)," by Bethel Music; "All My Hope," by Hillsong; "Trust in Me" and "Come Unto Me," by Gail Mangeri; "How Great Is Our God" and "Holy Is The Lord," by Chris Tomlin; "When Grace Calls You Out," by Laura Kaczor; "Hope of the World," by Hillsong Live; "Above All," by Michael W. Smith; "Revelation Song," by Kari Jobe; "Intimacy," by Jonathan David Helser; "As the Deer," by Marantha! Music; and "In the Garden," by various artists.

What worship song spoke most to your heart? What things did you see as you closed your eyes and made the lyrics a prayer from your heart? What other song in your life has the Lord used to give you hope?

Experience the Story

Sleepy eyes begin to focus. The child stretches and senses the warmth and security of a loving embrace. A muffled sound grows more and more distinct. The child hears what seems to be a faint rhythm echoing his tired, beating heart. Another heart is heard beating in perfect unison, rising and falling with the child's every longing, and responding to his every fear and sorrow.

The child looks up from the chest that holds and consoles him. Within the eyes gazing down into the child's eyes is a love far deeper than the fathomless oceans. The eyes of the One holding him are smiling compassionately and sparkling so joyfully, for the child, and for him alone. Waves of mercy begin to surge and then surround the child's broken heart, flowing into every empty place, drowning every fear and sorrow. He bows his head and closes his eyes. As he snuggles into the arms that hold him so tenderly and securely, the child senses for the first time the warm, wonderful, and loving Presence of the One who came to heal broken hearts. The child breathes deeply. An emerging smile brightens his once-downcast face. Like a warm, incoming tide, grace rises up to wash and soothe his troubled soul.

♫ Listen to the Music

A Miracle of Hope

Hope is the innocent freedom/ Found in the eyes of a child
Trusting that Love's all around them/ Facing their fear with a smile

Somehow the years make us colder/ Careful to cover our hearts
Only the hope of a Savior/ Will keep us from falling apart

Chorus:
Oh, we need Your hand of healing/ We are broken and alone
Like a rushing wind/ Stir our hearts again
With a miracle of hope!
You promise never to leave us/ You know the places we hide

Calling us out of the darkness/ Offering grace and new life
How can we run from Your mercy?/ Why do we run from Your love?
When will we learn to be faithful?/ Trusting Your love is enough
You alone can save us/ You alone can set us free!

Vocals by Kristen Vail. Written by Michele Wagner & Trevor Morgan.
©1999 Safe Place Music (ASCAP) All rights reserved. Used by permission.

Meditate upon Truth

- *Let the beloved of the Lord rest secure in Him, for He shields him all day long, and the one the Lord loves rests between His shoulders.* (Deuteronomy 33:12 NIV)
- *This I recall to my mind, therefore I have hope. Through the Lord's mercies we are not consumed, Because His compassions fail not. They are new every morning; Great is Your faithfulness. "The Lord is my portion," says my soul, "Therefore I hope in Him!" The Lord is good to those who wait for Him, To the soul who seeks Him. It is good that one should hope and wait quietly For the salvation of the Lord.* (Lamentations 3:21–26)
- *The Lord is near to those who have a broken heart, and saves such as have a contrite spirit … and binds up their wounds.* (Psalm 34:18; 147:3)
- *"I know the plans I have for you," says the Lord "They are plans for good and not for disaster, to give you a future and a hope."* (Jeremiah 29:11 NLT)
- *A father to the fatherless, a defender of widows, is God in His holy dwelling. God sets the lonely in families, He leads forth the prisoners with singing.* (Psalm 68:5–6 NIV)

- *Hope deferred makes the heart sick, But desire fulfilled is a tree of life.* (Proverbs 13:12 NASB)
- *"... those who hopefully wait for Me will not be disappointed" ... "Those who hopefully wait for Me will not be put to shame" ... Christ in you, the hope of glory.* (Isaiah 49:23 NASB; Isaiah 49:23 NASB; Colossians 1:27)
- *Now may the God of hope fill you with all joy and peace in believing, that you may abound in hope by the power of the Holy Spirit.* (Romans 15:13)

(See also Joel 2:25–27; Psalm 130:5–7; Proverbs 3:5–6; Romans 5:5.)

Life Principle:

The healing journey is just that—a journey, a process. We can rest on this *truth*: our healing will be found in the journey as long as we listen to Jesus' words of truth and love, and believe that it is through His death and resurrection we are healed of the wrongs done to us and the wrongs that we have done. Jesus is our only Hope.

Seek Truth:

1. What thoughts or pictures came to mind as you read the allegory and listened to "A Miracle of Hope"? What is Jesus saying to you?

2. What Scripture verse in this journey meant the most to you? Why? What do you think Jesus wants you to know? Please cross-reference the verse and seal this truth in your heart and mind. List two or three ways to apply the verse to your life. Remember to always personalize and speak aloud these verses.

3. In your life experience, what took away your childlike innocence, your implicit trust in God?

4. From what sins, habits, addictions, or compulsions (all evidences of a heart bound by pain) would you like to be free? Tell Jesus how these things make you *feel.* What does Jesus think about your feelings?

5. How would freedom from the problems you listed in question 4 change your life? What would this new freedom look like?

Hope deferred makes the heart sick, But desire fulfilled is a tree of life (Proverbs 13:12 NASB). Hope deferred, or a delay in something for which we anxiously await, causes disappointment in life. Disappointments are a very fertile soil for lies. The enemy of our souls uses disappointments to make us question the goodness of God. Then we are vulnerable to the lies that God does not really love us, that we are not significant or valuable. As seen in Eden, Satan attacks our identity by causing us to question what God thinks of us and what He has said to us—His words of truth and love. Hence every lie of the enemy contains a false claim about who God is (attacking God's goodness) and who we are in Him—His beloved child, designed in His image. When we listen to those lies, we become sick, first emotionally and spiritually, and then physically. *Beloved, I pray that you may prosper in all things and be in health, <u>just as your soul prospers</u>* (3 John 1:2).

However, when Jesus lives in our heart, we have absolute and certain hope, because He is our hope (1 Timothy 1:1), our hope of glory (Colossians 1:27). God's glory is the manifestation of Jesus in our life; when we hear His words of truth and love and sense His peace (manifestations of Jesus), we have absolute hope—a confident expectation in God's goodness. Through hope, all impossibilities become possibilities. Hence, if hope in God's goodness is absent in any area of our life, then we can know we are imprisoned to a lie. Hope deferred makes us sick; hope restored makes us and keeps us healthy because the by-product of hope is peace, the antidote to stress and all its illnesses.. Peace is proof that we are truly living in God's Presence, in the confident and joyful expectation of God's goodness and faithfulness in our lives. To the world, peace is merely the absence of things that cause fear, but to the Christian peace is the powerful Presence of the One who banishes all fear.

Healing of life's disappointments comes as we pour out our hurt to Jesus. Whenever your heart breaks as you write out a response to any of these questions, talk to Jesus about the *feelings* you are experiencing. The feelings are more important than the events. For example, in your responses to question 3 and question 5 above, what painful feelings did this bring up? Try to summarize your heartache using single-word descriptions (I feel guilty; I cannot trust; I feel defeated; this makes me feel abandoned; I feel so lonely, etc.). Whenever you share pain and disappointment with Jesus, wait and listen for Him to respond. Always write down the thoughts of truth and love that Jesus brings to your mind. Note with what lies the enemy had deceived you. Never leave the Presence of Jesus until His peace has been restored in your heart.

6. What is it about Jesus that gives you the greatest sense of hope?

Blessed are they whose delight is in the law of the Lord,
and in His law they meditate day and night.
Blessed are they who trust in the Lord
and have made the Lord their hope and confidence.
They shall be like a tree planted by the rivers of water,
whose roots reach deep into water, whose leaves will never whither,
but will always stay green and fruitful.

(Paraphrased from Jeremiah 17:7–8 NLT and Psalm 1:2–3)

Journey 3: True Beauty

Pray to Invite the Intimacy of the Presence of Jesus

Also, ask Jesus to reveal any scars hiding in your heart.

Worship Him

Suggestions: "Captivate Us," by Watermark; "My Beloved," by Kari Jobe; "The Beauty of This Man," by Tim Reimherr; "None But Jesus," by Hillsong United; "All I Have," by Charlie Hall; "What Am I Without You," by Twila Paris; "I've Seen I Am," by Jonathan David Helser; "His Glory Appears," by Hillsong; "Oh Lord You're Beautiful," by Keith Green; "More Precious Than Silver," by various artists.

What song most communicates to you the beauty of the Lord's love for you, and can you feel His love as you listen to the song? If not, ask Jesus to manifest His love to you. He promised He would do this (John 14:21).

Experience the Story

The child rises to his feet. His eyes are filled with wonder and awe. This was not a dream. No, it wasn't! But how could this be possible? How could his wandering heart, so lost in mountains of disappointment and so alone in streams of sorrow, encounter such amazing hope? The child looks again into the tender eyes now fixed upon him.

At first glance, the child sees in those eyes what seems to be the shimmering reflection of a slender, rather indistinct figure. Amazingly, the figure starts to glow and then glisten amid the fiery tears of the One who had held him. The beauty the child beholds in that glistening form is like the brilliance of a diamond enflamed with sunlight. His mind is ablaze with wonder. Stepping closer to look even deeper into the tender eyes, the child gasps in utter astonishment. It just can't be! Could this be true? It is the child's own reflection! He rubs his eyes in disbelief, and yet the closer he looks, the brighter and brighter becomes the child's treasured reflection. Yes, it is certainly true. Never before did the child realize how Jesus sees him.

Looking into the eyes of his Savior, the child saw what transforms him: the refining fire of His radiant love. As that fire blazes, it consumes his ashen heart and miraculously forms a brilliant, shining, and beautifully priceless creation.

Jesus' scars of perfect love uncovered the child's scars hidden deep within his heart, then freed his mind of lies, and filled his heart with truth . . with the radiant beauty of the love of Jesus.

♫ Listen to the Music

You're Beautiful

You line up your failures and count them again / Is there one more second chance?
You've made good first impressions
But their big expectations brought fear along the way
So you hide your dreams you cover your scars
You're afraid someone might know you
But spiritual freedom comes from believing / You're loved as you are

Chorus:
You're beautiful like a diamond in the sun
You're so beautiful, and you're becoming brighter
You're beautiful, and the world needs so much to see
All the treasure in your soul, You're beautiful!

We all are imperfect most insecure / We're afraid of who we are
It's hard to imagine this world that we live in / Could need us at all
But we must be worth something for Jesus to bear / The scars of perfect love
And begin the refining until we are shining / A jewel in His care

Vocals by Michele Wagner. Written by Michele Wagner & Timothy K.S. Norris ©1989 Ariose Music (ASCAP)(adm. at CapitolCMGPublishing.com), New Spring (ASCAP), Paragon Music (ASCAP). All rights reserved. Used by permission.

Meditate upon Truth

- *And God said, "Let us make man in Our image, according to Our likeness" ... put on the new man created to be like God in true righteousness and holiness ... put on the new man who is renewed in knowledge according to the image of Him who created him.* (Genesis 1:26; Ephesians 4:24 NIV; Colossians 3:10)
- *We all, with unveiled face, beholding as in a mirror the glory of the Lord, are being transformed into the same image from glory to glory, just as by the Spirit of the Lord.* (2 Corinthians 3:18)
- *I praise you because I am fearfully and wonderfully made.* (Psalm 139:14)

- *The King will greatly desire your beauty; Because He is your Lord, worship Him.* (Psalm 45:11)
- *"The Spirit of the Lord GOD is upon Me, because the Lord has anointed Me to preach good tidings to the poor ... to heal the brokenhearted, to proclaim liberty for the captives, and the opening of the prison to those who are bound ... to comfort all who mourn ... to give them beauty for ashes, the oil of joy for mourning. the garment of praise for the spirit of heaviness" ... and by His stripes we are healed.* (Isaiah 61:1–3; 53:5)
- *For our citizenship is in heaven, from which we also eagerly wait for the Savior, the Lord Jesus Christ, who will transform our lowly body that it may be conformed to His glorious body.* (Philippians 3:20–21a)
- *He is like a refiner's fire ... and His eyes like a flame of fire.* (Malachi 3:2; Revelation 1:14)
- *Perfect love casts out fear, because fear involves torment.* (1 John 4:18)
- *God has not given us a spirit of fear, but of power and of love and of a sound mind.* (2 Timothy 1:6; see also Psalm 139.)

Life Principle:

Journey 3 involves seeing yourself through your heavenly Father's eyes and embracing that *true* picture of yourself. Truly, the cross is the ultimate revelation of our immense worth and significance.

Seek Truth:

1. What thoughts or pictures came to your mind as you read the allegory and as you listened to "You're Beautiful"? What is Jesus wanting to say to you?

2. Which Scripture verse in this journey meant the most to you? Why? Seal this verse of truth in your heart and mind. Always talk to the Lord about the way the verses touch you. An example: If John 4:18 ("Perfect love casts out fear, because fear involves torment") opened your heart, list the fears that Jesus revealed there. How does His perfect love cast out each of these fears? Ask Jesus to do this.

3. What disappointments have you encountered in life that caused you to hide your dreams? Tell the Lord how this feels. What dreams do you think Jesus has for you? Meditate on Psalm 37:4.

4. Do you know that you are truly beautiful in the Lord's eyes? If not, tell the Lord how you feel about the scars you are hiding. Are these scars based upon truth or lies? If you are uncertain, ask Jesus. Have you ever truly contemplated the scars that Christ endured and now carries for you?

A miracle in healing occurs when the Lord reveals to us *why* we feel negative emotions or feel bad about ourselves. If you feel ugly or shameful or not good enough, or if you struggle with sins, depression, or an addiction and you don't know why, you have become imprisoned to a lie or lies about yourself. If that is the case, or if this unknown surfaces anywhere else in your responses to the questions in this book, read the article "Lies Hurt and Truth Heals," under "Prayers That Can Change and Heal," Section II at the end of the last journey, Journey 8. Then meditate on the sample prayer that follows. Journal this journey and note what Jesus said and did. (Remember that Jesus can reveal His words of truth to you in Scriptures, thoughts, memories, pictures, songs, and even those rare audible words that He brings to your mind.)

5. What characteristics of Jesus are most beautiful to you? When you contemplate the truth that you are designed in His image, can you see this beauty in you? Ask Jesus what He loves most about you.

Journey 4: Immeasurable Worth

Pray to Invite the Intimacy of the Presence of Jesus

Also ask the Lord to show you your immeasurable worth in His sight.

Worship God

Suggestions: "At the Cross," "Mighty to Save," and "We the Redeemed," by Hillsong; "Our God Reigns," by Chris Tomlin; "Song of Solomon," by Martin Smith; "For the Glory of It All," by David Crowder; "Because I Love You," by Graham Cook; "Your Name is Glorious," by Jesus Culture; "Here I Am to Worship," by Chris Tomlin; "Amazing Grace," by Judy Collins; "Broken Vessels" (Amazing Grace), by Hillsong.

What song clearly tells you Jesus loved you so much He died for you? Have you ever thanked Jesus for dying a terrible death so that He could send His Spirit to live inside you and tell you how much He loves you? If not, why not do it now?

Experience the Story

The child begins to weep. Never before has he experienced such love. Never before has he realized that the immense value of his life is found in the love of the One who died for him. The child looks up again into that amazing face. Wonder fills his eyes as he listens to Jesus speak His words of love and hope to him:

> *[Your name], My child, I have loved you with an everlasting love. Yes, I chose you when I planned creation. I knew you even before you were conceived. I knit you together in your mother's womb. You are fearfully and wonderfully made. You were made in My image and My likeness. In Me you live and move and have your being. You certainly were not a mistake, for all your days are written in My book. I determined the exact time of your birth and where you would live. I am familiar with all your ways. I know when you sit down and when you rise up. I even know the number of hairs on your head. I shower My love on you simply because you are My child and I am your Father. I offer you more than your earthly father ever could. I am your provider, and I will meet all your needs. I am your greatest encourager. For I am the perfect Father. I am able to do for you more than you could possibly imagine. I want to show you great and*

marvelous things. Every good gift that you receive comes from My hand. I will never stop doing good for you. I am the Father who comforts you in all your troubles. When you are brokenhearted and feel unworthy of anyone's love, I am close to you. As a shepherd carries a lamb, I have carried you close to My heart. My plan for you has always been to give you a future and a hope. You are My treasured possession. I will never leave you nor forsake you. I will quiet you with My love, and I will rejoice over you with singing. Delight in Me and I will give you the desires of your heart, for it is I who gave you those desires. Your name is written on the palms of My hands! With all My love, your heavenly Father***

(*Paraphrased from the following verses, in order of appearance : Jeremiah 31:3; Ephesians 1:11; Jeremiah 1:5; Psalm 139:13; Psalm 139:14; Genesis 1:26; Acts 17:28; Psalm 139:15-16; Acts 17:26; Psalm 139:3; Psalm 139:2; Matthew 10:30; 1 John 3:1; Matthew 6:31-33; Matthew 7:11; 2 Thessalonians 2:16-17; Matthew 5:48; Ephesians 3:20; Jeremiah 33:3; James 1:17; Jeremiah 32:40; 2 Corinthians 1:4; Psalm 34:18; Isaiah 40:11; Jeremiah 29:11; Exodus 19:5; Deuteronomy 31:8; Zephaniah 3:17; Psalm 37:4; Philippians 2:13; Isaiah 49:16; **A *wonderful* YouTube video that also communicates the above is "God's Love Letter To You.")

This has to be a dream! The longing to know and embrace this love draws the child closer and closer to Jesus' side. The closer he sits to Jesus, the more His peace envelops the child. And the longer he sits listening to Jesus, the more the child longs to be with Him, to be like Him.

But with this longing comes the stirring of a new emotion, of contemplative yet perplexing thoughts. The child hears that familiar echo of his heart beating once again as he sits with Jesus. However, this time there seems to be an unusual heaviness to the rhythm. It sounds almost ominous, like a grieving lament. Doubts, then fears, inside the child's heart begin to swell, blurring Jesus' words of hope, deafening the beating of His heart. What is wrong? Sensing the rising of a feeling of unworthiness in the Presence of Jesus, the child's little heart becomes erratic. He listens intently, anxiously. The echo fades. Then he sobs and cries out, "Where did You go?"

Waves of sorrow bring streams of compassion cascading from the heart of Jesus. The nail-scarred hands reach down and tenderly pick up the tearful, trembling body and carry the child in loving and merciful arms to a place called Calvary.

♫ Listen to the Music

Someone Worth Dying For

Feelings of doubt question your worth / And hang like storm clouds above you
Silent voices cry out, "Look what you've done! / How could Jesus still love you?"
But you're not the nothing they say you are /Remember His scars!

Chorus:
He knew you were someone worth dying for / No one could ever love you more
You're precious to Him, a shining gem / It was for you He paid the price
He knew you were someone worth dying for
Forever a priceless jewel for the Lord
He considered the cost then went to the cross
Oh you must have been someone to Him!

Once you see yourself through His hopeful eyes / I know you'll start believing
There's incredible wealth found in your life / You were bought for a reason
His death was the path His love just had to take / Your soul was at stake!

Bridge:
You may never have the world's affirmation / But here's a truth too hard to ignore
Your heart was valued at the price of salvation / Worth God Himself dying for

Ending:
Oh, you must have been someone to Him!

Vocals by Kristen Vail. Written by Michele Wagner & Mark Hauth ©1992 Meadowgreen Music Company (ASCAP)(adm. at CapitolCMGPublishing.com), New Spring (ASCAP), Paragon Music (ASCAP). All rights reserved. Used by permission.

Meditate upon Truth

- *"My sheep hear My voice, and I know them, and they follow Me" ... and he calls his own sheep by name and leads them out ... He will feed His flock like a shepherd; He will gather the lambs with His arm, And carry them in His bosom, and gently lead those who are with young.* (John 10:27, 10:3; Isaiah 40:11)
- *See what great love the Father has lavished on us, that we should be called the children of God!* (1 John 3:1)
- *In this the love of God was manifested toward us, that God has sent His only begotten Son into the world, that we might live through Him. In this is love: not that we loved God, but that He loved us and sent His Son as the propitiation*

[atoning sacrifice] *for our sins.* (1 John 4:9–10; see also John 3:16).

- *Jesus said to him, "I am the way and the truth and the life. No one comes to the Father except through Me."* (John 14:6)
- *... that if you confess with your mouth Jesus as Lord, and believe in your heart that God raised Him from the dead, you shall be saved; for with the heart man believes, resulting in righteousness, and with the mouth he confesses, resulting in salvation.* (Romans 10:9–10 NASB)
- *God saved you by His grace when you believed. And you can't take credit for this; it is a gift from God. Salvation is not a reward for the good things we have done, so none of us can boast about it.* (Ephesians 2:8–9 NLT)

(See also Ephesians 3:17–19; Psalm 139; John 15:13; Hebrews 2:9.)

Life Principle:

Journey 4 is understanding with our minds and embracing in our hearts the *truth* that God is good. He knows and wants what will bring us complete contentment—intimacy with Him. And because no one in our lives can model the love of God perfectly for us, our journey into the depths of God's heart for us can be hard to comprehend and can take time.

Seek Truth:

1. What thoughts or pictures came to your mind as you read the allegory and as you listened to the song? Has Jesus repeated Himself yet? What has He said about His love for you?

2. What Scripture verse in this journey meant the most to you? Why? Please cross-reference it. What did Jesus want you to know about His heart? Seal this verse in your heart through meditation and prayer. What is the practical application of this verse to your life?

3. Do you think you have failed the Lord in any way? How? How does it make you feel? Please tell Jesus, and then listen to Him. What is God's heart toward you now? Ask Him. What truth did the Lord bring to your mind?

4. Have you experienced times when you felt God let you down? What was the outcome?

5. Do you believe that you are a child of God and that your heavenly Father wants you to have a good future? How do you know you are a child of God? If you are uncertain in the slightest that you are His child, ask Jesus this question: Jesus, did You die for me? When He responds with a thought or picture in your mind, please pray the sample prayer to receive Jesus as your Savior found at the end of Journey 8.

If you have already prayed this or something similar in the past but struggle with the truth that your heavenly Father wants you to have a "good future and a hope" (Jeremiah 29:11), tell Jesus why it is hard for you to believe this. What feelings are associated with these thoughts? What would Jesus say about these thoughts? What would He have you do?

6. To you personally, what is it that makes Jesus worthy of your praise and your worship?

The reason many people do not hear God's voice is because of a wall surrounding their hearts. Before that wall can be torn down, the first question to be addressed concerns the individual's salvation experience—was it real? True repentance means having sorrow for sin, turning away from it, and resolving by God's grace never to return. *For the kind of sorrow God wants us to experience leads us away from sin and results in salvation. There's no regret for that kind of sorrow.* (2 Corinthians 7:10 NLT). When we truly repent with a "godly sorrow" (2 Corinthians 7:10), our way of thinking changes. We now start thinking, acting, feeling, and desiring with God's perspective. An important example is seen in the individual making Jesus the Lord of his or her life. The individual desires to turn from life as it has been—ruled by self—to life where Jesus alone is now Lord. (See Romans 10:9–10.) *Every tongue should confess that Jesus Christ is Lord* (Philippians 2:11). Repentance and Lordship needs to be clearly understood and embraced.

When we choose to give up control of our lives (and other people's lives) and make Jesus the Lord of our life, Jesus honors that prayer. His Spirit takes control and gives us the enabling power to do so, when we ask Him (Chapter 12). Satan wants everything we learn about Jesus to stay in our heads so that our salvation experience is merely intellectual. Hence, when we choose to give Jesus lordship over everything and everyone in our life, the enemy loses control and is defeated.

An excellent illustration of the importance and truth of the above happened while I was working in India with Alice Shevenek. Alice had been a missionary in China for twenty years before she went to India, where she has been ministering for over forty years. We traveled from village to village, meeting and praying with churches whose pastors had become Christians under Alice's ministry. The people walked for miles just to hear Alice preach. Her knowledge and understanding of God's Word was simply remarkable (she would respond to my every question with four or five memorized Scripture verses), and her love for the people of India was precious and beautiful.

At all our meetings, whenever Alice finished sharing God's Word, she would invite people to pray with her to receive Jesus as their personal Savior. That was the peaceful part of the ministry. These Indian people were delightful—very polite, respectful, kind, and, despite their poverty, very hospitable. They were thankful to pray this prayer. (I remember one time standing in a street in India praying for a young mother's child only to look up after the prayer to see a long line had formed with more eager and hungry hearts waiting for me to pray for them.)

After Alice prayed with people for their salvation, she then asked if they would choose to also make Jesus the Lord of their lives. Since Hindus have thousands of gods (manifestations of Brahmin), she made it very clear that for them to be set free from the emptiness and torment that comes from worshiping idols, they needed to understand that their decision meant they would "have no other gods before the Lord God" (Exodus 20:3). Contemplation of that cost was evidenced on many faces, and several people did leave. But it was during this second prayer to be empowered by the fire of Holy Spirit to make Jesus the Lord of their lives, that my theology was startled and my heart gasped. I witnessed evil spirits violently attacking *many* of these people. They were thrown down on the ground screaming, some writhing, some becoming sick. At first it was terribly frightening and disturbing to me. However, I watched Alice walk around the room among those poor imprisoned people and calmly command in the name of Jesus that the evil spirits leave. The people's bodies and minds were put to rest *instantly*. Their countenances changed. The atmosphere in the room changed as peace exuded from healed minds and bodies. (I share more about the ministry of deliverance in Part 2, Section VI.)

My understanding of the salvation experience changed in India. The enemy, I witnessed, has no problem with people praying the simple "sinner's prayer" (i.e., "Thank you, Jesus, for dying for me"), but he attacks mercilessly when people specifically repent of the idols in their life and make Jesus their Lord. However, when people pray and ask God to send the power of the Holy Spirit upon them, Satan will always be defeated in that person's life by the One who crushed Satan on Calvary. That choice and prayer renders Satan powerless to harm those who have stepped down from the throne of their lives to let Jesus regain His rightful position. And as you will see later in this book, that prayer is also the key to pursuing the greatest intimacy we could ever experience in our lives.

Journey 5: Holes in Hearts and Hands

Pray to Invite the Intimacy of the Presence of Jesus

Also, ask Jesus to show you the extent of His love and sacrifice for you.

Worship God

Suggestions: "I am the Bread of Life," by John Michael Talbot; "Lord of Lords" and "At the Cross," by Hillsong; "Come to the Altar," by Elevation Worship; "Grace to Grace," by Hillsong worship; "At the Foot of the Cross," by Kathryn Scott; "How Great is our God," by Chris Tomlin; "Sing to Jesus" and "O Sacred Head Now Wounded," by Fernando Ortega; "This is The Air I Breathe," by Kathryn Scott; "Be Still My Soul," by Katherine Jenkins; "A Beautiful Exchange," by Hillsong; "Touch the Sky," by Hillsong United; "The Old Rugged Cross," by Sandi Patti; "And Can it Be That I Should Gain?" by Marantha! Praise Band; and "Come Thou Fount of Every Blessing," by Mormon Tabernacle Choir.

What song in your life has helped you the most to see your need to seek the mercy and forgiveness of Jesus? Does the song help you feel or sense His mercy in your spirit? Please do not forget to worship in song every day of your life.

Experience the Story

Black clouds gather, darkening the heavens, shadowing the entire earth. As he stands all alone, the child is transfixed by what he sees. The One who carried him to Calvary's hill, now hangs battered and bleeding on a splintered wooden cross. Around the cross, angry crowds mock and jeer. Soldiers spit and slander the innocent Man, who is wrapped in unspeakable agony. As the child's bewildered, horrified gaze turns from Jesus' face to His hands and feet, the child is startled by what he sees. The jagged iron nail in His hands seem to melt and become like a black abyss inside the torn and bleeding hole. A gasp of pain from Jesus causes the abyss to ripple, allowing the child to peer into the depths of the blackness. Held speechless by the sight, the child sees images of hidden sorrow and darkness entangling the child's heart.

Overwhelmed by feelings of pain and shame, the child's mind begins to reel. Pictures from his past advance, and he begins to reflect reluctantly upon those memories. Many times others had hurt him, even those who should have loved him the most. Abuse, neglect, and rejection from family and friends wounded

the child more deeply than the attacks of any enemy; he had not h
assaults well. Anger and unforgiveness lay buried in the deepest, darkest
of his heart. For the first time in his life, the child sees that he has suffered more torment from his sinful responses to the wrongs others had done to him than from the wrongful act itself. They, too, were the reason his newfound best friend and Savior had to die.

The child's bitterness swirls from this deep hidden darkness and seems to buffet the tormented body of Jesus, now hanging limply on the cross. Pain is etched in His face. Crimson streams trickle from His thorn-pricked brow and flow from the blackened nails into the depths of a wellspring called life, at the foot of the cross.

The child looks up. The eyes of his Savior look down at him from His lonely cross, and the child's heart seems to stop. Pangs of conviction pierce to the core of the child's being and his frail legs begin to shake beneath the weight of sorrow and sadness. He whispers, "Forgive me, Jesus," and falls to his knees, hiding his face in his hands.

Ominous clouds gather. Lightning cracks. A strange stillness emerges, quieting the groanings of creation. An eerie silence resounds.

The excruciating torture causes Jesus to gasp, heaving His bleeding chest. Eternity pauses. Suddenly, the endless moment of silence explodes. Jesus' soul-wrenching, victorious cry tears away the veil across heaven's throne and breaks in two the hands of time: "It is finished!"

♫ Listen to the Music

Until You Forgive

You've been wronged / You have wounded
You've been hurting for so long / And you've learned to hide your feelings
As you struggle to be strong / But you can't leave the past behind
There's just no moving on

Chorus:
Until you forgive, I know you'll search for joy
You'll long for the peace to fill your void
You'll wait for the healing of your soul
And look for the love you'll never know
Until you forgive

God is longing to hold you / For He knows how much you ache
All the bitterness inside you / Causes His own heart to break
But in His patience, in His love / He'll wait as long as it takes.

Bridge:
A love that will not let you down / A love that can't be found

Vocals by Kristen Vail. Written by Michele Wagner Jacobsen, Dwight Liles ©2002 Ariose Music (ACSAP) (adm. at CapitolCMGPublishing.com), Safe Place Music Publishing. All rights reserved. Used by permission.

Meditate upon Truth

- *How can I know all the sins lurking in my heart? Cleanse me from these hidden faults.* (Psalm 19:12 NLT)
- See *to it that no one misses the grace of God, and that no bitter root grows up to cause trouble and defile many.* (Hebrews 12:15 NIV)
- *"See, I have inscribed you on the palms of My hands; your walls are continually before Me."* (Isaiah 49:16)
- *... and do not give the devil a foothold ... get rid of all bitterness, rage, and anger, brawling and slander, along with every form of malice. Be kind and compassionate to one another, forgiving each other, just as in Christ God forgave you.* (Ephesians 4:27, 31, 32)
- *All of us like sheep have gone astray, Each of us has turned to his own way; but the Lord has caused the iniquity of us all to fall on Him.* (Isaiah 53:6 NASB)
- *If we confess our sins, He is faithful and just and will forgive us our sins and to cleanse us from all unrighteousness.* (1 John 1:9)

Life Principle:

The journey is understanding the *truth* that bitterness leads to bondage; repentance and forgiveness lead to inexpressible freedom. Although forgiveness is an instantaneous choice, the healing of the pain and shame inflicted upon our hearts (by the wrongful acts of others and by our own unforgiveness) many times can be a journey.

Seek Truth:

1. What thoughts or pictures came to mind as you read the allegory and listened to the song? What truths did Jesus want to communicate to you?

2. What Scripture verse in this journey meant the most to you? Why? Please cross-reference it and seal this truth in your heart and mind. Pray aloud this Scripture. Has Jesus talked to you before about this truth?

3. Have you been wounded more by abuse, neglect, rejection, or abandonment? In what ways? Describe to Jesus how these wounds made you feel, allowing yourself to grieve freely. Tell Jesus about the fears these wounds produced in you. How does Jesus defeat fear? Listen to His response. How did your perspective about your fears change after listening to Jesus?

The wounds others have inflicted upon us above have caused much pain. However the real problem is not about the sins of others but how we have responded. If we don't take our pain and resulting fears (lies) to Jesus for healing, we will become angry and unforgiving. When we respond in this way, the real problem we are struggling with in life is our wrongful, sinful response.

4. What sins* do you harbor that impede your ability to hear Jesus and feel His love? (*actions or attitudes that are inconsistent with the heart of Jesus)

Looking deeper into anger and unforgiveness:

A) Depression and Anger:

Many have called depression "frozen rage." If you struggle with depression, ask Jesus, "Why am I so angry?" Be open to His voice reminding you of people that have hurt you, people you have hurt, or situations that trigger your anger. Pour out your painful feelings to Jesus and listen to His response.

Secondly, depression can be related to a hidden traumatic or tragic event that has been buried or denied in your heart for a long time. See "Prayers That Can Change And Heal," at the end of the Journey 8.

Thirdly, depression can be caused by not doing the work or not living in the place that God intended for you. At the very least, we need to live in community with others who love God. God created us with spiritual DNA. If we are not loving God and loving others with His love, we will despair of life.

Finally, depression can be caused by the oppression of evil spirits. You will read about this problem in Part 2, Section VI and the story of the young suicidal woman whose heart Jesus healed. As with all attacks by the enemy, we need to ask Jesus what gave the enemy of our souls the opportunity or "legal" entry for his demonic army to harm us.

Anger and disappointment with God: When we allow Jesus to work on our anger, keep in mind that the most harmful anger of all is anger toward God for what has happened in our life. Very often, we either don't know this anger exists or we deny it. Ask the Lord to help you keep your heart open to this possibility.

If you discover you are angry at God or if you already know you are disappointed in Him, please remember the following:

- If things did not turn out our way, it does not mean God is not working all things together for our good (Romans 8:28). Because God *is* good, that would be an impossibility. Without a solid, unwavering understanding that God is good, we will continuously flounder and be defeated in our christian walk. When Moses asked to see God's glory - the manifestation of who He is - God said He would show Moses His glory in His *goodness* (Chapter 11).

- Because God is good, we must never accuse Him of unfaithfulness or wrongdoing as we tell Him honestly how we feel about an event. Example: If I rested on a promise of His in the Bible, and things did not turn out the way I thought they should, I can say to Him (honestly) that I know He is faithful and true, but it seems He did not keep His word to me in this situation, etc. Instead of asking Him the why question, ask the Lord what is it about His heart and your heart that He wants you to lean from this experience, and now do about it? Nothing is impossible with God, so every problem is allowed to help make us more like Him so that we can experience His joy.

- Go to His Word and read and read His words of truth until you hear Him speak to you about the pain your poured out to Him. Psalms is the most honest book in the Bible and is very helpful during times we struggle with disappointment in God. Also meditate on the list of healing Scriptures in the appendix (Appendix B).

- When the Lord reveals to you a lie you have embraced about Him or your situation, repent of that lie, and then confess out loud truths about Him that pertain to that situation. Worship Him with songs that declare His faithfulness and power. Offer to Him a sacrifice of thanksgiving. *Let them sacrifice the sacrifices of thanksgiving, and declare His works with rejoicing* (Psalm 107:22). You will know that your heart has experienced deep healing and is no longer angry with God when you are able to honestly say, "thy will be done." ♫ Please listen to the very powerful song, "Thy Will" by Hillary Scott.

I remember praying about my divorce, and once again asking Jesus to help me get out all the terrible pain. As I was telling Him how much it hurt, I asked Him why He had never healed my marriage. "Isn't this why You died?" I lamented. While I cried out this pain to Jesus, His Spirit opened a door to a room I did not know existed in my heart. When I realized it was filled with anger toward Him, I told Jesus how sorry I was for not believing His word, for not trusting Him. And as I spoke those words, the overwhelming peace of His Presence surrounded me. I cannot describe the freedom I found in the Lord's forgiveness, and the love that flooded my heart when my walls of anger came crashing down.

Veiled within our deepest loss or disappointment will be the doorway to our victory—to our destiny. Thus the times we spend in repentance at the feet of Jesus will be some of the most intimate times of all with Him. Our sins are what separate us from the love of God, so when we repent and seek forgiveness, there is nothing in our lives that can hold back the outpouring of His love upon us and through us!

5. Are you disappointed in the Lord for allowing painful things to happen in your life? Could this disappointment really be anger toward Him? What lie had taken root?

B) Unforgiveness:

Are you harboring any bitterness or unforgiveness? If so, against whom? Whom do you need to forgive from your heart that you have trusted in the past? If you are uncertain whether or not you are harboring unforgiveness, ask the Lord to show you. Ask, "Jesus, do I have unforgiveness in my heart toward _______ (his/her name)?" When you say this name, wait to see if the Lord's Spirit reveals a negative emotion about that person. If so, then tell Jesus all the pain this person has caused you and how this pain has affected you—the feelings associated with the pain. Listen to Jesus respond to the feelings you described for Him.

Be sure to ask Jesus to forgive your bitterness, and then ask Him to give you His eyes to see this person (or people) as He does. (A very powerful "picture prayer" to help you in your forgiveness journey is entitled "The Woman Caught in Adultery." It is located at the end of Journey 8, under "Prayers That Can Change and Heal," Section III)

In His healing ministry, Jesus focuses on our unforgiveness, not on the sin of the one who hurt us. Sometimes this can be a long journey. The anger I held against my husband blinded me for so long to my own sin of self-righteousness. After the Lord opened my heart and eyes to His healing words of truth, I was able to see and understand, for the first time, that He "hated" my own sin of pride. (Pride is listed first in the seven sins that God hates in Proverbs 6:16–19.) How Jesus deals with the person who wronged us is not our concern. It is when we confess and repent of our own sin that the Lord forgives us and heals the pain caused by those who hurt us. Jesus replaces our brokenness with a new and compassionate heart—His heart. *Then* we are able to forgive from our heart those who have hurt us, even when they remain unrepentant. This is a miraculous working of the Holy Spirit. He enables us to do what we humanly cannot not do. If you feel unable to seek another's forgiveness or repent of your wrongdoing, or provide restitution for materially harming another, ask the Holy Spirit to work in your heart and help you do this. Healing cannot happen outside of repentance. A heart that remains unrepentant will bring about physical and emotional sickness and disease.

Jesus said in Matthew 5:23–24, "*Therefore if you bring your gift to the altar, and there remember that your brother has something against you, leave your gift there before the altar, and go your way. First be reconciled to your brother, and then come and offer your gift.*" This is a very powerful and profound command. It can and should be read two ways: (1) from the perspective that you have wronged another and (2) from the perspective that you are the innocent party. Even if you think you have done nothing wrong, you are to go to the person who has a problem with you and seek his forgiveness. For what? To correct the misunderstanding that harmed the relationship. Hence, never wait for the other person to ask for your forgiveness. Note that at Calvary, Jesus forgave those who crucified Him as they were mocking Him.

This is the heart of Jesus—the ministry of reconciliation. It is why Jesus died and what He is living to do—to bring reconciliation to broken relationships, first in our relationship with our heavenly Father, then with others. You will know that you have finally forgiven from your heart those who hurt you when you are able to feel compassion for them whenever you think of them. That is the compassion of Jesus that has been released inside you as a result of His healing love.

C) Final Points about Forgiveness:

Forgiveness is *not* saying the event did not matter or was not important; nor does it relieve the wrongdoer of the consequences for his behavior.

Forgiveness *is* choosing not to hold the sin of the wrongdoer against him anymore and releasing him for Jesus Himself to judge. We need Jesus's help to live with the consequences of the wrongdoer's sin and faith to believe that He will turn our ashes into beauty. *Forgiveness is becoming more like Jesus.*

A prayer for forgiveness includes:

- Telling the Lord everything that upsets you about an individual. (Allow yourself to grieve fully.)
- Describing to the Lord how the individual's wrongful actions made you feel.
- Sitting quietly and letting Jesus respond with His words of truth and love.
- Repenting of resentment and feelings of revenge
- Telling the Lord that you choose to forgive the individual for what he/she did or did not do and that you choose not to hold on to resentment. (Healing of the pain cannot commence until you choose to forgive.)
- Thanking Jesus for healing your pain and setting you free from the lie's prison of bitterness. Worship Him in song.
- Verbally blessing those who have hurt you, with the Presence of Jesus. (Please know that until the offender repents and evidences a truly repentant heart in his/her actions, you will need to protect your heart, and maybe your body, with "boundaries." A very good resource on this important topic is a book titled *Boundaries*, by Dr. Henry Cloud and Dr. John Townsend.)

Jesus said, *"Judge not, and you shall not be judged. Condemn not, and you shall not be condemned. Forgive, and you will be forgiven"* (Luke 6:37). When we forgive and pray for those who hurt us, we free them from the bondage of our judgment, and release them to a place where God can deal with them. Then we are set free from the pain (emotional and physical) and the prison of unforgiveness that binds our hearts.

Finally, many counselors quote to those who have been wronged, "*Vengeance is mine, I will repay," says the Lord* (Romans 12:19–21; Deuteronomy 32:35) as words of comfort and assurance that injustice will be remedied. True, righteousness and justice are the foundation of God's throne (Psalm 97:2). However, I have found the most powerful position, meditation, and prayer in regard to injustice in one's life is this: *Let my vindication come from Your Presence* (Psalm 17:2). Remember, God's justice is always deployed against anything that interferes with our love for Him.

A book suggestion for you on this important subject is *Total Forgiveness*, by R.T. Kendall.

Journey 6: The Miracle of Forgiveness

Pray to Invite the Intimacy of the Presence of Jesus

Also, ask Jesus to reveal hidden sins, anything that is not like Jesus inside of you, and help you become so close to Him that your hearts beat as one.

Worship God

Suggestions: "Forever," by Kari Jobe and Brian Johnson; "All Hail King Jesus," by Jeremy Riddle; "How Can it Be," by Lauren Daigle; "Not Guilty," by Mandisa; "Lord Have Mercy," by Michael W. Smith; "Our God," by Chris Tomlin; "Holy One," by Michele Wagner; "Man of Sorrows," "More than Life," and "A Beautiful Exchange," by Hillsong; "Turn Your Eyes Upon Jesus," by Helen Lemmel; "Wonderful, Merciful, Savior," by Selah; "Stricken, Smitten, and Afflicted," by Fernando Ortega; "And Can It Be?" by The London Fox Choir; "Because He Lives," by Kristin Chenoweth; and "There is a Redeemer," by Keith Green and various artists.

What has been your most favorite worship song thus far? Why? What worship song makes you the most thankful for the freedom that Jesus' forgiveness brings to your heart and life?

Experience the Story

The child grimaces against the cold, hard ground. It seems that days have passed since he was able to move. His best friend had died. No one else had ever loved him or could ever love him as much. No one else could reach into the depths of his heart and rescue him from the things that hide there. Only Jesus could touch those places with true healing. Only His words could truly comfort the child. And now that best friend was gone. Overwhelming sadness surrounds the child, attempting to suffocate him.

Rustling leaves. The breath of a warm breeze. Something stirs nearby. The child feels a wonderful warmth next to him. He turns and sees a resemblance of the One who was hanging from the cross, sitting right beside him. He looks again. Is his mind fabricating pictures? Is his heart being deceived by his emotions? Jesus reaches out to gently stroke the trembling child's hair. The child closes his eyes, basking in the comfort of that gentle touch, reveling in the tenderness and warmth of indescribable love. The strong, calloused, nail-pierced hand gently lifts the child's face so that the he can look into the brilliance of eyes radiating the grandeur and joy of life-giving love. The child once again sees his own bright and beautiful diamond-like reflection in Jesus' tears of jubilation. It truly is Jesus, so alive and so real. Oh how long has He been waiting there?

The child sees in Jesus' eyes a longing to hold him. The warmth of mercy and compassion radiates from His face. But the child turns away from the tender, forgiving eyes, so filled with grace. He ponders Jesus' death for him and His love that lives to forgive and heal him. Contemplation compels conviction. The child begins to think of those he hurt unintentionally—the ones he loved and cared for most. As he reflects on the ways he wrongly treated others because of the pain he had unknowingly held inside for so long, remorse and shame stir in his heart. His hurtful actions should have warned him of something wrong inside. But no one had ever told him what would happen if he did not give his pain to Jesus. So many wounds were left open to fester. So many relationships were left unrestored. So much time was wasted running from pain and from the only One who could give him rest.

Hearing the silent cries of the child's heart and seeing the sadness on his face, Jesus tenderly lifts the child into His arms and holds him very close to His heart. Resting against His chest, the child feels His warm breath upon his face. Then Jesus speaks softly into the child's ear. "Father, forgive this child, for he did not know what he was doing." The most amazing, astonishing words of mercy and love, first spoken from a cross of tortuous injustice, enter the child's heart, now opened by brokenness. Compassion and forgiveness flow from the heart of Jesus, filling the child's soul. The walls the child once needed to protect his wounded heart begin to crumble. Painful memories melt away. Freedom erupts, destroying the hollow of guilt. Mercy and compassion flood into his being. The child's repentant and tender heart now weeps for the sins, shortcomings, and woundedness of others. Amazed by the compassion and peace overflowing from his heart, the child wonders, "How long has Jesus been holding me?"

Very slowly, very softly, the faint rhythm that had once echoed in his heart returns. This time the pulse rises, pounding with a passionate crescendo until there is only one powerful beat heard—much more powerful than before. The child's heart has finally become as one with Jesus, its beat rising and falling with His every longing, responding to His every word, overwhelmed by His love, and finally resting in the peace of His Presence.

♫ Listen to the Music

Lord Forgive Them

"My God My God, why have You forsaken Me?
I know it's time that I must die / For all your children
I wear their shame, I bear their pain / That they might gain Your love and Your life
I know that there's a reason for this darkness / I know there's a reason for this day

Chorus:
Lord, forgive them, for they know not what they do
Their hearts are torn in two/ They're living a lie
Your forgiveness can heal their hearts within / And free them from their sin
That they may have Your life / Oh, I pray they have Your life

They laugh at Me, say that I'm not King of Kings / I feel alone and so afraid
They stare at Me while they pierce My hands and feet
Yet do not see the love in My eyes
My love is strong enough that I will die for them
This love could love no other way

Bridge:
With love, the veil has been torn in two
With love, I cry and commit My spirit to You!"

Vocals by Evan Schoombie. Written by Michele Wagner Jacobsen ©1999
Safe Place Music Publishing (ASCAP). All rights reserved. Used by permission.

Meditate upon Truth

- *As God's chosen people, holy and dearly loved, clothe yourselves with compassion, kindness, humility, gentleness, and patience. Bear with each other and forgive whatever grievances you may have against one another. Forgive as the Lord forgave you. And over all these virtues put on love, which binds them all together in perfect unity.* (Colossians 3:12–15 NIV; see also Mark 11:25)
- *The sacrifices of God are a broken spirit, a broken and contrite heart—these O God, You will not despise.* (Psalm 51:17)
- *As far as the east is from the west, so far has He removed our transgressions from us.* (Psalm 103:12)
- *"I, even I, am He who blots out your transgressions for My own sake; And I will not remember your sins."* (Isaiah 43:25)

- *"I have swept away your sins like a cloud. I have scattered your offenses like the morning mist. Oh, return to Me, for I have paid the price to set you free."* (Isaiah 44:22)
- *There is therefore now no condemnation to those who are in Christ Jesus, who do not walk according to the flesh, but according to the Spirit.* (Romans 8:1)
- *If our heart condemns us, God is greater than our heart, and knows all things.* (1 John 3:20)

Life Principle:

Journey 6 is understanding the *truth* that, if denied or not dealt with, our wounds will not only harm us (and even destroy us) but will also harm those who had nothing to do with our being wounded.

Seek Truth:

1. What thoughts or pictures came to your mind as you read the allegory and as you listened to the song? Where could you picture Jesus?

2. What Scripture verse in this journey meant the most to you? Did you meditate upon a truth that you never knew before? Please seal this truth in your heart and mind. As you pray this Scripture, what other verses or thoughts did Jesus bring to your mind?

3. How have your sins* or selfishness interfered with your relationship with the Lord? How have they affected others in your life that you love?

(*Sin means falling short of God's glory, or living contrary to the heart of Jesus [Romans 3:23]. We were designed in our Father's image to behold and radiate His attributes and character so that we could live in relationship with Him and others. Hence, because we are spiritual beings made in God's image, when we sin we live "ingloriously," or void of the radiance and manifestation of God's Presence, separate from Him and others. Sin always leads to death—emotionally, spiritually, and physically.)

4. Do you have any regrets regarding your treatment of yourself? What about your self talk; how do you talk to yourself? What words of love would Jesus say about you? What should you do about any negative judgments you have made about yourself?

Not taking our pain to Jesus buries our pain and holds us imprisoned to judgment, control, bitterness, addictions, etc. Hence it greatly hurts not only us but also the people around us. "No man is an island, entire of itself (unto himself)" (*Meditation XVII*, by John Donne). When I finally realized how much my woundedness had hurt others, I became very remorseful. Because I did not know I needed to give my pain to Jesus, I had only forgiven "from my head," and not "from my heart" those who had hurt me. Freedom came when I repented—when I told Jesus how terrible I felt about hurting innocent people (especially my children)—and when I listened to His compassionate response. Then His love descended and surrounded me in such an amazing way. During times of sorrowful repentance, nothing can stop His love from consuming us. There is no limit to His mercy and grace!

5. What would be necessary for you to feel free from guilt and condemnation?

Please always remember that Jesus never condemns us; nor does He heap guilt upon us—only the enemy of our souls does that. The conviction of the Spirit of Jesus produces *godly sorrow*, which leads to repentance and total freedom (2 Corinthians 7:10). Please meditate upon the words Jesus spoke while He was suffering on Calvary.

Journey 7: The Renewed Path

Pray to Invite the Intimacy of the Presence of Jesus

Also, thank Jesus for His enveloping peace and ask Him to bring a renewed expectation of your glorious future.

Worship God

Suggestions: "I Will Lift My Eyes," by Bebo Norman; "No Longer Slaves," by Bethel Music; "Mountain," by Bryan & Katie Torwalt; "Heart of Worship," by Matt Redmond; "Hosanna," by Brooke Fraser; "None but Jesus," "Healer," "You Are Worthy," "The Power of Your Love," and "Where the Spirit of the Lord Is," by Hillsong; "Closer" and "You Make Me Brave," by Bethel Music; "Give Thanks," by Don Moen; "A Mighty Fortress," by Amy Shreve; "Because He Lives," by Nicole C. Mullen.

What "song of deliverance" do you think has helped you the most in the valley experiences of your life and brought Jesus' beacon of hope to your heart?

Experience the Story

The truth of Christ's words and His love begin flooding the caverns of unforgiveness hidden beneath the crumbling walls that had surrounded the child's heart. Healing waters heave and surge into every hidden place, drowning the anger, fear, and sorrow that had bound the child inside his merciless prison. For the first time in his life, the child feels the exhilaration of true freedom!

The valley no longer looks dark and ominous to the child. He starts to run and leap down the path. Lightning becomes a brilliant, fascinating sight to the child, dazzling the sky with excitement. Thunder is a resounding joy, like the hands of heaven clapping together! The child sees in the clouds a smile of pleasure on the face of his Creator. In the stars, he sees a radiant glory shimmering and reflecting the joy sparkling from his Savior's eyes. The pouring rain becomes a cleansing, quenching shower, drizzling through the trees. Not far off the path, by still and peaceful waters, the child watches sheep gather to rest, safe and secure, in the presence of their Shepherd. Flowing beds of flowers planted by the Shepherd break through the rich soil, adorning the green, luscious valley.

The once downcast, wandering child fixes his gaze above. He looks to the hilltop and listens and waits. Listens and waits. Then he hears his Shepherd's voice! Jesus calls the child to come and watch Him paint the morning sky with the child's favorite colors. The rising sun has never looked more beautiful or felt so warm. In the light of dawn and in the heart of the child, there is an enveloping peace, an assured expectation.

♫ Listen to the Music

Light in the Valley

We call it a valley, our tears fall like rain
We're worn from the journey and weary from the pain
The lonely shadows fall as we descend to the valley

The stars are appearing above the distant hills
We rest by still water in lush, growing fields
The shepherd watches as the sheep lie still, in the valley

Chorus:
In the morning, the Sun of righteousness
Rises to lead us forth with healing in His wings
And in the valley, the Sun is shining bright
I see a ray of hope, with joy my spirit sings
There's light in the valley

We look to the hilltop and hear the Shepherd's cry
He's calling us upward to meet the morning sky
For by His grace and by His strength we climb from the valley
Do you see His light? Oh, there's light in the valley!

Vocals by Kristen Vail Connell. Written by Michele Wagner Jacobsen, Dwight Liles
©2002 Universal Music-MGB Songs / Safe Place Music Publishing (ASCAP)
All rights reserved. Used by permission.

Meditate upon Truth

- *"Every valley shall be exalted, And every mountain and hill made low; The crooked places shall be made straight, And the rough places smooth."* (Isaiah 40:4)
- *"For you who revere my name, the Sun of Righteousness will rise with healing in His wings. And you will go free, leaping with joy like calves let out to pasture."* (Malachi 4:2 NLT)
- *The Lord is my shepherd ... Even though I walk through the darkest valley, I*

will not be afraid, for You are close beside me; Your rod and Your staff protect and comfort me. (Psalm 23:1, 4 NLT)

- *"I will instruct you and teach you in the way you should go: I will guide you with my eye."* (Psalm 32:8) *The steps of a good man are ordered by the Lord, And He delights in his way.* (Psalm 37:23). *You will show me the path of life; In Your Presence is fullness of joy; At Your right hand are pleasures forevermore.* (Psalm 16:11)
- *Then Jesus spoke to them again, saying, "I am the light of the world. He who follows Me shall not walk in darkness, but have the light of life."* (John 8:12)

Life Principle:

Journey 7 is understanding that only God's light of *truth* spoken into our hearts can break the bondage of the darkness that surrounds lies.

Seek Truth:

1. What thoughts or pictures came to mind as you read the allegory and listened to the song? Have you ever seen light radiating from or surrounding Jesus as you picture Him in this journey, or at some other time in your life?

2. What Scripture verse in this journey meant the most to you? Why? Do any of the above verses remind you of another verse or passage of Scripture? What truth does Jesus want you to seal in your heart and mind? Please make this verse a prayer to Jesus.

3. What were the valley experiences in your life that helped you climb mountains; helped you become stronger or experience His love and truth in a new way? Did Jesus ever speak to you in a valley experience with a song?

4. A line from the music says: "We look to the hilltop and hear the Shepherd's cry." *He calls His own sheep by name and leads them out ... "My sheep hear My voice, and I know them"* (John 10:3, 27). Looking back on your life, in what ways has Jesus pursued you? Is He pursuing you the same ways now? In what ways has Jesus called you "by name"?

There are many examples in the Bible of broken people floundering in the valleys of their lives. But that is where they met Jesus, the patient and passionate Pursuer. I encourage you to go through the Gospels (the first four books of the New Testament) and meditate on everything you see about healing in those books. Note what Jesus sees, how He sees people, what He says or does, and the many ways He heals—there is no formula. Note the word "touch" in the healing miracles of Jesus. Note, too, the role of family and friends—how they were used in taking their loved ones to Jesus.

The following are a few examples of Jesus seeking the brokenhearted:

The blind man: In John 9, after Jesus healed the blind man, the man was thrown out of the synagogue by the religious leaders. Then Jesus went looking for him and touched the man's heart as He had his eyes—with healing.

Mary Magdalene: Jesus had healed Mary of terrible emotional oppression (Mark 16:9). And when He died, Mary suffered greatly. So Jesus went to comfort Mary as she was weeping at His tomb. Mary heard Jesus call her by name, and His words restored hope to her soul (John 20). (Book suggestion, *When God whispers Your Name*, by Max Lucado.)

Thomas: Thomas's refusal to believe that Jesus had risen from the dead brought Jesus to the room where Thomas was hiding. Jesus showed Thomas the scars in His hands and side. Then Thomas worshiped Jesus as his risen Lord, who had suffered and died for him (John 20).

Peter: Peter grieved terribly and suffered much guilt and shame for having denied Jesus. Notice how Jesus heals Peter's pain of that awful memory: Jesus recreates the John 18:18 fire. How heartbreaking that must have been for Peter! But now he sees Jesus next to the fire. Three times Peter denied Jesus, so Jesus, full of mercy, talks to Peter three times about Peter's love for Jesus.

The disciples: Two of Jesus' disciples, unaware that He had risen from the dead, grieved as they walked together on the road to Emmaus. Jesus went to them and asked them to share their conversation, their thoughts, with Him. Blinded by grief, the men did not recognize Jesus. Then Jesus opened the Scriptures and showed them many truths in God's written Word. After that, Jesus dined with them. Then, when Jesus blessed the bread, broke it, and gave it to the disciples, their eyes were opened and they recognized Him, the One, whose body had been broken for them. The Presence of Jesus and the words He spoke to the disciples made their hearts "burn" for Him (Luke 24, especially verse 32).

Every time you read these accounts and others in the Gospels, and in the rest of the Bible (e.g., Adam and Eve, Cain, Hagar, Elijah, Daniel), you will see something wonderful about Jesus' compassion for our broken hearts and bodies. Truly, He is our passionate Pursuer. So let God be God and let Him speak to you, heal you, and love you however and whenever He desires.

Journey 8: Indescribable Freedom

Pray to Invite the Intimacy of the Presence of Jesus

Also, ask Jesus to manifest to you, in whatever way He chooses, God's amazing glory.

Worship God

Suggestions: "Here's My Heart," by Lauren Daigle; "Glorious," by Brian and Katie Torwalt; "I Will Rise." by Chris Tomlin; "You Are My All In All," Maranath! Music; "Walk With Me," by Jesus Culture; "Waste It All," "Pursuit," and "I Surrender," by Kim Walker-Smith; "None but Jesus," by Hillsong Live; "She Gave Her All," by Michele Wagner; "No Borders," by Ginny Owens; "I Give You My Heart," by Hillsong; "Deep In Love with You" and "All I Want," by Michael W. Smith; "I Am Yours," "Let Me Love You More" and "Lovesick," by Misty Edwards; "Do I Love You First?" by Michael Wagner; "I Exalt Thee," by Alleluia Worship Band, Jesus Culture, etc.; "I Love You Lord," by Kelly Willard; "Come to Jesus," by Chris Rice; "I Surrender All," by Helena; "Like an Avalanche," "More Than Life," "Love Is War," and "Oceans," by Hillsong United; "Every Praise," by Hezekiah Walker.

Please do not forget to worship in song every time you get alone with Jesus, throughout your day, and for the rest of your life. Never leave your time alone with Jesus until you have heard Him speak to you.

Experience the Story

The night ends. The light of day, that radiance of new and abundant life, has finally dawned. The wandering and searching are over. There is no more bitterness, no more emptiness. The child has fallen in love with Jesus—his Savior and Healer, and the One who brought him to the Father he had always longed for. While resting in His arms, looking into His loving eyes, and listening to the only voice that shatters all lies and dispels all fears, the child is filled with penetrating peace. Complete security. Unquestionable identity and worth—he is his heavenly Father's child!

Living in the light of God's Presence, the child revels in the joyful inner laughter of indescribable freedom. That freedom sings of his Father's glory—the love of his Father as manifested in the majesty and beauty of Jesus. As his songs build a rising crescendo of thanksgiving and adoration within the depths of the child's soul, the flame that flickered in his heart now becomes an unquenchable fire consuming his very being, impassioning the child to love others with the love of his adoring Father. Clothed in robes of royalty, the child is empowered with his Father's glory to climb unimaginable heights, to fight any foe, to conquer the impossible, and to be a compassionate instrument of hope and healing for the broken and weary hearts of others.

The child's once desperate dream of a safe, warm, loving home and refuge is now fulfilled and forever sealed in the Presence of the Lover of his soul, whose voice is unmistakable, whose love will never fade, nor ever fail, and whose peace is constant and unshakable. Hope assured, eternally.

♫ Listen to the Music

With My All

The night is done the day has come / The darkness slowly melts away
The past is gone my heart is won / I'm never going to be the same
Lord, I have looked into Your eyes / And I have seen Your love for me

Chorus:
With my heart, with my will
With my mind and strength until my life is done
I will love You with my all
With my dreams, with my hopes
I will stay and never go because You are the One
I will love You with my all

So take me now into Your world / And I will take You into mine
I want to give each day I live / To You until the end of time
For You have bound my soul to You / And You have set my spirit free

Bridge:
All I have, all I am, all I want to be is Yours

Vocals by Kristen Vail Connell & Michele Wagner Jacobsen. Written by Michele Wagner Jacobsen & Dwight Liles ©2000 Safe Place Music, Universal Music-MGB Songs. All rights reserved. Used by permission.

Listen also to the song, "I Surrender," by Jesus Culture, by Hillsong Live, and by Celine Dion (imagine Jesus is the You to whom Celine is singing!)

Meditate upon Truth

- *Therefore, if anyone is in Christ, he is a new creation; old things have passed away; behold, all things have become new.* (2 Corinthians 5:17)
- *Jesus replied, "Anyone who loves Me will obey My teaching. My Father will love them, and We will come to them and make Our home with them."* (John 14:23 NIV)
- *And He said, "My Presence will go with you, and I will give you rest."* (Exodus 33:14)
- *Jesus said, "Now remain in My love. If you obey My commands, you will remain in My love ... I have told you this so that My joy may be in you and that your joy may be complete"* (John 15:9, 11 NIV). *Your word have I hidden in my heart, That I might not sin against You.* (Psalm 119:11)
- *"You shall know the truth and the truth shall make you free ... Therefore, <u>if the Son makes you free</u>, you shall be free indeed."* (John 8:32, 36)
- *And behold, I am sending forth the promise of My Father upon you; but you are to stay in the city until you have been clothed with power from on high.* (Luke 24:49 NASB).
- *If you spend yourselves in behalf of the hungry and satisfy the needs of the oppressed, then your light will rise in the darkness, and your night will become like the noonday.* (Isaiah 58:10 NIV)
- *Only fear the Lord, and serve Him in truth with all your heart; for consider what great things He has done for you.* (1 Samuel 12:24)

Life Principle:

Journey 8 is remembering that Jesus is *truth*. Hearing Him speak His words of truth and love is what sets us free from ourselves (from our selfishness, control, bitterness, addictions, and lies) to love Him and to love others as He does, unconditionally.

Seek Truth:

1. What thoughts or pictures came to mind as you read the allegory and listened to the song? Have you ever felt the intimate, unconditional, and pure love of Jesus?

2. What Scripture verse in this journey does Jesus want you to meditate upon? Did He bring other thoughts of truth to your mind with this verse? If so, He is wanting to have a conversation with you. Remember to always personalize and speak aloud these verses.

3. Have you been made a "new" creation in Christ? If so, describe this newness.

Scriptural evidences and descriptions of that new life in Christ include unconditional love, a joy that no man can take away, a peace that passes understanding, a "longsuffering" or patient spirit, forgiveness, sacrifice, meekness and kindness, goodness and generosity, compassion and gentleness, truthfulness, and faithfulness.

4. What does it mean to you to enter into the intimate Presence of Jesus? How does obeying the Lord enable you to live in His love and abide/stay in His Presence? God's peace is the litmus test of living in His Presence. Whenever we do not sense the peace of the Prince of Peace inside of us, we can go to the feet of Jesus, ask Him why we don't, and have His peace restored as we listen to and obey His words of truth and love. (Book suggestion: *Hosting the Presence*, by Bill Johnson.)

If after making a conscious and determined choice to obey God you still find obedience hard, tell Jesus how hard it is. Then ask for His help. (How Jesus empowers us is the subject of Chapter 12.) But remember this: Our struggles with obedience, faith, trust, sacrifice, etc., are not always our real problems. Our real problem is a love problem. That's why this journey is all about falling in love with Jesus—daily entering into His Presence, worshiping Him, listening to His words of truth and love, and experiencing the wonderful manifestation of His Presence touch our spirit. The peace and love that fill us each day as we spend time alone with Jesus will produce a confidence and trust in Him so strong, so secure, that nothing can shake or defeat us in life. As King David—the Bible's most passionate worshiper—said, *I have set the Lord always before me. Because He is at my right hand, I will not be shaken* (Psalm 16:8).

5. Has God's love ever flooded your heart through the Holy Spirit? Have you ever sought, waited, and wrestled with God for that sudden, tangible evidence of His Spirit coming upon or moving within your spirit? *"Call to Me, and I will answer you, and show you great and mighty things, which you do not know"* (Jeremiah 33:3).

Worship God

Ecclesiastes 3:1 and 4 states, *To everything there is a season, A time for every purpose under heaven ... a time to weep, and a time to laugh; a time to mourn, and a time to dance*. Now that you have entered the garden and refuge of His Presence, I encourage you to dance with Him! Suggested dancing songs: "I am Free" and "Something Wonderful," by the Newsboys; "In the River," by Jesus Culture/Kim Walker Smith; "Glorious," by Brian and Katie Torwalt; "Rooftops," "Your Love Never Fails," "King of Glory," and "Dance (Live)," by Jesus Culture; "Eden" and "This is Amazing Grace," by Phil Wickham; "Adonai," by Paul Wilbur; "Chasing You," by Bethel Music; "Overcomer," and "Shackles," by Mandisa; "Price of Love" and "Dancing Girl," by Heather Clark; "The River is Rising," by Michael W. Smith; "Looking Forward," by Michele Wagner; "Like," by Mike Smith Band; "One Thing Remains," by Soul Survivor and by Melissa How; "King of My Soul," by Matt Redmond. Pray that a dance rises up around the world for Jesus—be sure to see the following YouTube videos: "Resurrection Sunday Dance," Budapest, Hungary (2010); and "Up to Faith Global Dance 2012," Bern, Switzerland.

Which song helps you rejoice in the love of Jesus or feel His love the most? What are your own favorite dancing songs?

You turned my wailing into dancing; you removed my sackcloth and clothed me with joy, that my heart may sing to you and not be silent. O Lord my God, I will give you thanks forever.

(Psalm 30:11, 12 NIV)

Prayers That Can Change and Heal

The journey is all about listening to Jesus. This chapter contains *sample* prayers that can help us talk with Jesus about the walls in our heart and the wonders of His heart.

I. Prayer to receive Christ as your personal Savior:

The most important decision you will ever make in life is to make Jesus your Savior and your Lord. The amazing life that can be yours—listening to Jesus, hearing His words of truth and love fill your mind and heal your heart, and feeling His love and peace surround you—requires the Holy Spirit to be living inside you. If you have never asked Jesus to send His Spirit to come and live inside your heart, please do so today by praying this prayer. Then follow Jesus' example and command and be baptized in water (Matthew 3:16; 28:19). Baptism is a public declaration of a personal conviction, regarding Christ's death and resurrection, and a commitment to live for the Lord. And, like Jesus' baptism, it can be a very powerful encounter with the Holy Spirit. As we go down into the water, we confess that we have died to our sins, and when we come up out of the water we avow that we have been risen to new life in Christ (Colossians 2:12). Making Jesus our Savior and Lord means giving Him our life, in exchange for His.

Father, open my heart to Your precious Holy Spirit. I believe that Your Son, Jesus Christ died a terrible death on the cross to shed His blood for my sins, for my selfishness. I believe that He rose from the dead and is alive and is seated at Your right hand. Please forgive me of my sins and cleanse me from having lived life my own way, outside of Your Presence. I repent of and I am sorry for ________________________. Help me to forgive others as You have forgiven me. Please change the way I think. Reveal any lies hidden within my heart and heal me.

Jesus, I believe in my heart and confess with my mouth that You are my Savior and my Lord. May the power of Your Holy Spirit living in me help me surrender completely to You so that You may always rule and reign in my life, making my heart just like Yours. I want to always hear Your voice —Your words of truth and love—above every other voice in my life. I want Your goodness and kindness, Your love, joy, and peace, Your faithfulness and purity, and other fruits* of Your precious Holy Sprit to be powerfully manifested in every aspect of my life.

Thank You for seeing me as Your very special child; as someone worth dying for. Please fill me so full with Your Spirit that Your love overflows my heart into the hearts of my family and friends. I want to live and sing in Your Presence each day of my life. In the name of Jesus I ask this.

(A prayer to be clothed with the glory of God will be presented in Chapter 12.)

Please meditate upon these important Scriptures:
Romans 3:10; 6:2; Isaiah 53:6; 1 John 1:9; Romans 10:9-10 NASB, 13; Matthew 10:32; Acts 4:12; 1 Timothy 2:5; Ephesians 2:8-9; 1 John 5:11-13; John 10:27-30; Luke 11:13; Fruits* of the Spirit - Galatians 5:22-23 and 1 Corinthians 13.

II. Prayers to heal the wounds in your heart:

(See Isaiah 61:1; 53:5; Matthew 8:16–17; Luke 4:18; Psalm 107:20; 147:3.)

Important note: The Lord can heal a heart in any way He desires. These prayers are simply aids. Let the Holy Spirit guide you in prayer, leading you as *He* (vs. the prayer) directs. If possible, pray with someone who has experienced the Lord's healing touch. Before you pray, please listen once more to the song "He Knows," from Journey 1.

A. When you are suffering because of a painful event:

Ask the Holy Spirit, now living within you, to open the doors of your heart to the Lord and His love for you. *The spirit of man is the lamp of the Lord, searching all the inner depths of his heart* (Proverbs 20:27). Think of your deepest burden or fear, and ask Jesus to release the pain that is buried there. Honestly and truthfully tell Him how you *feel* about this heartbreaking event. Try to describe your feelings with single words, and write them down on paper.

If the Lord reveals any hidden anger in your heart toward Him (an unknown wall in many people's hearts), pause and reflect. Do you need to ask Jesus where He was when this heartache occurred, how He could have let this happen, whether He really loves you, etc.? Consider any other questions that are unique to your experience and pour them out to the Lord. Whenever you feel pain, allow yourself to grieve freely and fully. Please know that, *The Lord is near to all who call upon Him, to all who call upon Him in truth* (Psalm 145:18).

Thank Jesus for His closeness, and ask Him to speak to you about the feelings you poured out to Him. Sit quietly and wait patiently, believing Jesus is with you. Listen for Him to respond to what you just told Him. What truth does Jesus reveal in response to your words describing how this heartache feels? What was Jesus' response if you told Him you were fearful or lonely, etc.? How did Jesus respond if you told Him you doubted His love for you? Jesus' words are always words of truth and love. Write His responses next to your list of words and the questions above. Look up the words He spoke to you in the Bible. Memorize the verses that are most on point regarding your situation, and apply them to your life. Whenever you talk with Jesus, remember that He, too, experienced the same pain here on earth. "He knows all the struggles you are going through; He knows the pain you're feeling" (See the song "He Knows," as well as Hebrews 4).

While thinking about the words of truth and love that Jesus just spoke, believe that Jesus is very near you, and wait patiently until He does something. Look into His eyes to see the depths of His love for you while you are waiting. Be patient. If you have never seen Jesus do something before in your prayers or worship, then ask, "Jesus, what do You want to do?" If His arms are reaching out to you, will you let Him hold you? As you sit there watching Jesus, can you see His love for you in His actions? If you have harbored anger or resentment against others or against Him in your heart concerning this pain, confess it and ask for His forgiveness. Ask Him to help you forgive the one who hurt you. And if you have broken someone else's heart, tell the Lord you will ask for that person's forgiveness, and ask the Lord to help you do this.

Remember to always write down whatever Jesus says and does when you are with Him.

B. When you struggle with depression or addictions and you don't understand why:

Please read the following article before you meditate on the prayer:

Lies Hurt and the Truth Heals

By Dennis and Melanie Morgan-Dohner

©Big God Ministries, Inc., Lafayette IN. All rights reserved. Used by permission.

"And you shall know the truth, and the truth shall make you free" ...

—John 8:32

We react to life and interpret life events through our past experiences. In fact, most of our emotional reactions are formed before we are eight years old. In our early years, we learn about fear. We come to conclusions which become judgments, we make vows that we think will protect us, and we hear many lies from the enemy. Satan watches for times and places where we are vulnerable, and he speaks into our situations and experiences, lending his own twisted explanation for things that happen. Much of what we come to believe becomes hidden, as we grow up and those experiences fade into our memories. But, even while hidden from our conscious minds, those beliefs [lies] go on to motivate and influence our behavior—and they cause pain to be re-lived.

People think their pain is coming from their present, but it is coming from their past. The past is shadowing, or obscuring, truth that could lead toward resolution of the present. Our brains associate current things with past things. For example: a situation at work has similarity with a childhood incident with a brother, and suddenly we are acting as if we are involved in a sibling fight. Or an employer says something to us, and instantly we are attributing the characteristics of an angry parent to that person. Something that was said or done today reminded us, on a deep level, of something we learned much earlier.

The problem is what we usually learned [in painful situations] was based on lies, rather than truth. Every time we heard and believed statements like; "You're no good," "You'll never be worth anything," "I wish you weren't here," lies were planted. When we have believed we were abandoned, unwanted, or unloved, we have believed lies. Why are these lies? Because Jesus has been beside us, has loved us and will never stop loving us. In a way that a human parent or friend could never do, He stands ready and willing to fill the depth of love needs that we have.

Some of us had loving parents, while others of us grew up in horrendous and abusive situations. Either way, there were events that shaped us, and things we came to believe. Even in the most healthy and loving home, there are times when a parent is tired or irritable or overwhelmed, and things are said and done which cause pain—the pain of feeling separated, unworthy or unloved. Why does it still hurt? What is it that hurts? If a man was hit by his father, thirty-years ago, he does not still feel physical pain. The place where the blow struck does not still hurt. But if thinking about it is painful, there is an emotional wound—unhealed. Perhaps he believed that this signaled the end of his father's love, or that it was a more true representation of his father's feelings for him than the rest of the day. That is where the pain comes from—what he came to think he knew, from the event.

When the past is healed, the present is restored. Jesus speaks truth—the truth that has been missing—and His words dispel the lie. In fact, His words begin to unravel the web of lies that has been built upon as different life circumstances seemed to reinforce them. The memories don't change, but the person's interpretation does. What he comes away with is a different belief. When the man mentioned above hears Jesus tell him that He has always been there, and has always loved and valued him, his heart becomes healed.

Our inner-most self craves affirmation and relationship that no human can sufficiently provide. That our parents, or siblings or people in authority. etc., left us with sore and hurting places is not a shameful thing - it is a human thing. In the worst cases of human abuse, knowing that Jesus has love and hope, and being able to hear Him talk about the hurt (and forgiveness) brings a redemptive healing so profound that many people later feel only sorrow or pity for the perpetrator, where before there had been only hate and unforgiveness. God stands outside of time and space as we know it. He knows every root place where we have believed a lie, and He will meet us there.

Jesus is, and has been, speaking words of Life to us and over us. If we are hearing and believing things other than what He is saying, we are accepting lies. What hopelessness says is not true anywhere in the universe, except for the demonic. Always, there is an answer. Always, there is hope. Jesus has paid for all our sins and all sins committed against us—He has peace and healing for us—and He is generous with it. Our hope and freedom are in Him alone.

Ask the Holy Spirit, now residing within you, to shine His light of truth into the hidden places of your heart. Listen to a song about the Lord that touches you deeply or makes you cry for His love. Then make a list of the deepest feelings or fears you are experiencing. (You do not need to describe the events or circumstances associated with these feelings.)

Because depression and addictions are due to unresolved pain in our lives, ask the Holy Spirit to show you how the feelings began. When did you first sense this feeling? What was going on in your life? Who was in your life at that time? Wait patiently on the Lord; He is your wonderful Counselor and gentle Healer. When you see, hear, or feel a memory or a picture, release your emotions surrounding this memory or picture and pour out all the pain to Jesus. Write down all the feelings that surface. Note especially how these feelings made you think about yourself. Allow yourself to grieve fully and freely.

Identify the lies: Ask Jesus to respond to each feeling you listed with His words of truth and love. When He does, note the wrongful, imprisoning thoughts that you had believed about yourself or someone else because of this experience. What wrong vows or condemning judgments did you make (e.g., "I'll never be like him/her," "I will never amount to anything in life.")? Next to every lie you believed about yourself, write down Jesus' words of truth that shatters that lie.

Ask the Lord to forgive you for believing lies, making wrongful vows, or speaking condemnation. Listen to His words of grace and mercy, including "Father, forgive her for she did not know what she was doing" (Luke 23:34). (Remember to always write down/journal whatever Jesus says to you or shows you.) Look up verses in the Bible relating to the words Jesus spoke to you. Memorize the verses that are most on point regarding your situation and apply them to your life. God's truth alone breaks the power of lies. If someone's words or actions harmed you, leading you to believe lies, ask the Lord to help you forgive that person also.

Summary of "Prayers That Can Change and Heal"

Pour out to Jesus the deepest burden you carry—tell Him how this burden makes you feel, allowing yourself to grieve fully and freely.

Quietly wait and listen to Jesus respond to your cries with His words of truth and love.

Confess and repent of your wrongful thinking and actions.

Embrace forgiveness.

Then Jesus said to those who believed ... "And you shall know the truth, and the truth shall make you free ... therefore if the Son makes you free, you shall be free indeed." (John 8:31, 32, 36)

He sent His word and healed them; And delivered them from their destructions. (Psalm 107:19, 20)

III. Picture Prayers

(Written for this ministry by Betsy Lee, Prayer Ventures, Bloomington, MN prayerventures.org)

A. The Healing of Peter's Heart:

Read and reflect on John 21:1-19:

After these things Jesus showed Himself again to the disciples at the Sea of Tiberias ...

But when the morning had now come, Jesus stood on the shore; yet the disciples did not know that it was Jesus ... Then that disciple whom Jesus loved said to Peter, "It's the Lord! ..."

As soon as they had come to land, they saw a fire of coals there, and fish laid on it, and bread ...

Jesus said to them, "Come and have breakfast" ...

So when they had eaten breakfast, Jesus said to Simon Peter, "Simon, son of Jonah, do you love Me more than these?" He said to Him, "Yes Lord; You know that I love You." Jesus said to Him, "Feed my lambs."

Jesus said to him again a second time, "Simon, son of Jonah, do you love Me?" He answered, "Yes, Lord, You know that I love You." Jesus said to him, "Tend My sheep."

Jesus said to him the third time, "Simon, son of Jonah, do you love Me?" Peter was grieved because Jesus said to him the third time, "Do you love Me?" He said, "Lord, You know all things; You know that I love You." Jesus said, "Feed my sheep"... And when Jesus had spoken this, He said to him, "Follow me!"

The Prayer:

Picture yourself as Peter, the strong, passionate disciple. It is early morning, just before dawn. You are worn out from fishing all night. Your mind wanders as you rock back and forth on a gray, sullen sea. It wanders back to another predawn morning. You are huddled in front of a coal fire in a Roman courtyard where Jesus is about to be tried. Strangers sitting around the fire recognize you as Jesus' friend. "I don't know the man!" you insist. Suddenly, a cock crows, and you remember Jesus' words: "Before the rooster crows today, you will disown me three times."

Disown Jesus? How could you have betrayed your closest friend? Only hours before, you had sworn that you would never desert Him. "Even if I have to die with you," you boasted, "I will never disown you." Yet you did.

Jesus had looked straight at you as the soldiers took Him away. The sadness in His eyes pierced your heart. Filled with remorse, you turned away and wept bitterly. How could you ever erase that terrible memory from your mind?

Suddenly you are jolted from your thoughts by an outcry on the boat. Someone is pointing toward the shore and shouting, "It's the Lord! It's the Lord!" What? Your friends must be imagining things. It has been a long night. Everyone's tired … and a little crazy.

In the distance, you see a man standing on the beach. A stranger? An apparition? As you head closer toward shore, you are astonished. You strain to see for yourself. Can it be? Yes … it really is Him!

As you come ashore, Jesus stretches out His hand to you and the others. He smiles, putting you at ease. "Come and have breakfast," He says. He invites you to sit down and eat the food He's prepared.

You can hardly believe it. It's just like old times, sitting around a campfire with a small circle of friends, sharing a meal and listening with wonder to Jesus. Oh, how good it is to be with Him again.

Your own joy is tinged with sadness. You glance at Jesus and then look away. It is hard to look into His face. You stare instead at the burning coals, shame burning within you.

After the meal is finished, Jesus draws you aside from the others. He invites you to go for a walk. The water beside you is quiet, spread out, still. The waves gently lap the shore.

At first there is silence. A long silence. You bask in that silence, enjoying the physical presence of Jesus, the sense of His being there. Jesus breaks the silence with a question. "Peter, do you love me?"

You're stunned. You love this man more than you've loved anyone else. He understands you as no one else ever has; He accepts you as no one else ever could. "Yes, Lord, you know that I love you."

Jesus asks not once, but three times: "Do you love me? Do you love me?" Each time, He searches deeper. "Do you love me?" You remember the crow of the cock and bitter tears of betrayal, yet there's no hint of accusation in Jesus' voice, but only grace, forgiveness, like waves washing over the sand, erasing the footprints behind you.

The affection in His voice is reassuring, gentle. "If you love me," Jesus says, "follow me. Leave the past behind—the mistakes, the failures." Jesus stops walking. He turns to you and rests His hands on your shoulders. "If I kept a record of wrongs, Peter, who could stand? My love covers a multitude of sins."

Now you know why He asked the piercing question "Do you love me?" It was not to condemn you, but to restore what had been lost between you. Three times you denied Him; three times you were given a chance to reaffirm your love for Him.

As the Lord touches you, you feel His forgiveness flow into you and feel a sense of sweet release. You can look into His eyes now, freely, without reservation. The heaviness in your heart seems to lift like the darkness around you dissolving with the light of day.

"If you love me, Peter, feed my sheep," Jesus says. "As you have received, gladly give. Let my love flow out to others."

As you walk on together, you notice the nail marks in Jesus' hands and feet. You know so little of what real love is.

"If you love me," Jesus says, "feed my sheep."

How can you love as Jesus does? You are just a fisherman. Your hands are calloused, not tender; your words rough, not compassionate. How could *your* hands heal? How could *your* words offer hope to a hurting world?

You feel a longing in your heart, an expectancy. Perhaps there is something of the Shepherd in you, for you yearn to see people touched by Jesus as you have been touched; to know His love, His forgiveness, His grace.

"Follow me," says Jesus. "Follow me. Give me the ordinary things of your life, and I will do something extraordinary."

* * *

Peter did follow Jesus, and God did do extraordinary things through him. He served the Lord faithfully, performed healing miracles as Jesus did, resurrected someone from the dead, and wrote letters (now two books of the Bible) to encourage believers to stand fast and true in the midst of persecution and trials. In 1 Peter 5:7 he writes of the Lord's compassion that he knew so well. *Cast all your anxiety upon Him, for He cares for you* (NIV). Was Peter someone worth dying for? Of course. Are you? Follow Him and see.

The Healing of Peter's Heart—Personal Reflection

Do you doubt whether you are worthy of God's love? Where do these doubts come from?

Is guilt over past sins a problem for you, as it was for Peter? Where is this guilt coming from?

In the picture prayer, Jesus heals pain from the past in Peter's life. Jesus recreated the scene of the betrayal by making a coal fire just like the one from the painful memory. Then He asked Peter three times to reaffirm his love for Jesus to erase the guilt of the three denials. This created a new, positive memory. You might try the following prayer to heal a hurtful memory. Here are three steps:

1) Ask the Holy Spirit to bring to mind a painful memory that He wants to heal.

2) Recall as vividly as possible the scene of the memory. Let yourself grieve this event. Tell Jesus how this pain made you feel.

3) Ask Jesus to show you where he was when the event happened. What does He do? What does He say? As the incident unfolds, Jesus does what love does—He shatters the lies that have brought you so much pain. Write down the words of truth he brought to your mind.

In healing prayer, the facts of the memory remain the same, but the painful feelings coming from the lies associated with the memory can be released through receiving truth in prayer. It is released if Jesus' love absorbs all the darkness of that moment and it can no longer spill out into the rest of our lives. *"By His stripes we are healed"* (Isaiah 53:5). Did Jesus bring a song to your mind? Let Him sing it to you.

A thought to hold on to: Nothing you do or don't do will cause God to stop loving you. *I am convinced, that neither death nor life, neither angels, or demons, nor things present nor things to come, nor powers, nor height nor depth, nor any other created thing, will be able to separate us from the love of God, which is in Christ Jesus our Lord* (Romans 8:38,39 NASB).

B. The Woman Caught in Adultery:

Read and reflect on John 8:2–11:

Now early in the morning He came again into the temple, and all the people came to Him; and He sat down and taught them. Then the scribes and Pharisees brought to Him a woman caught in adultery. And when they had set her in the midst, they said to Him, "Teacher, this woman was caught in adultery, in the very act. Now Moses, in the law, commanded us that such should be stoned. But what do You say?" This they said, testing Him, that they might have something of which to accuse Him. But Jesus stooped down and wrote on the ground with His finger, as though He did not hear.

So when they continued asking Him, He raised Himself up and said to them, "He who is without sin among you, let him throw a stone at her first." And again He stooped down and wrote on the ground. Then those who heard it, being convicted by their conscience, went out one by one, beginning with the oldest even to the last. And Jesus was left alone, and the woman standing in the midst. When Jesus had raised Himself up and saw no one but the woman, He said to her, "Woman, where are those accusers of yours? Has no one condemned you?"

She said, "No one, Lord."

And Jesus said to her, "Neither do I condemn you; go and sin no more."

The Prayer:

Picture yourself as an onlooker in the temple courts. Suddenly you find yourself caught up in a great commotion. A woman is thrust before the crowd, half-clothed, shivering in the cold. She has been caught in the act of adultery. The Pharisees demand to know what Jesus will do.

Adultery is a serious offense. The people around you are seething with anger. "Guilty!" cries the crowd, and they take up stones. Without thinking, swept along with the emotion of the moment, you become one of the accusers in that crowd. Your hand grips a stone, hard and heavy. That's how your heart feels: hard and heavy. Angry. Hateful.

The crowd presses in, bearing down on the woman, on Jesus. Despite the tension in the air, the growing violence, Jesus is calm, composed. Instead of answering the accusation of the Pharisees that this woman surely should get what she deserves, He bends down and writes in the dust. There is a stillness about Him, a composure that will not be hurried. He looks at the woman with compassion, and then He looks up at the crowd. His words penetrate to the core of every heart. "Whoever is without sin among you, let that one throw the first stone."

The crowd grows quiet. Some look away; others bow their heads. *Thud.* A hard rock hits the ground. *Thud. Thud.* Another and then another. One by one, the woman's accusers walk away.

You turn to walk away too, but for some reason you pause, linger, and decide to stay behind. If you slip behind a pillar in the courtyard, perhaps you won't be noticed. Jesus and the woman are alone now. You watch from a distance, anxious to see what Jesus will do.

The woman is shaking and sobbing with fear. Jesus draws close to her and puts His hand on her shoulder to comfort her. Then He does an amazing thing. He reaches out and lifts her chin up with such tenderness that it takes your breath away. He smiles and wipes away the tears that stain her cheeks.

It seems strange, but as you watch Jesus put His hand on the woman's shoulder, you almost feel as if He is putting His hand on your shoulder. When He lifts her chin up and smiles, it is as if He is smiling at you; for, like that woman, you too have sinned and have needed to be forgiven, restored, set free.

The woman looks at Jesus with great gratitude. She seems somehow to change right before your eyes. Her shoulders straighten. She is no longer shaking but now is more certain of who she is. She walks away with new dignity, new hope.

You are glad for the woman. Then you wonder, *Why am I holding a hard stone in my hand?* It was not so long ago that you played the part of the accuser. The Pharisee. The self-righteous judge.

As you gaze at the stone in your hand, ask yourself honestly what you would do if faced with someone who really hurt you. Think for a moment about a specific person in your life who has hurt you. Hurt you deeply. Say that person's name. Picture your offender standing in front of you.

In prayer, remember Jesus' soft eyes of mercy. Tell Him about the pain this person has caused you. Give Him all your pain. Confess any resentment or bitterness you have harbored toward the person. Receive the free gift of His forgiveness.

Now imagine Jesus looking at your offender with the same love in His eyes that He had for you. "As I have forgiven you," says Jesus, to you, "can you not forgive this one who has wounded you? Can you not see (____________) with my eyes? Release (____________) as I have released you. Extend your love to (____________) as I have extended my love to you." You may begin to feel a river of mercy flowing inexplicably out of your heart toward this one whom you have kept at arm's length.

Open your hand, drop the hard feelings, and begin to bless the person who has hurt you, wishing him or her God's best and extending as much love as you can. Little by little, your heart will change. God promised, "*I will give you a new heart and put a new spirit in you, I will remove from you your heart of stone and give you a heart of flesh*" (Ezekiel 36:26 NIV).

Note: you might find it helpful to hold a real stone in your hand as you think of forgiving someone. Literally let the stone go as you forgive.

The Woman Caught in Adultery—Personal Reflection

In the foregoing prayer, you were asked to forgive a person who hurt you. Forgiveness is a process. You may not have been able to forgive completely, but you may be aware that this first expression of forgiveness has brought a change of attitude, however small. Thank God that He who began a good work in you will carry it on to completion (Philippians 1:6).

Is there a specific action you can take to demonstrate your forgiveness? A loving gesture? Write a note. Make a phone call. Bring a gift. If the person you need to forgive is dead, this does not prevent you from expressing your feelings. You can write a letter or imagine the person there and then address him or her in prayer. To take the act of forgiveness one step farther, begin to *bless* the person you have just forgiven. Write or pray a blessing, asking God's best for that person.

A thought to hold on to: "It is not on our forgiveness any more than on our goodness that [the healing of the world] hinges," said Corrie ten Boom, "but on God's. When He tells us to love our enemies, He gives, along with the command, the love itself."

CHAPTER 9

My Eyes Have Seen Holy

Blessed are the pure in heart, for they shall see God.

— Matthew 5:8

My journey, and yours, continues …

A few days after my time with Jesus in Gethsemane, I celebrated His resurrection in a sunrise service held at the site of the Garden Tomb in Jerusalem. Because it was a celebration of everything I had experienced in Gethsemane, it was the most powerful Easter memorial I had ever attended. That early morning at the Garden Tomb, I felt the joy of Christ's resurrection. The Bible says that the angels rejoice when one comes to know Jesus as the Savior (Luke 15:10). Can you imagine then, their celebration after we, who have experienced the fellowship of Christ's sufferings, come to know Jesus as the lover of our souls? Jesus, who experienced our pain and sorrows, is alive, living inside our hearts to restore the love and the joy for which we were created. (Please listen to the victorious song, "Victor's Crown" by Darlene Zschech.) In Gethsemane, a renewing joy entered my life when Jesus turned my focus from the pain in my heart to the person who heals my heart.

After the sunrise celebration, I was invited to attend an Easter feast held at the Mt. Zion Fellowship home where Karen Dunham, an American missionary ministering in Jericho, spoke to us about the amazing and miraculous things the Lord was doing in Jericho. How I wanted to be part of that work! The following October, Stefania and I returned to Israel to work at Karen's base, the Living Bread International Church in Jericho, and to attend the Feast of Tabernacles in Jerusalem.

More Reasons to Celebrate

The Feast of Tabernacles is also known as the Feast of Ingathering and the Festival of Shelters. The Jewish people call this celebration the Festival of Sukkot ("Sukkot" means "booths" or "temporary shelters"), and it is one of the most joyous celebrations of the Hebrew year. The Lord told the Israelites that they were to build booths each year and live in them for seven days to remember how God miraculously rescued them out of slavery, provided their every need for forty years in the wilderness, and brought them safely into their Promised Land (Leviticus 23:33–44).

The Lord said the Festival of Shelters was to be observed from generation to generation "forever" (Leviticus 23:41). Four times in Exodus 12, the Lord also tells Israel to never forget to celebrate Passover, the Feast of Unleavened Bread. Like the Festival of Shelters, it was to be a feast celebrated to the Lord "forever" (Exodus 12:14). Another "forever" festival is the Feast of Harvest, also called the Feast of Weeks and the Day of the First Fruits. Today Jewish people celebrate it as Shavot, which Christians call the Day of Pentecost, the day the Old Testament fire of God came down upon the New Testament believers. The fire that consumed sacrifices made on the altar of the temple in the Old Testament would now burn in the hearts of Christians, whose bodies are the new temple of God's Holy Spirit (1 Corinthians 6:19).

In the evenings, I loved to walk through the Jewish orthodox community of Ma Sharim. As I watched with fascination the Jewish families eating and praying together in their booths, I contemplated what life must have been like in the wilderness for the Jews. Their sandals never wore out, their food fell from heaven, and they drank water from rocks. The Lord directed Israel step-by-step in a cloud by day and in a fire at night. He never left her side or sight. What a vision that must have been! It is hard for me to even imagine what it must have been like for Israel to watch God's fire consume the sacrifice for sins on the altar, to hear God speak out of His fire, to watch His glory part a sea, or to feel the glory of His Presence shake a mountain!

My experience in Ma Sharim inspired thoughts about my own Christian faith and life. Why shouldn't my Christian community have feasts or festivals throughout the year to commemorate analogous events in our Christian life (e.g., being saved *[sozo]* from the slavery of sin through the blood of the Jesus, God's Passover Lamb, and being clothed with the fire of God's glory)? We can celebrate these things every day, but how good it would be to communicate the Lord's faithfulness visibly and tangibly to our children and others! (Those feasts certainly provide a powerful alternative to the world's Santa Claus and Easter bunny.) After the Lord parted the waters and Israel crossed the Jordan River on dry ground, He commanded the Israelites to pick up twelve stones and pile them on the other side of the Jordan. Then when their children asked, "What are these stones?" their parents could tell them of the Lord's miraculous power in providing dry ground for them to cross both the Jordan River and the Red Sea. Everyone would know that "*He did this so all the nations of the earth might know that the Lord's hand is powerful, and so you might fear the Lord your God forever*" (Joshua 4:24).

The "Wilderness" Worship Service

I never ever dreamed or even imagined that I, too, would experience what Israel did in that land. It changed my entire understanding and perspective regarding the Bible and my life.

During that week in Jerusalem, Stefania and I met two other women who were missionaries. They also were traveling and ministering from place to place, wherever the Lord led them. I had a long discussion with one of them about my favorite subject—the Presence of the Lord. I told her that I sense the sweetness of the Lord's Presence, His love and His peace, when I pray for the healing of a broken heart. I also communicated to this woman my love for worship music. She emphatically agreed about the importance of worshiping God and then smiled and asked, "Would you like to attend what could be the most powerful time of worship of your life?" To me, that is like asking a bird if it would like to soar, or asking a horse if it would like to be let out of its stall.

The next day, the four of us took a Palestinian bus to a condominium community about twenty minutes outside Jerusalem. We walked another fifteen minutes or so to the home of an older female American missionary, who would lead the worship gathering. To get to her door, we walked down several flights of stairs and then down even more steps into her basement, where people had gathered to worship. This meeting room was intimate and beautifully adorned with Hebrew decor.

The missionary entered the room, smiled at us, and sat down at her keyboard. Her face was amazingly radiant with peace. Our small group sat silently, waiting for the music to begin. As we waited, the woman sat there looking down at the keys. I glanced around the room a few times and saw everyone else praying, not surprised by the length of the silence. So I waited, and I prayed again. I earnestly prayed that we would hear Jesus speak to the depths of our hearts.

We waited in silence, but it seemed quite a while. Finally, the missionary began to play a beautiful melody unlike any other music I had ever heard. I imagined it was like the music the angels sang around the throne of God. It was so beautiful that it seemed to infuse the room with an unusual, pervading peace.

After a while, our worship leader began singing one line at time from her song. She sang about God and His majesty and glory. She sang about the names of Jesus: Adonai, El Shaddai, Jehovah Rapha, and the Lion and the Lamb. After each line, she repeated the music and we all sang the same line together. Then we waited for her to sing the next line. There were no books or handouts or overhead projections of lyrics. But there was something else that was very different in this worship music. There seemed to be an expectation or anticipation with every stanza that there would be another revelation or communication about the Lord that was even more wonderful than the last. However, I certainly wasn't expecting what happened next. Suddenly, there came an undeniable Presence of God in the room. It is very difficult to describe in words, but it felt something like a slight pressure upon my shoulders that made me want to bow. It must have been obvious to the other worshipers, because all those in the room went to their knees or fell prostrate next to their chair. I had never been in a worship gathering where *everyone* felt the sudden and undeniable weight of Lord's Presence at the same time. Then an aura of holiness permeated the room.

As my eyes welled up and overflowed with tears, the first thing that came to my mind was to ask the Lord to forgive me of anything in my heart, known or hidden, that would ever separate me from *this* presence, His holy Presence. I felt no condemnation or guilt from Jesus for the things His Spirit revealed to me; I only sensed my deep sorrow for having displeased Him. As I lay there, I asked Jesus to reveal anything in my life that would keep me from always entering this place with Him, and staying there. After this confession and plea, I felt His love come down upon me and envelop me. It was a love deeper than any I had ever experienced before in my life. The music continued, and His love deepened. I didn't want to leave that place, and I felt as though I was not physically capable of leaving. The atmosphere of His Presence was purifying, immensely healing, and very intimate. After worship ended, people slowly got to their feet and wiped the tears from their eyes, but not the wonder and joy from their faces.

After most of the people left, I talked with the missionary who had led our worship time. As I described my experience, she made no comment; she just smiled. Then I asked her, "How do you write such beautiful music? What influences in your life bring about the lyrics to your songs?"

She smiled again, her face radiating the love and peace of Jesus. She told me that she had not written or sung, before that day, the music we heard her sing. She said that as she waited on the Lord while sitting at her keyboard, she heard the music in her mind. So she just began playing what she heard. And as she played, the words began to flow from the melody into her mind. So she sang those words from her heart. All she did was to listen to Jesus. When He spoke to her of His love, we could hear it in the music of her song. And as we sang the words to the song, we could feel His Spirit descend tangibly and touch our hearts with His love. She explained that this descent of God's Spirit, this tangible awareness of His manifested Presence, is sometimes called the manifest weight of His glory or the power of the Holy Spirit. (♫ Paul Wilbur's song "Let the Weight of Your Glory Fall" certainly holds a new meaning for me now.) She encouraged me to reread my Bible in light of the glory of God and note its evidence or manifestation in His Presence, His voice, His light, His fire, and His holiness and power, especially as seen in the life of Jesus. I was to note how His glory suddenly, undeniably appeared to people. To me, God's "glory" had been just a term that included all the definitions of God's character. I had not known that it also included the tangible, personal, and intimate communications or manifestations of His love through Jesus living in my heart; through Christ in me, the hope of glory (Colossians 1:27). The realization that my spirit had been tangibly touched by my Savior, the healer and the lover of my soul, set me on a brand new quest in life—to plumb the depths of the love found in His Presence. ♫ Please listen to "Pursuit," by Jesus Culture / Kim Walker-Smith.

The All-Consuming Love of Jesus

That worship experience touched my heart as profoundly as had witnessing, as a young girl, the minister cry in the tent meeting as he talked about the depths of the love of Jesus. That morning, God ignited a fire in my soul, a desire to live where I could encounter that tangible expression of the Lord's love for me. It is a holy place—a place where I desire with all my heart to be free of any sin, both known or hidden, that would keep me from the Lord's Presence. *But only the high priest ever entered the Most Holy Place, and only once a year. And he always offered blood for his own sins and for the sins the people had committed* <u>*in ignorance*</u> (Hebrews 9:7 NLT). Truly, it is our hidden sins that keep us from the most intimate place of all. Jesus' death tore the veil in the temple from across the entrance into the Most Holy Place so that we can enter into that refuge with Him—that place of healing and safety. It is an all-consuming place. Nothing can stand there other than Jesus in all His beauty and power. There is no room for fear, doubt, loneliness, or sorrow. It is devoid of pain. It is a place filled with the enveloping and transforming love of Jesus. This truth is powerfully proclaimed in Kim-Walker Smith's song, "Still Believe."

Once again, with the passion of a child in a tearful tent meeting, I said, "I want this so much. I want to be so close to Jesus that my spirit can sense the intimacy of His manifested Presence *every* time I worship in song, *every* time I meditate on God's Word, and *every* time I listen to His heart as I pray." God heard that prayer. This tangible, most intimate and consuming encounter with the Lord's Presence was later to become part of my everyday life. God designed it for everyone who loves Jesus—it is to be not just a once in a while occurrence, but our lifestyle.

When I was taught by religious leaders that God stopped talking personally and directly to people when the Bible was completed and that my salvation was not about feelings but about faith, I was robbed of the intimacy with Jesus for which I was created and for which I longed. True, my salvation came about through faith, but what about the fruit of that faith? That fruit includes God's love, His joy, and His peace. Romans 14:17 states, *The Kingdom of God is ... righteousness and peace and joy in the Holy Spirit.* Doesn't this verse say that two-thirds of the Kingdom can be felt? I certainly do not want to be controlled by feelings of depression, loneliness, anger, etc.! Hence, if I do not feel His peace, I stop everything and go away with Jesus to listen to Him tell me what has stolen it. When He tells me, I repent of my thoughts or actions that robbed me of His peace and it is instantly restored. God's peace is our litmus test as to whether we are abiding in His Presence. I need to sense this peace in my heart *continuously*. It is not an emotion; it is a state of being. It is the peace of the Prince of Peace, whose Holy Spirit is living inside of me. Jesus Himself expressed deep feelings in Gethsemane, at Lazarus's tomb, over people's grief, over Jerusalem's rejection of Him, and in the depth of His love for His Father and His Father's love for Him. If we are created in His image, filled with His Spirit, and think what He thinks, won't we also feel what He feels? No other love on earth compares to the love of Jesus. It is an intimacy that can be felt, and sensed most powerfully, when we are worshiping Him.

My Personal Sukkot

I have learned that when the Lord is trying to get my attention or communicate something to me, He *always* repeats Himself. A few months later, when I was back in the States, my sister Kristen Mary invited me to a conference in New York about the glory of God. At the conference, I heard what the Lord had shown me in Israel—the importance of worship in the Christian's life. Again and again my heart responded most strongly to the Lord's Presence when worship became a time of listening to the Lord's heart. When the worship leader finished leading us in singing the lyrics of a song, he continued playing its melody. As the music continued, the worship leader would either sing new words to the song or just let us listen to Jesus speak to our hearts. Having time to listen to Jesus in the services was wonderful, and vital. The Lord used that conference to confirm what the worship leader had said to me in Jerusalem and to set me on a passionate quest to discover what God Himself said about His glory, and what relation the word "glory" had to intimacy with Him.

I longed for so much more of the love of Jesus. So deep was this longing that after I returned home, I resolved I would go into the wilderness with the Lord and fast and pray for the manifestation of His Spirit to touch my spirit in such a powerful way that I would become very sensitive to His Presence, even to His whispered *still small voice* (1 Kings 19:12) in my daily life. This forever changed the way I looked at the Bible, at the glory of God, and at worship. And it gave me a new understanding about the destiny of our journey: every time we are "touched" by God's glory—every time God's manifests or reveals His glorious Presence to us—we experience His healing, fall deeper in love with Him, and become more like Him. Both the Bible and my experience told me that it is impossible to encounter God's Presence and not be affected by it. Never before in my forty years as a Christian had I ever heard that one of "the riches of God's glory" is the touch of the fire of His all-consuming love, which purifies and heals us. With every encounter we become more like Jesus—a radiant bearer of His love, a vessel filled with Him. This is the life God intended for us to live and why He tells us to go *from glory to glory* (2 Corinthians 3:18). After we enter into this garden, this refuge, we will never want to leave.

♫ "My Eyes Have Seen Holy" expresses my heart's response to the manifest weight of God's glory during worship. It was a place of conviction, not condemnation, where I desired with all my heart to be free of anything that separated me from sensing His Spirit touch my spirit and "lift my soul" into His arms, to be carried into the refuge of His strength and rest. Please listen to this song by Bebo Norman on YouTube.com.

My Eyes Have Seen Holy

Am I unfit for You?/ Remember me, the one who turned from You
I come in rags tattered by the fall
And all the earth, a witness to my crime

Chorus:

Mercy, weep over me / Let Your tears wash me clean
Majesty, be merciful with me / For my eyes have seen Holy
Hear my prayer at night / Let the morning find me alive
For I am tired and weakened by the fall
Let all the earth bear witness to my cry

Musical Bridge:
Let the Amen sound from Heaven as You lift my soul.
Let the Amen sound from Heaven as You lift my soul.
Let the Angels sound from Heaven, "Holy is the Lord!"

By Jeffrey Stephen "Bebo" Norman / Jason Ingram ©2006 New Spring, Inc./
Appstreet Music / Peertunes, Ltd.& Windsor Way Music (Peertunes Ltd. admin. on behalf
of itself & Windsor Way Music for the World.)All rights reserved. Used by permission.

CHAPTER 10

The Intimacy That Jesus Desires

I am my beloved's, and my beloved is mine.

— Song of Songs 6:3

The conference in New York had communicated to me yet another incomparable treasure—the precious privilege and importance of encountering the tangible manifestation of the love of Jesus every day of my life. Now, back in the wilderness in Ohio, I would stay with Him for extended times of prayer, seeking to understand more of the power of His Presence and how to make that touch, a manifestation of His glory, a lifestyle. I was filled with much expectation and anticipation. After all, Jesus promised me He would manifest His love to me (John 14:21).

It seemed as though I had embarked on a treasure hunt. Every day I would get up and worship with intimate worship music that spoke of God and His glory—listening, and seeing with my eyes closed, the many ways He communicates His majesty and His love. I loved the song "You are Worthy" from Hillsong Music. "Let the Weight of Your Glory Fall" and "Your Name is Holy" were my favorite songs by Paul Wilbur. Twila Paris's songs "Lamb of God" and "Sanctuary," although written many years ago, touched my heart afresh and took on a new and much deeper perspective. Songs like these helped me to enter into the place I longed to go.

(♫ It is interesting to observe that around the mid 2000's, Christian music started focusing much more on God's glory and the intimacy of the love found in His Presence. Some examples include; "Revelation Song" and "Let the Heavens Opens," by Kari Jobe; "Holy Sprit" and "Show Me Your Glory/Majesty," by Kim Walker-Smith and Jesus Culture; "Victor's Crown" by Darlene Zschech; and music by Bethel Music, Hillsong, Vineyard, Gateway Worship, and IHOP-KC. One of my favorite songs of God's majesty was recorded by Anna Blanc when she was a worship leader with the 24/7 worship ministry of the International House of Prayer in Kansas City. To me, "You Reign," on YouTube, is one of the most powerful worship songs I can meditate upon when I am in the midst of a very difficult battle. And it is the desperate daily need to listen to His words of truth and love that draws my soul to songs that powerfully invite the Lord's Presence, e.g., "Waiting Here for You," by Christy Nockels; "Walk with Me," by Jesus Culture; and "Holy Spirit / Your Presence Lord," by Brian and Katie Torwalt. A wonderful and effective way to discover this new worship music, other than on YouTube, is through custom internet radio stations such as Pandora.com and iTunes Radio.)

Every day I would pray for that sudden awareness of the Lord's Presence to be revealed to me in whatever way He chose. But nothing tangible or perceptible happened for many days. I learned all I could about God's glory. I found that "glory" referred to the manifestation of God's beauty and character—it is the radiance of His love, it is the manifestation of Jesus. So I searched the Bible for the many ways the Lord communicated and manifested that glorious Presence to people. I noticed that throughout the Bible the word "suddenly" preceded an appearance of God in some form or manner. And whenever God suddenly appeared to men and women, they knew it was Him; there was no doubt! As I searched, the Bible became a brand-new book to me. I discovered a theme that had eluded me for my entire Christian life; From Genesis to Revelation, I saw that everything related to the revelation of God's glory, the perceptible manifestation of His love for His creation. The intimacy of that love would always be seen or heard or felt while in His Presence, listening to His voice.

The Heart of Jesus for Us

One day in the wilderness, when I was reading in John 17, I saw the heart of Jesus unlike I had ever seen it. I was amazed to see Jesus, knowing that His torture before Pilate and on Calvary was imminent, was spending much time with His Father, praying *for us*. He wanted us to understand that eternal life is so much more than life with Him in heaven—it is also an abundant life, or intimacy, with Him on earth. This has always been God's plan for us. Again, we need to simply look at life in Eden.

Jesus says in John 17:3, "*This is eternal life, that they may know You, the only true God, and Jesus Christ whom You have sent.*" The word "know" expresses much more than knowledge of God. It refers to loving, revering, obeying, and showing affection for God—being involved in an intimate, growing relationship with Him. The Greek word translated as "know" (*ginōskō*) in the verse above is the same word used to describe the intimate relationship between a husband and wife that results in the birth of a child. Genesis 4:1 uses the Hebrew counterpart of *ginōskō*, called *yada*, in saying that Adam "knew" his wife and she bore him a son. Accordingly, when Jesus continued His prayer for intimacy for us in John 17:21–23, He prayed that this intimate knowledge of His heart would result in a oneness with Him and His Father. Ephesians 5:30–32 states that becoming one in Christ is likened to a man who leaves his parents and becomes one flesh with his wife. Verse 32 states that this is a great mystery, but it is to illustrate the "oneness" Jesus desires with His bride, the church (followers of Christ). Truly, it is a mystery to those who do not know Jesus intimately. However, those who know Jesus as the lover of their soul discover that their new life in Christ is birthed through intimacy with Him, not just through confession of Him as Savior. (Two songs that describe the depth of love our hearts desire are "Intimacy," by Jonathan David Helser, and "Lockstep," by United Pursuit Band. One of the most powerful songs about becoming one with Jesus is "Yield My Heart," by Kim Walker-Smith.)

Our Heart for Jesus

Jesus wants us is to *know* Him as the Lover of our souls so that we will become as one with Him. In that oneness with Jesus, we are intimately aware of His voice, and we will hear Him call us by name (John 10:3, 27). Jesus said in John 8:47, "*He who is of God hears God's words*"—His spoken or *rhēma* words. When we hear Jesus speak to us personally and individually, we are hearing Him call us by name. Jesus said this is the essence of our lives—it is how we truly are able to live and enjoy life (Matthew 4:4). This oneness with Jesus becomes so precious to the Spirit of God inside us that whenever Jesus speaks, our heart confidently cries out, "It is the voice of my beloved!" Only a song could begin to communicate the depth of the intimacy Jesus desires with us, and its stanzas are found in Song of Songs.

It is the voice of my beloved!
My beloved spoke, and said to me: "Rise up, my love, my fair one, and come away.

For lo, the winter is past ... the time of singing has come ... Let me see your face, Let me hear your voice, for your voice is sweet, and your face is lovely."

(Song of Songs 5:2; 2:10–12, 14)

♫ After Jesus led me to this discovery, as though to confirm what He was saying to me, He brought me many songs whose lyrics contained verses from Song of Songs, e.g., "My Beloved," by Kari Jobe; "Faint With Love," by Heather Clark; "You Won't Relent" and "Lovesick," by Misty Edwards; and "Song of Solomon," by Martin Smith. These songs became intimate prayers for me, and as I prayed to become as one with Jesus, the song "Unstoppable Love," by Kim Walker-Smith, became a joy to me. Truly His love is unstoppable, and it is intensely loyal. Please also listen to "Loyal," by Lauren Daigle.

Wonderful books, including studies on the Song of Songs, about growing in our passion for Jesus through intimacy with God, are written by Mike Bickle. Mike is the Director of the International House of Prayer in Kansas City. For men who find the subjects of intimacy with Jesus and identifying as the Bride of Christ hard, Mike Bickle (a former boxer) is your author.

The Father-Heart of God

Finally, in John 17, I saw the foundation of intimacy with Jesus flowing from the Father-heart of God. *"Father, I desire that they also whom You gave Me may be with Me where I am, that they may behold My glory which you have given Me; for You loved Me before the foundation of the world"* (John 17:24). The entire reason Jesus came to earth was to show us what the Father's love for us looked like and to reconcile our broken relationship with Him so that we could live in His Presence. There is no powerful way God could have possibly communicated the utter depths of His love than through the sacrificial death of His Son. *God so loved the world that He gave His only begotten Son, that whoever believes in Him should not perish but have everlasting life* (John 3:16). Since the beginning of time, our Father planned to radiate His love for us in His Son. And for all time that love would be communicated to us through His Holy Spirit. The oneness of God would bring us into oneness with Him and magnificently fulfill His creative purpose for our lives.

Unfortunately, many people only understand the love of their heavenly Father in their head. They really don't *know* His love, because they have never felt it in their hearts. I was one of those who had only an intellectual knowledge of my heavenly Father's love. Like so many people (including Christians), I had an inaccurate perception of the word "father." To me, father was the parent who laid down guidelines for obedience and ensured punishment for disobedience. I never really understood God as a merciful, loving Father and protector. I had no idea what it meant to be loved unconditionally, to be encouraged unceasingly, and to be held tenderly. So I feared God and His punishment. That fear became the foundation of many other fears and insecurities in my life.

When I discovered that Jesus died to heal my broken heart and speak His words of truth and love to me, the walls of fear started crumbling. When I heard Jesus tell me that He delighted in me and that I was precious in His sight, I no longer believed the enemy's lie that I was unlovable and not valuable. I was God's beloved child! John 3:16 became a new verse to me. I saw that Jesus' death brought me into a brand-new family with a brand-new Father, and I felt His love surround me. Jesus set me free from the orphan spirit that had bound me. He promised, *I will not leave you orphans; I will come to you.* As the Bible explains, *You did not receive the spirit of bondage again to fear, but you received the Spirit of adoption by whom we cry out, "Abba, Father"* (Romans 8:15).

Discovering the father-heart of God is an essential part of the healing journey. The more we understand and experience the father-heart of God, the more secure our hearts will be in our heavenly Father's promises to provide, to protect, and to love us, no matter what we have done or not done. I encourage you to read more on this important subject.[7] ♫ Some of my favorite songs about my Father's heart are "My Father's Chair," by David Meece (Chapter 3); "The Father," by Heather Clark; and "He Knows My Name," by Anna Blanc. YouTube has many songs about our Father by Brian Doerksen including, "I am Your Father," and "Father Me," and also see the very powerful all scripture video, "God's Love Letter to You."

Living Within the Heart of Jesus

As I journeyed onward, I saw that the more I listened to Jesus, the more He revealed His heart to me. Like most people who try to emulate those they admire, I found myself wanting to become more like Him. I wanted to love and help people the way He did. So I asked Jesus to give me His heart. He did, in fulfillment of a promise made long ago.

As I pursued the heart of Jesus, I became more and more sensitive to the sufferings of others. This also included animals. I could no longer watch an

---

7 A very good overview of the subject is the article written by John Dawson, "The Father Heart of God," available at lastdaysministries.org. Another resource is *The Father Heart of God*, a book written by Floyd McClung Jr., available at YWAMpublishing.com and Amazon.com. You can also find videos on this subject by Mr. McClung and others on YouTube.com.

African animal kill another animal, whether it was on TV or as I sat on an African plain. One day I was in a library and a large black bird landed outside on the window ledge directly in front of me. He had a little chipmunk in his mouth. When the bird started to kill the chipmunk, I put my hands over my face and cried. Honestly, I was a little worried about myself. I had been in the mission field in Africa, India, and Israel, living among terrible poverty and very distressing circumstances. So I thought that my tears for the chipmunk meant that I was losing it. Then a more frightening thought came: perhaps I still had not been healed from all the heartache I had been through.

A few months later, I attended a YWAM discipleship training school (DTS) on Kona, Hawaii. Many people had told me that I was wasting my time and my talents (legal) in the mission field, so, listening to those voices, I went to the YWAM Justice School as the first step toward applying to be legal counsel for their Center for International Justice in London. There I hoped to work on issues such as child trafficking, child soldiers, abuse of women, etc.

While I was studying justice issues, I also prayed with many brokenhearted people on Kona. Then the Lord very clearly closed the door to YWAM's justice center. There was no doubt that I was already doing what He wanted me to do. He kept my focus on sharing the Presence of Jesus—listening to His voice and loving Him—as the answer to our problems.

My favorite class at DTS was on hearing the voice of God, as you might imagine. It was taught by a precious woman, Donna Jordan, who has been teaching and writing on the subject for many years.[8] One morning, Donna came into the classroom and told us to get out a piece of paper and pen. Then she told us to ask Jesus what He thought of us. "Wait until He puts His words into your minds, then write them down," she said. I didn't hear one word from Jesus.

The night before this class, I had attended a movie about how a dysfunctional family coped with their problems amid the "functional" families around them. One member of this dysfunctional family struggled with pornography. At one place in the movie, a pornographic picture flashed across the screen. When I saw it, I felt like I had been hit in the stomach. The blow resounded into the depths of my soul. I got up and left the movie and went out into the night and cried out my anguish to Jesus. Pornography has destroyed so many marriages and so many lives.

Now, as I sat in the classroom with that picture still in my mind and sorrow in my heart, I was completely deaf to the Holy Spirit. Donna then asked each of us to share what Jesus had said. We listened to each other share, many times with tears,

---

8 Donna has written a manual called *Listening to God*. There is also a wonderful children's book on this subject, entitled *Children Can You Hear Me*, by Brad Jersak. Both are available at ywamassociates.com.

the precious words that Jesus had spoken. I was the last one in the room to share that day. Still, I had not heard one word from Jesus. I just sat there overwhelmed with sadness. So when it was my turn, I told Donna I would like to pass on sharing that morning. She saw the tears in my eyes and asked everyone to pray quietly for me. Then again she asked me to share, assuring me of the support that I had in the room and encouraging me to get out what was so heavy in my heart. So in front of all my classmates, I cried as I shared the previous night's heartache.

Beholding His Glory

I couldn't stop the tears. Instead of going to the rest of my classes that day, I left the campus to be alone with Jesus. I rode my motorcycle as fast as it could go to a favorite beautiful coffee plantation overlooking the ocean. When I arrived, I hurried to a lone setting of chairs where no one could see me. I sat there alone with Jesus, pouring out my heart to Him but listening to the enemy. As each wave slammed against the rocky shore, the thought that I still wasn't healed slammed against my heart. Weren't last night and today proof? I truly had lost it. I was a real basket case, as proven by the memory of that day in the library when I saw that helpless little chipmunk.

I couldn't get those thoughts out of my head; they were so powerful and seemed so true. The only thing I could do was cry out, "Help me, Jesus! Please help me." Suddenly, a stillness began to surround me. It was like a calm in the storm. Then Jesus spoke the loudest, clearest words that He had ever put into my mind. "I *have* healed you, Loren. You are not a basket case. There is nothing wrong with your heart. I have given you a brand-new heart. I have given you My heart. You are weeping over the things I weep over. I never intended for animals to kill each other, for children to be abused. I, too, weep over the ugliness and destruction of pornography. I made all things beautiful. I intended that you live in beauty, always beholding beauty. Loren, I made *you* beautiful."

The ocean was never more spectacular to me than it was that day. It seemed to sparkle like the stars in heaven. That assurance of my healing, spoken by Jesus Himself, was so profound that all I could do on that hillside was cry tears of happiness and sing and dance for joy. (♫ The song "Awesome God," by Rich Mullins or Michael W. Smith, etc., and Wayne Watson's song "Almighty God" are wonderful songs to celebrate the Lord's faithfulness.) *"But for you who fear my name, the Sun of Righteousness will rise with healing in his wings. And you will go free, leaping with joy like calves let out to pasture"* (Malachi 4:2 NLT). Jesus was true to His word. He did what He said He would do. *"I will give you a new heart and put a new spirit in you; I will remove from you your heart of stone and give you a heart of flesh*" (Ezekiel 36:26 NIV). This is how Jesus heals the broken heart, how He sets the prisoner free. He gives us His heart, and then we love Him and others with His love. We love what He loves, and we weep over what He weeps over.

♫ A few lines from the chorus of Hillsong's song "Hosanna" communicates this so well: "Heal my heart and make it clean, Open up my eyes to the things unseen, Show me how to love like You have loved me, Break my heart for what breaks Yours, Everything I am for Your Kingdom's cause."

Since that day at the ocean with Jesus, and because of that day, I learned something very important about our healing journey. After Jesus brings the walls down around our heart, and as we fall deeper in love with Him, we can experience times when we feel despondent when there really is no reason. At those times I have found that after I have asked Jesus if there are any lies I am believing, or if there is any unforgiveness hiding in my heart, and He does not reveal any of these things, then He is calling me to go to another place with Him, physically, emotionally, as well as spiritually. The enemy wants us to doubt the healing work Jesus has done, but Jesus will turn that deception into our very great advantage and a wonder-filled victory. *"My beloved spoke, and said to me: 'Rise up, my love, my fair one, And come away. For lo, the winter is past, The rain is over and gone"* (Song of Songs 2:10–11). *"I have loved you with an everlasting love. With unfailing love I have drawn you to myself"* (Jeremiah 31:3 NLT).

Hearing Jesus speak His heart is a most precious and vital treasure, an immeasurable gift. When His words became "spirit and life" to me, I began to see glimmers of the radiance of God's original plan, to embrace us in the glory of His Presence, throughout the Bible. That plan was first communicated in the Genesis account of creation. Thousands of years passed between Eden and the birth of Jesus, the one whose death and resurrection would open the gate for us to return to the garden of God's Presence. Thus, I was surprised to see that God's restoration plan was communicated in the very next book after Genesis. Exodus, chapter 33, glisters the mystery, the intimacy, and the transforming power of that plan. I had read that passage many times over the years, read commentaries about it, and heard sermons on it. I was always fascinated, intrigued and very desirous to experience what Moses experienced with God that day on Mt. Sinai, but my heart remained bewildered. However, the present and passionate journey I was now on would take me to places in the Lord's heart I had never before ventured—into once hidden and mysterious rooms, behind doors that were formerly closed to me. And He (Jesus) said to them, *"To you it has been given to know the mystery of the Kingdom of God; but to those who are outside, all things come in parables,"* (Mark 4:11).

CHAPTER 11

The God Whose Love Can Be Felt

Scarcely had I left them when I found him whom my soul loves;
I held on to him and would not let him go...

— *Song of Songs 3:4a (NASB)*

Of all people on earth, no one experienced more miracles, signs, and wonders, nor attended more religious meetings than Moses: crossing the Red Sea on dry ground, eating food fallen from heaven every day, being led with a cloud by day and a fire at night, drinking water that flowed from a rock, witnessing the cloud of God's glory fill a tabernacle and the fire of His glory consume a sacrifice, feeling God's Presence shake a mountain, and speaking to God face-to-face. Yet after all that, Moses still pleaded with God to show him His glory. What?! What was he saying? There must be something, something more to Moses' request than the desire to witness other evidence of God's majesty. So I asked the Lord, "What was it that Moses was really asking You?" And my journey with Moses began. I was amazed to see that journey chronicle the healing path of the broken heart into the very depths of the love of God: Moses poured out the pain in his heart to God, listened to God respond with His words of truth and love, and hungered for more. He wanted what we all want, what we all were created for—to have the love of God embrace us.

Exodus 33 and 34 recount Moses' fourth trip up Sinai and his second forty-day experience alone on the mountain with God. This was something I needed to see. There simply is no short cut into the depths of the heart of God. And whenever our pursuit becomes passionate, the enemy will attack. It was while Moses was alone on the mountain with God that the children of Israel committed a most grievous sin in worshiping another god—a god made by human hands. Their god of gold represented the god of this world (and Egypt's god Apis)—power and prosperity. Israel had broken her covenant with God not to have *any* idols in her life. Because of this, God told Moses He would no longer accompany Israel on the rest of her journey into His promised land. I can't even imagine how distressing that had to be for Moses. However, Moses responded in a remarkable way—the way I know I should have responded when I was confronted with disappointment in God.

Moses was able to persevere because of his devoted worship and honest communication with God. He moved his place of worship (tabernacle of meeting) outside the camp, away from those whose hearts were not devoted to God. God honored Moses and sent His glory down in a pillar of cloud and stood at the door of the tabernacle talking with Moses. It was very interesting for me to see that when the people observed this, they too worshiped God (Exodus 33:7-10).

Moses talked with the Lord, in the midst of His glory, *face-to-face, as a man speaks to his friend* (Exodus 33:11). The term "face-to-face" is figurative, meaning that Moses talked directly with God on a very favored and special basis. He had spent much time talking with God about laws, altars and sacrifices, incense and oils, the order of worship, purification, holy garments, kosher foods, the tabernacle construction project, and all those discontented and disobedient people he was leading, etc. However this conversation was unlike any other. This present situation was probably the worst Moses had encountered since leaving Egypt. This problem went to the core of Moses' soul—a troubled soul, as revealed by the tenor of his words. It seemed God was being unfair and inconsistent to say He knew Moses by name and yet would not tell Moses whom He would send on the rest of the journey with him (Exodus 33:12). I believe that Moses, faced with feelings of abandonment, was questioning and maybe even doubting God's faithfulness and goodness. His identity was crumbling, and he needed reassurance. He needed to hear God say He cared about him; that He was pleased with him. And most of all he wanted to know God's love for him. So Moses said to God, *"If You are pleased with me, teach me Your ways so I may* <u>*know*</u> [yada] *You and continue to find favor with You"* (v. 13 NIV). God, the essence of compassion, responded to Moses with words of intimate reassurance: *"My Presence will go with you, and I will give you rest"* (v. 14). However, Moses was not able to grasp the intimacy of what God was saying to him. In this conversation, God was revealing to Moses

His *perfect* plan for all mankind, for ages to come. Moses' heavenly Father was talking about His Son, the Messiah.

When God said His Presence would go with Moses, God was literally saying His face would go with Moses. The Hebrew word for presence, *paniym*, means "face." God's perfect and wondrous plan would be for all to see His glory, *His radiant love*, revealed in the face of Jesus Christ (2 Corinthians 4:6). Because Moses lived before the birth of Christ, and because no man can see the face of the heavenly Father (Exodus 33:20), Moses could not understand the intimacy in God's promise. Therefore Moses interpreted God's promise as simply assuring Moses that He would not abandon Israel—that His Presence would continue to provide for and protect Israel. To Moses, God's Presence is what distinguished Israel from all nations of the earth (Exodus 33:16). He could not see it was the place of passionate interaction with his God.

The same holds true for God's promise to Moses that He would give Moses rest. Moses' daily responsibilities would had to have paled those of any pope or president. Unending sacrifices, rendering of legal decisions, journaling of God's words, preparing for the construction of the tabernacle, and traveling with over one million people[9] and their livestock certainly would have overloaded Moses' days and nights. Also Moses, the lawgiver, only knew of the one-day-a-week Sabbath rest. Hence, as seen in the passage, Moses did not even acknowledge this promise. That unending, pervading, and very intimate rest God promised would only be found in the peace of Christ's glorious Presence, alive in the heart that knows (*yada/ginōskō*) Him. Jesus promised, *"Come unto me you who labor and are heavy laden and I will give you rest"* (Matthew 11:28).

Moses remains somewhat bewildered and unconsoled by God's words of intimacy. So God, the compassionate and wonderful counselor, returns to the heart of the conversation—the insecurities in Moses' heart—and communicates the depths of His love for Moses; *"I will do the very thing you have asked, because I am pleased with you and I know you* [yada] *by name"* (Exodus 33:17 NIV). God assured Moses that He was delighted in Moses and that He loved him—words that Moses' heart longed for and words his ears were created to hear.

Isn't it wonderful to know that when God is trying to communicate with us, He will always repeat Himself? He knows we are made of dust and that our finite minds cannot even begin to approach the heights of His thoughts, but He faithfully pursues because He, too, deeply desires a very intimate relationship with us. *My beloved spoke and said to me ... "O my dove, in the clefts of the rock, In*

9 There were 603,550 Hebrew soldiers (Numbers 1:46), plus young and old non-soldier males, the Levites, women and children, and non-Israelites (foreigners).

the secret places of the cliff, Let me see your face, Let me hear your voice" (Song of Songs 2:10,14). Hence, and thankfully so, the Lord will keep bringing a subject to our attention until we grasp it. This truth is wonderfully seen in the story of Moses. God was relentless in His pursuit to pierce the lawgiver's legalistic mind and his yearning heart with His words *"I know you by name."*

I am certain that these words were of great comfort and healing for Moses. But the heart that has heard the Lord's healing words of truth and love will always desire even more—that heart will want to be *embraced* by God's love. Now there was no one else on earth, other than Moses, who knew better that God always revealed Himself through His glory. So Moses, seated in the midst of God's glory, talking with Him face-to-face, emboldened with God's words of love "*I know you by name*" sealed in his heart, cries out *"Please show me Your glory"* (Exodus 33:18)! What more profound and powerful way could God possibly reveal His love for Moses than through His glory?! Truly, Moses, who, like each of us, was created in the image of God to experience the love of God, longed for that glorious, tangible intimacy to be realized in his life. *My soul yearns, even faints, for the courts of the Lord; my heart and my flesh cry out for the living God* (Psalm 84:2). ♫ Please listen to the song, "Show Me Your Glory/Majesty," by Jesus Culture. It is a very powerful communication of the most powerful plea our heart could ever entreat of our heavenly Father.

God's Plan for Intimacy with Him

Because of the cry of a yearning heart, God revealed an aspect of His glory that no human being outside of Eden had yet experienced—the manifestation of His intimate Presence. Through His response to Moses' cry, God revealed His plan for us all to encounter His all-consuming love. It is the most profound experience in life. No human love can even compare to the love of God. As I meditated on Exodus 33:18–34:9, I saw that I experienced in Jerusalem, for the first time in my life, what Moses had experienced on Sinai for the first time in His life. And the result in both our lives was radiant!

The Lord told Moses that the intimacy of His glory would be seen in the revelation of *His goodness*, and He would pass that goodness in front of Moses. Truly, this is one of the most foundational beliefs that we must always guard within our hearts. Without an understanding and conviction that God is good, we will be perpetually buffeted by doubts and fears and unable to rest in the peace of His Presence. (♫ Please listen to "Good, Good, Father," by Chris Tomlin.) So important is our understanding of God's goodness that God adorned its revelation with His names. As all His goodness passed before Moses, the Lord proclaimed the names of His intimate glory—merciful, gracious, long-suffering, abounding in loving-kindness and truth, faithful, and forgiving. Moses knew that each name of God revealed an attribute of His character, His glory. Moses knew well the names Elohim (God the Creator, Preserver, mighty and strong), El Elyon (God the Most High), Adonai (Lord and Master), El Shaddai (the all-sufficient God), Jehovah-Jireh (the Lord will provide), El Roi (the God who sees), Jehovah-Rapha (the God who heals emotionally, spiritually, physically), etc. However, the names of God's intimate glory were new names to Moses, the old covenant lawgiver. These were new covenant names of grace, revealed and personified in God's Son, Jesus, whose name is above all names (Philippians 2:10). And these names would one day be given to us—as the names of the fruit of His Spirit living inside of us. Jesus would manifest the glory of God in His words and radiate it in His life. *The Son radiates God's glory and expresses the very character of His God* (Hebrews 1:3a NLT). *We have seen His glory, the glory of the one and only Son, who came from the Father, full of grace and truth* (John 1:14 NIV). Absolutely all the goodness of God is revealed in the Son of His love, Jesus. Therefore, to experience the intimate glory of God, Moses would have to encounter the triune God. It would be impossible for Moses to understand the depths of the Father's love for him without seeing and experiencing the manifestation of His love for Son, and in His Son.

As the glory of God surrounded Moses, he found himself sheltered and embraced in the "cleft of the rock." God said to Moses, *"Here is a place by Me, and you shall stand on the rock. So it shall be, while My glory passes by, that I will put you in the cleft of the rock, and will cover you with My hand while I pass by"* (Exodus 33:21–22). God stood beside Moses at Horeb when Moses feared that Israel would stone him because they had no water and God provided water for the people, from a rock. I am sure Moses remembered that miraculous experience of provision in this present conversation. But this time, the cleft of rock becomes a refuge of security, and intimacy. God Himself lovingly puts Moses within the rock and covers him with His hand. Never before has Moses been cradled by God. The powerful hand of God that brought Israel out of Egypt becomes a source of great comfort, and joy. *Even there Your hand shall lead me, And Your right hand shall hold me* (Psalm 139:10). *My soul clings to You; Your right hand upholds me* (Psalm 63:8). *You will show me the path of life; In Your Presence is fullness of joy; At Your right hand are pleasures forevermore* (Psalm 16:11).

When the fullness of time came (Galatians 4:4), when God became a man, that Rock of security, protection, and provision was revealed to be Jesus, the tangible communication of God's love for us. 1 Corinthians 10:4 recounts the presence of Jesus throughout Israel's desert experience: *For they drank of that spiritual Rock that followed them, and that Rock was Christ.* In the cleft of the Rock, in Jesus, we are saved (*sozo*), steadfastly loved, and protected. Jesus is seated at the right hand of God, and we are seated right beside Him (Luke 22:69, Ephesians 1:20, 2:6)! We will never be snatched out of God's hands when we listen to the words of Jesus. *"My sheep hear My voice, and I know them, and they follow Me. And I give them eternal life, and they shall never perish; neither shall anyone snatch them out of My hand. My Father, who has given them to Me, is greater than all; and no one is able to snatch them out of My Father's hand. I and My Father are one"* (John 10:27-30).

As the Father's glory passes by, Moses is permitted to see only the back of His Son—the unforgettable and powerful picture of the protective strength and shadowing embrace of God's shoulders. The Bible states that God is a Spirit and that no man has seen God at any time (John 4:24, 1 John 4:12). Not even Moses? Whenever God manifested Himself on earth in the form of a man, as revealed many times in the Bible, He did so as the second person of the Trinity, God the Son. Therefore, that day on Mt. Sinai, amidst the glorious wonder of it all, Moses is shown the back of Jesus, who is the epitome of the love of God and from whom the intimate, tangible love of God flows. Because the fullness of time had not yet come for God to become a man, the face of Jesus was hidden that day. However, a few days later (in man's time approximately 1,500 years) at the transfiguration of Christ, Moses was allowed to see the full revelation of the cry of his heart when he saw the "front" of God—the face of God revealed in Jesus (Mathew 17:1-3). The intimate glory of God would forever be manifested in and through Jesus. *For God, who said, "Let light shine out of darkness," made His light shine in our hearts to give us the light of the knowledge of the glory of God in the face of Christ* (2 Corinthians 4:6 NIV).

The love of God is always powerfully felt when Jesus heals the painful effects of sin in our hearts with His words of truth and love. When the guilt and shame and other heartaches of sin are healed, our souls are set free from sin's terrible burden to feel the Love that died for us on Calvary—the love that is alive and living in our hearts in the Spirit of Jesus Christ. Not only does the love of Jesus heal us, but it also lovingly clothes us in His glory (Luke 24:49)—the clothes God has always intended for us to wear (Genesis 2:25). All of this could never happen under the old covenant animal sacrifices (Hebrews 9:9; 10:4). Hence the love that Moses longed for and felt that day flowed from the Father heart of God into the wellspring of the heart of His Son, whose love became the healing balm for Moses' soul. When this love was poured out into the heart of Moses by the Holy Spirit (Romans 5:5), the glory of God overshadowed and enveloped him. How do I know? When the love of Jesus touches us, it will always be seen or heard or felt (John 14:21).

Did Moses Actually Feel the Love of God?

Yes, emphatically, yes. There are three reasons we can know that Moses felt the love of God when God's glory passed by. First, notice Moses' new vocabulary. It was Moses who wrote this blessing, *"Let the beloved of the Lord rest secure in Him, for He shields him all day long, and the one the Lord loves rest between His shoulders"* (Deuteronomy 33:12 NIV). Moses talked about resting between the Lord's shoulders because of his intimate experience that day on Mt. Sinai when he saw the powerful back of his loving God (Exodus 33:23). He could not understand the word "rest" in his conversation with God, until he experienced it in the midst of God's glory.

Notice too Moses' vocabulary in the way he described Israel's relationship with God before and then after he encountered God's intimate Presence. Before that time, Moses described the relationship in terms of God's "blessings" upon Israel. But after his intimate experience on Sinai with God, Moses spoke more of God's love for His children and His children's need to love Him with all their heart and mind and soul and strength (Deuteronomy 33:12, 6:5). As with Mary Magdalene, when a heart is touched with the healing love of God, that love cannot be contained. Moses, too, could not remain silent. His soul was touched by God's glory, and it affected his thoughts and his vocabulary. (Romans 12:2 states we too are transformed/transfigured by the renewing of our minds—our souls.)

Second, look at the physical change in Moses. The face of Moses, just like the face of Jesus at His transfiguration, glowed (Exodus 34:29–30). The Bible says that as Jesus talked with His Father (Luke 9:29), Jesus' face shone like the sun (Matthew 17:2). When Jesus was transfigured, and also when He was baptized, Jesus heard His Father say, *"This is my beloved Son in whom I am well pleased"* (Matthew 3:17; 17:5). Note that since the beginning of time, Jesus listened to His Father's words of love for Him.

You loved me before the foundation of the world (John 17:24). *When He* [God] *prepared the heavens, I was there; when He set a compass upon the face of the depth; when He established the clouds above; when He strengthened the fountains of the deep; when He gave to the sea His decree that the waters should not pass His commandment; when He appointed the foundations of the earth; then I was by Him, as one brought up with Him; and I was daily His delight, rejoicing always before Him* (Proverbs 8:27–30). (Colossians 1:15-17 states that Christ, who is the visible image of God, existed before God created anything and is the one through whom God created and holds together everything in heaven and earth.)

After Moses talked with God and encountered His intimate glory, Moses' face also became radiant. I am sure Moses glowed for the same reason Jesus glowed. In the midst of God's Presence, they both heard the Father speak words of love to them. And what can make our own faces glow more than to know that our sins are forgiven, to know that God is pleased with us, to hear that we are deeply loved, and to actually feel the love of God? *They looked to Him were radiant, And their faces will never be ashamed* (Psalm 34:5 NASB). Truly when the love of God touches (heals) our souls, our physical bodies will be greatly affected (Psalm 84:2). *Beloved, I pray that you may prosper in all things and be in health, just as your soul prospers* (3 John 1:2).

Note that although Moses wonderfully radiated the glory of God, it would eventually fade away (2 Corinthians 3:7–13). However, the radiance of the glory of God emanating from the resurrected and ascended Spirit of Jesus Christ living inside of us will never fade. In fact, as we obey God's Word and go "from glory to glory" (2 Corinthians 3:18), it will increase, because every time we encounter the healing love of Jesus, we become more like Him.

Third, look at Moses' spirit, as seen through his actions. I was fascinated to see that I had a very similar reaction to God's manifested Presence in Jerusalem as Moses did on Mt. Sinai. When the "weight" of God's glory came into our meeting room and upon us, my first reaction was to bow on my knees and repent. As His love enveloped me, I desired to worship God with all my heart, forever. My spirit sensed God's glorious Presence and immediately responded. Exodus 34:8–9 recounts the response of Moses: *So Moses made haste and bowed his head toward the earth, and worshiped. Then he said, "If now I have found grace in Your sight, O Lord, let my Lord, I pray, go among us, even though we are a stiff-necked people; and pardon our iniquity and our sin, and take us as Your inheritance."*

It was fascinating for me to see that God had revealed at the burning bush, in His very first conversation with Moses, His plan to draw Moses into His heart—His original plan for us all. At that time Moses didn't even know God's glory when he saw it. (However, he certainly didn't miss it!) But God would never relent of His plan for His children to experience the love for which they were created. When God appeared in the fire of His glory to call Moses to lead Israel out of Egypt, Moses declined the offer, citing his insufficiency and unworthiness for such a task (Exodus 3:11). The Lord responded, *"I will be with you"*—words of truth and love that assured Moses his competence and worth would be found and secured in his relationship with God alone. Also, God further promised that Moses would understand why God had called him to this task, that he would know what the journey of life was all about, that he would understand his purpose and importance in life and see that it all had been planned, when he worshiped God "on this mountain," Mt. Sinai (Exodus

3:12). When Moses worshiped God on Sinai in the midst of the *intimate* glory of God (Exodus 33, 34), all his questions were answered and the very deepest needs of his soul were met.

And the Lord spoke to Moses, saying; "Speak to Aaron and his sons,
saying, 'This is the way you shall bless the children of Israel. Say to them:
"The Lord bless you and keep you (God the Father); The Lord make His face shine
upon you, And be gracious to you (God the Son);
The Lord lift up His countenance upon you,
And give you peace (God the Holy Spirit)."'
(Numbers 6:22-26)

As I reflected on my meditation in Exodus, I saw in the life of Moses three very important truths. One, I needed to pursue intimacy with the Lord above *all* else. Despite all the amazing things Moses saw and did in his life (including serving God), his heart still needed so much more. Until I return to the place where I was created to live, within His intimate Presence, and daily seek to be *filled* with His love for me, my heart will still wander, and ultimately follow counterfeit affections.

Secondly, the fulfillment of God's intimate love for me will be found in His love *overflowing* from me to others. When Moses encountered the glorious manifestation of God's intimate love, he was impassioned to pray for Israel and to communicate God's love for her. After the Holy Spirit came upon Jesus, and thereafter upon His followers, their lives could be described in a three-word phrase: sacrificially loving others. As I meditated upon this, I saw that the sudden descent of God's manifested Presence upon us is not only for us to experience the most powerful love of all and become sensitive to the ways in which God's Spirit communicates to us, but also for us to experience the contentment and reward in loving others with the love of God. They also need to be touched by His love.

Thirdly, before Moses died, he recorded his final instructions to Israel in a song (Deuteronomy 32)! We are to teach and admonish one another in songs, *singing with grace in our hearts to the Lord* (Colossians 3:16).

This is God's simple plan for our lives: love God, love others, sing to Him. However until our love for God becomes intimate, it will lack the passion and power needed to touch and heal the hearts of others. This, I discovered, was the real destiny of my journey in the wilderness. Yes, I needed to return to the garden of God's Presence for intimacy with Him, but I needed to "change my clothes" to be able to stay there. That tangible and perceptible touch of God's glory that

I was pursuing came from not only a new voice, but also a new wardrobe. There would be no doubt, not the slightest uncertainty, when those royal robes clothed me. This is the story in the last chapter of our journey together.

♫ In closing I would like to share with you some of the many wonderful songs about God's face and His glory. Have you ever noticed that the most intimate and comforting worship songs sing about God's face? Some examples include "The More I Seek You," by Kari Jobe; "My Desire," by Kelly Willard; "Captivate Us," by Watermark; "Light of Your Face," by Misty Edwards; Anna Blanc's "He Knows My Name," the first song of Anna's August 2011 worship set on YouTube; "Savior of My Heart," "Hope," and "Benediction," by Shelia Walsh; "Show Me Your Face," by Paul Wilbur; and "Intimacy," by Jonathan David and Melissa Helser. Songs that sing about God's Presence and His glory are "Waiting Here for You," by Passion Worship Band or Christy Nockels; "In Your Presence," by Paul Wilbur; "Show Me Thy Glory," (about Exodus 33) by Marty Goetz; and "Show Me Your Glory," by Jesus Culture. As you listen to some of these songs, be sure to ask the Lord to give you a vision of His glory and to touch you with the wonderful revelation and manifestation of His intimate and precious Presence.

CHAPTER 12

Dance with Me

You turned my wailing into dancing; You removed my sackcloth and clothed me with joy, that my heart may sing to You and not be silent. O Lord my God, I will give You thanks forever.

— Psalm 30:11, 12 (NIV)

On Easter, I had to end this wilderness experience, this extended time of meditation and prayer alone with God as I pursued a deeper understanding of the work of His glory (the Presence of God manifested in power). I would be leaving the following day to visit my daughter Victoria for a week in Colorado before I returned to the mission field. Although I had not experienced one of those sudden movements of God's Spirit (a "suddenly," as described in the Bible), I felt closer to Jesus than I had ever been in my life. Also, I had complete assurance from God's Word that my spirit *would* unmistakably encounter the tangible manifestation of the love of God, as a lifestyle, when He clothed once again with His glory. This had been my Father's plan since the beginning of time and Jesus Himself specifically promised His royal robes would do this.

The Resurrection Plan

After Jesus' resurrection, Jesus came to His disciples and showed them His hands and His side. They were exuberant! Jesus also bountifully blessed them with His promise of peace. *And when He had said this* ["Peace be with you"], *He breathed on them, and said to them, "Receive the Holy Spirit"* (John 20:19–22). The breath of life that breathed (*emphysaō* - Septuagint) His life into Adam to live with Him in Eden, now breathes (*emphysaō* - only appearance in New Testament) the life of His Holy Spirit into His followers to return with Him to a new garden, *to live*. With the breath of life living inside, hearts could be healed of the effects of sin—its guilt and shame, its bitterness and fear. Now the heart could stay pure. As Jesus went about breathing His Spirit into His followers after His resurrection, I saw His ministry now focusing on the healing of broken hearts (Mary at the tomb, the disciples on road to Emmaus, Peter by the sea, etc.)

Jesus told His followers they were to stay in Jerusalem and wait for "the Promise of My Father." In Eden, the Father's love adorned His children with garments of His glory—the radiance of the purity and power of an adoring Parent. And ever since Adam and Eve discarded their royal robes, our Father has passionately pursued His plan, through His son Jesus, to restore His children to His original design—bearers of His image, clothed with the glorious power of His love. Jesus said, *"And behold, I am sending forth the promise of My Father upon you; but you are to stay in the city until you have been clothed with power from on high"* (Luke 24:49 NASB). (The NKJV says *"endued" with power* which literally means in the Greek (*endyō*), "to sink into a garment.") Jesus said His Father promised that the Holy Spirt would do this. Through the Holy Spirt, the fire of God's glory would come upon us to clothe us with our Father's love, purity and power. Note that the Greek word for the "power" we would receive is *dynamis*—supernatural, miracle working power. Truly, this would be a glorious power, enflamed with the love of God inside us, overflowing in miraculous, wondrous ways to others. But Jesus told His followers that they would have to wait for that power to clothe them. It would come with a cost.

In order for His followers to receive this baptism[10] of power, Jesus had to undergo the most excruciating baptism of all.

"I have a baptism to undergo, and how distressed I am until it is completed."

(Luke 12:50)

Surely He has borne our griefs and carried our sorrows; But He was wounded for our transgressions, He was bruised for our iniquities; The chastisement for our peace was upon Him, and by His stripes we are healed.

(Isaiah 53:4a–5)

10 Greek - *baptizō*: to immerse, to cleanse, to overwhelm

Jesus became God's sacrifice for our sicknesses and our sins: *For all have sinned and fall short of the glory of God* (Romans 3:23). We were designed in God's image to be full of God's glory, and Jesus' baptism of brokenness, an immersion in agony, would finally reclaim God's originally intended plan through the work of Christ's glorified (enthroned) Spirit, enflamed with God's love.

A baptism of brokenness pours out a baptism of fire. In the Old Testament, God's fire came down and consumed the broken sacrifice upon the altar. That fire, God's glory, then filled the temple (2 Chronicles 7:1). The fire of God's glory, kindled from heaven (Leviticus 9:24), was *never* to be put out (Leviticus 6:9, 12–13). And it always fell down on sacrifices that pleased God. The question to me, then, was what kind of brokenness in Jesus' followers pleased God and brought down the fire of His glory upon them? I pondered much upon the hearts that day in an upper room in Jerusalem during the feast of Pentecost. Although Jesus had appeared to 500 people after He rose from the dead, only 120 went to the upper room as He had instructed. They were the ones who loved Him—the ones who would sacrifice for Him. "*For the gate is small and the way is narrow that leads to life, and there are few who find it*" (Matthew 7:14).

I can only imagine the prayers and the tears that flowed as Jesus' devoted followers waited and waited, and prayed and prayed; and many, I believe, fasted, for what—power? I am sure there was much discussion about that power; what exactly did Jesus mean, and what in the world would that power look like? But oh, how they must have cried as they thought more about the Person than they did about the power. What a terrible death Jesus had suffered for them! They had seen the terribly tortured body of Jesus, witnessed His horrible crucifixion, and now were contemplating Jesus' words that they, too, must take up their own cross to follow Him—they, too, needed to lay themselves down upon an altar and die, to themselves. *How* would they be able to do this without Jesus? The most loving Man they had ever known, the most loving Man that had ever lived, was gone. I am sure many travailed about His promise to never leave them or forsake them, wondering how His promise of power could ever replace Him and the love they felt in His Presence. Yes, it was wonderful to have seen Him alive after His resurrection, but now He was gone. They couldn't see Him anymore or lean against His chest or sit at His feet and listen to Him speak His words of hope and love to them. They could no longer watch Him heal blind eyes and leprous bodies. They could no longer walk along a road with Jesus and feel His words burn in their heart, or sit by the garden tomb and hear Him call them by name. They couldn't weep with Jesus about their betrayal of Him and listen to His words of love restore them to His side. Thus, I believe with all my heart that while they waited for the promised power, their greater desire was for His

Presence. Oh, how they must have prayed that their best friend, their Savior and Healer, would return! Truly these broken, pleading hearts were a pleasing sacrifice to God (Romans 12:1) and were worthy to be filled with His glory. An imploring heart is a humble heart—emptied of self and burdened for others. And an imploring heart is a hungry heart, understanding of the need for God's Presence and empowering help. *The sacrifices of God are a broken spirit, A broken and a contrite heart—These, O God, You will not despise* (Psalm 51:17).

In the midst of this brokenness and desire, after at least ten days of tearful, fervent prayers and passionate songs (Mark 14:26), the breath of God blew the Old Testament fire of God's glorious Presence down from heaven to purify, impassion, and empower the New Testament temple—the bodies of the followers of Jesus—just as had been promised. John the baptist, (whose baptism was limited to repentance) said,*"He will baptize you with the Holy Spirit and fire"* (Luke 3:16; Matthew 3:11). Jesus said, *"I came to send fire on the earth, and how I wish it were already kindled!"* (Luke 12:49). Now, finally, we could be purified by His fire and clothed in His glory, filled with God Himself, just as it had been planned from the beginning of time! The Shekinah glory of God has been and will always be the dwelling place of a dwelling God. Oh, how tears of brokenness always become tears of joy when we experience that deep oneness with Jesus. ♫ Rejoice in this truth with "Yield My Heart," by Kim Walker-Smith, and "Hands to the Heavens (Live)" and "Let the Heavens Open (Live)," by Kari Jobe. Our lives and our faces can once again become radiant with the fire of God's love—radiant when He heals our hearts, radiant when we hear Him call us by name, radiant when we feel His love fill us, and radiant as His love overflows from us into the hearts of others.

The Purpose of Resurrection Power

Now, clothed with the glory of God by the power of the Holy Spirit, we would be able to do greater works than Jesus had done on earth. Jesus had promised this too. He said this would be possible after He had gone to His Father (John 14:12). The glorified Jesus, seated at His Father's right hand, would send down the fire of His glory, and it would ignite the power of the Holy Spirit in us—His glory would do the work. *Christ in you, the hope of glory* (Colossians 1:27b). Now we, too, would watch His glory *"heal the sick, cleanse the lepers, raise the dead, cast out demons"* (Matthew 10:8). Amazingly, we would be able to witness God's manifested Presence fall from heaven in the midst of the cries of our prayers and the songs of our praise and see people healed and delivered simply as they stood there, singing to Him who sits upon the throne.

Truly, the greater works would be done by the greatest power of all—the glory of God. It was so interesting and exciting for me to observe in the mission field that the more we worshiped, the more our work would be done by God's glorious and miraculous power. This observation led me to always pray my seemingly impossible requests whenever the power of His glory tangibly appeared, and thereafter to watch my God make all things possible.

Jesus' followers heard, saw, and experienced that Jesus was true to His word. He did everything He promised He would do, yet so much more than they had ever imagined. They witnessed that the prayers of Jesus for them, their prayers for His Presence, and their songs of worship became the greatest weapon on earth to defeat the forces of darkness, and brought about the most powerful force of all to transform hearts and homes forever. Whenever they would gather together to pray, the glory of God fell upon them. It was unmistakeable. The fire of the Holy Spirit (Luke 24:49) would open the door to repeated outpourings of His glory, touching hearts with the overflow of His love. This empowerment would be repeated again and again in the lives of Jesus' followers until "going from glory to glory" produced a sensitivity to God's Presence so precious that it would become an empowered lifestyle (e.g., Acts 4:29–31; 12:5, 7; 16:13–14, 25, 26; 19:5–6.) *But we all, with unveiled face, beholding as in a mirror the glory of the Lord, are being transformed into the same image from glory to glory, just as by the Spirit of the Lord* (2 Corinthians 3:18). Truly Pentecost was not a day, but a feast. *He has brought me to his banquet hall, And his banner over me is love* (Song of Songs 2:4 NASB).

Glorious Proof

As I meditated upon the above, Jesus brought two thoughts to my mind: First of all, I saw that wherever, whenever, and however God appeared to man throughout the Bible, man *knew* it was God. There was no doubt. So it is in our lives. God's glorious Presence is always heard or seen or felt and it is manifested (communicated) in many ways, not just one way. (Many examples are given in Part II, Section V: "Seek the Light of His Fire.") In the upper room, God manifested His glory in several ways. First, a sound from heaven like a mighty rushing wind filled the whole house; this is reminiscent of the sound that came upon Mt. Sinai and the Old Testament temple when God's glory appeared. Then the eternal fire of God's glory descended upon the heads and filled the sacrificial bodies of the New Testament temple. The fire in Acts 2:2 looked like tongues, just like the fire of glory that *licked up* the water and consumed the sacrifice during Elijah's contest with Baal's idol worshipers (1 Kings 18). Thirdly, Jesus' followers were enabled to speak the language of another culture—a language they previously did not know. They were visibly empowered by the Holy Spirit to be all Jesus created them to be—lovers of God who could not restrain His love. Truly, absolutely *nothing* could constrain this love in their hearts—not language barriers, persecutions, famine, rejection, condemnation, or judgment. So in light of the above, the more important question in my life really becomes, not so much when did the power of the Holy Spirit come upon me (at salvation or thereafter), or what that event is called by religious leaders (the first or second or only baptism of the Spirit, the fullness or the filling of the Spirit, etc.) but how is the Holy Spirit's power manifested in my life? How is the Holy Spirit seen or heard or felt when I am alone with Jesus, and how does the overflow of that intimate and powerful time with Jesus touch and affect the lives of others?

The second thought, and maybe it was more of a burdened vision, came about as I reflected upon the lives of followers of Jesus after they had been clothed with God's glory. They simply were never the same again after that prayer meeting. Former betrayers of Jesus became martyrs for Him. They became radical lovers of God who sought nothing more than the Presence of Jesus and the power of His love falling upon them and working through them to touch the lives of others. Supernatural healings, deliverances, knowledge, and passion and boldness were a natural overflow of their love for Jesus. In the lives of these followers, I saw the church that Jesus died for, and I became even more burdened to pray, no matter how long it would take, that Jesus would send the fire of His love upon me and clothe me with His glorious Presence so that I, too, would be empowered to share the love of Jesus that could be seen or heard or felt.

The Resurrection Dance

I was not discouraged that Easter evening before I left for Colorado. No, not at all. Because I was armed with my Father's promise to empower me with the Holy Spirit, I *knew* His glory would suddenly appear one day to seal in my heart the daily touch of His Presence, if I only persevered. I made a little Easter meal to celebrate the amazing depth of love Jesus had communicated to me during this time of fasting, praying, and waiting. I grilled one lamb chop and three pieces of asparagus. Then I set the table for two and lit the candles. The candlelight reflecting from the candelabra created a starlight radiance in the room that glimmered upon the china and crystal. The final touch was dinner music—a selection of my favorite worship songs from the week spent with Jesus. ♫ While I was preparing dinner, Jason Upton's song "I Will Wait for You" played. I promised the Lord I would continue to wait upon Him as long as it would take until that descent of His glory, the fire of His all-consuming love, came upon me to become a lifestyle. As I prepared the meal, my stereo started playing another song I loved, Jason's "Let the Fire Fall."

As I enjoyed my meal, I turned to the place setting next to me and talked to Jesus with the same honesty and sincerity that I would use in talking to my husband or daughter or dearest friend. I told Him that even though I had not had a "sudden" encounter of the weight of His glory, it was wonderful to have spent all that time with Him. I felt closer to Him than I had ever been in my life, and I loved Him more than ever. I thanked Him for His love for me and all that He suffered for me in Gethsemane and on Calvary. And I thanked Him that He was alive, speaking His words of truth and love into my mind, and living within my heart, His home.

♫ Then "Dance With Me," by Robert Stearns, began to play. It had become my favorite worship song during this time. The lyrics are from one of my favorite books, the Song of Songs. Close your eyes and look at Jesus as you listen to the song on YouTube. I hope you too will dance with the lover of your soul.

As I sang this song to Jesus, suddenly, His glorious Presence filled the room and overwhelmed my heart! I felt an incredible "weight" of His Presence, a touch so tangible that I became prostrate next to my chair, hardly able to move, and not wanting to move one inch away from that place. So I remained there, amazed with wonder before Him. Just as during my Jerusalem worship time, tears came to my eyes as my spirit responded to His intimate Presence. Now I knew it was not a one-time event. Oh no, *it was to be a lifestyle.* Once again, I desired to be free of anything that would separate me from His wonderful closeness. So I asked the Lord to reveal and forgive me of anything in my heart that would prevent this. As I thanked Him for all He was doing to purify and impassion my heart to be like His, His peace and love consumed me.

I rested there a long time. It was a time of perfect peace, of absolute freedom. There was no doubt, no sadness, no worry, no loneliness, and no pain. It was more than a refuge. Within the arms of Jesus, I was strengthened. His joy brought joy into my heart. Then I began to pray. I sensed a very deep crying out in my spirit. As I prayed for my daughters and for my former husband, tears flowed from the depths of my heart and, I believe, from the heart of Jesus. They were tears for their healing and tears for a divorce that, had we known of the power of the all-consuming fire of God's love, would never have happened. From that day forth, while dancing within the arms of Jesus I experienced a miracle I never thought in the past would be possible—joy, unspeakable joy. Therein resides a formidable, supernatural power I had never before understood. Just as history's greatest worshiper and warrior,

King David, danced mightily before the Lord, so are we who dance with Jesus enabled to trample to death, the lies of the enemy.

♫ A wonderful song to dance to when the lover of my soul, the Healer of my scars has healed a recent heartache is by Kari Jobe, called "Steady My Heart." Look for the danceable official lyric version, as there is a softer acoustic version. (Also see other dance songs at the end of Journey 8.)

Waiting for Jesus

Since that day, whenever I wait for the Lord's intimate, glorious Presence to fall upon my spirit during my times of worship, the wait is no longer prolonged or extended, as my spirit is now very sensitive to the movement of His Spirit. Note too that after the power of the Holy Spirit finally came down upon Jesus' followers after at least ten days of waiting during Pentecost (Acts 2), there was no longer a lengthy wait for His glory to clothe them again. In Acts 4, when they prayed for boldness to speak and to believe God for miracles, signs, and wonders, their entire building immediately shook, just as Mt. Sinai shook when God's glory descended upon it. Then they were again filled with the power of the Holy Spirit to speak boldly for Jesus and display His healing power.

As noted above, when we have been clothed with God's glory, our spirit becomes extremely sensitive to His Spirit. Jesus at times moves in our spirit to get our attention when we should be more attentive about something someone has said to us or something we need to communicate. When I am talking with people and sense the Lord's Presence, I will pause and listen to Jesus tell me how He wants me to share His love. Many times as I listen to people talk about a heartache, the Holy Spirit will suddenly move in my heart and alert me to the real, deeper problem that has been hidden to them. Sometimes Jesus just wants to surprise us with His Presence in His unique and wonderful way. I can be riding my horse or watching the sun set when all of a sudden He manifests or communicates His love to me. Being sensitive to the movement of God's Spirit is not only an empowering experience but also a time of very deep intimacy with Jesus.

Worshiping God until His Spirit impassions and empowers me has become a wonderful lifestyle. I don't leave my daily time alone with Jesus until He has spoken His words of truth and love to me, and until I have communicated my love for Him. (I will talk more about this "love exchange" in Part 2.) This is what I believe is the life of going *from glory to glory* (2 Corinthians 3:18). When my spirit senses the Lord's intimate Presence, His peace, which is constant, becomes even deeper as tears appear— not from sorrow, but from the sense of His wonderful closeness and love for me. *Now* I understand the tears I witnessed as a young girl in the eyes of that minister at the tent meeting as he spoke of the love of the Lord Jesus. Whenever my eyes suddenly tear, I always thank the Lord for His precious Presence and ponder in utter amazement the reality of my faith—that I have a God who lives inside of me, talks to me and whose love I can feel! Truly, the good news of God's Kingdom on earth is real—it is a love so powerful that it cannot be contained.

Prayer to be Clothed with the Glory of God

I know of people who, as they were praying to receive Jesus as their Savior and Lord, had the fire of God's glory suddenly descend upon them. God is God, He knows all hearts, and He does whatever He pleases, whenever He pleases, including when He sends the fire of His love upon someone. And because He is God He will perceptively manifest that fire coming upon people and overflowing from them in whatever way, or ways, He choses (1 Corinthians 12:11, 30). As seen in several passages in Acts 2, when that fire of God's glory came down it was a perceptible event; a mighty wind blew (the breath of God!), the believers were immediately gifted with the ability to hear God's words and speak His heart boldly in the language of another culture, many signs and wonders were done. These manifestations were seen throughout the book of Acts in the supernatural ability to heal, to cast out demons, to prophecy, and to see dreams and visions of the glory of God, e.g., Paul and Stephen saw Jesus, and Stephen's face shone as an angel. I have seen people overcome with tears, joy, peace, warmth, and immense love as the fire of God's glory, with His healing and purifying love, comes upon them. (Note: the gifts of the Spirit are listed in 1 Corinthians 12:7-11, and the greatest gift of all is love, 1 Corinthians 13.)

Though many people have encountered the fire of God's glory suddenly coming upon them at the time of their salvation, most people experience a "wait" time—a time of realizing their great need and immense desire for even more of God and His love. This deep hunger, a form of brokenness, will bring down the fire of God's glory upon us, to clothe us. All we have to do is ask God for it. *"If you then, being evil, know how to give good gifts to your children, how much more will your heavenly Father give the Holy Spirit to those who ask Him"* (Luke 11:13). This event, this encounter with the Lover of our soul, opens the small, narrow gate into the secret place and refuge of His Presence (Psalm 91:1-2, 17:8, 27:5, 31:20, 32:7, 61:3-4, 62:8, 119:114; Song of Songs 2:14; Matthew 6:6; John 15:7,9. Please meditate on these scriptures.). It's like we have finally come home, to the perfect place of peace and rest. In this place alone, where our very deepest needs are met, we are empowered to face any foe in our heart or in the world, with the love of Jesus. This is the place of the *abundant* life in God's Kingdom on earth, just like it is in heaven, which Jesus promised. Below please find a sample prayer to be clothed/empowered with God's glory, if your heart so desires, if your soul so hungers:

Dear Heavenly Father, I desire with all my heart to know Your love in a deeper way and I want so much for Your love in me to be able to powerfully touch the hearts of my family and friends. Holy Spirit please show me anything in my heart and life that is not of Jesus so that I may repent and stand before you now, forgiven and free, to receive the fire of my Father's all-consuming love.

Come Holy Spirit send that fire upon me to purify, empower, and impassion me! Touch my Spirit so powerfully that I will always be sensitive to the movement of Your Spirit upon me, and in me, whenever and however You talk with me, sing with me, and love me. Take me into the deepest places of Your heart that I may learn of the mysteries, and live in the power, of Your Kingdom. Gift me mightily with the gifts of Your Spirit, and may those gifts be ministered to others within the powerful overflow of the fruits of Your Spirit in my life. Help me each day to go from glory to glory—staying in Your Presence, worshiping, until I have heard You speak Your words of truth and love, and have sensed Your arms around me. May those glorious times with You empower me to touch and mend many hearts, homes, and bodies for Your glory alone. Thank you Father, for clothing me with Your radiant glory! In the name of Jesus I pray.

♫ A song titled "Here With Me," by MercyMe, communicates very powerfully the essence of my experience and its reality in the Christian life. The first stanza to the song describes our heart's longing to be embraced by the Lord and to see His face. The chorus celebrates the answer to the cry of our hearts—the sudden and tangible descent of the Lord's Spirit that envelops us in the beauty and wonder of Jesus! Then the song describes the heart's response—total surrender to a holy and loving God.

The Overflow of God's Glory

The evidence that we have been clothed with the power of God's glory will be very evident as our love for Jesus touches others. Following is the story of the most wonderful example I could give you.

For several years I had been praying for a building in Italy, such as a monastero or santuario, to make into a mission base. I wanted a place in the country where people could get away from the busyness of life and experience what it means to behold and to be clothed in God's glory, experience the healing power of worship, and fall in love with the lover of their souls. My experience in Jerusalem and my study of Moses convinced me that if people could tangibly experience the fire of God's intimate glory, they would live the rest of their lives wanting nothing more than to fall deeper and deeper in love with Him. Then that love would overflow from their lives to touch others. This is God's perfect plan for us. It is His prescription for peace and contentment.

One morning while en route to see a monastery, Stefania and I were introduced to a Christian Italian man in a cafe. He asked me what I was doing in Italy, and when I told him, he paused, seemingly to contemplate what I had just said to him, and then asked me if I would pray for him and his wife. Tragically, they had just decided to divorce. They had sought help for their marriage for almost ten years, to no avail. Anger and depression plagued their lives. And, unknown to me at that time, his wife was contemplating taking her life now that their marriage was ending.

My heart broke for him, his wife, and their children. When I told him I would love to pray with them, he went and got his wife. The anger in the husband's eyes paled in comparison to the horrible, dark depression I saw in his wife's eyes. Her nose and eyes were red from crying, and black circles surrounded her eyes. I felt her awful pain of abandonment and rejection. There they stood, looking expectantly at me, their faces framed with sorrow, etched in hopelessness. Ten years of counseling had not helped them; what would I say in the few minutes I had with this couple? I cried out to the Lord for help. As I waited for Him to tell me, I asked them if they had ever heard how Jesus heals the broken heart or about the intimacy of His glory? Their response was no. I stood there wondering how to communicate in one prayer what had taken me so many years to learn and experience. Then the Lord responded to my cry. He told me to share just one thing—the fire of His love. So I shared with them that it was impossible to live the Christian life without the fire of God's glory coming upon them, clothing them. I asked them if they had ever prayed for Jesus to send the fire of His all-consuming love to burn up the chaff inside of them—their pride and anger and unforgiveness—and to give them His heart. Again, they said no. So we talked about the promise that Jesus will baptize us with the Holy Spirit and fire (Luke 3:16), giving us the needed power to follow Him (Acts 1:5, 8), if we earnestly ask Him. They said they wanted to pray for this. So the four of us held hands in a circle and prayed that the Lord would send the fire of His love to purify us, empower us, and impassion our hearts to be like His.

Over the years, I have observed many instantaneous physical healings. However, until that day, I had never seen an instantaneous healing of anyone's soul. God sent His glorious Presence into that cafe and into our hearts in a most powerful and amazing way. After our prayer together, the husband, so tall and strong, just stood there weeping. He told me he had never cried before and that he really did not believe in praying with women. When he asked me why he was crying, I explained that his spirit was responding to the fire of God's Holy Spirit, which had just come upon him. We all respond in different ways; his, like mine, was with tears. When I turned to his wife, I simply could not believe my eyes. She had literally transformed right before us. Gone were the red eyes and red nose and the black circles. It was absolutely incredible. She stood there with a smile on her face; honestly, her face radiated. I had never before seen this happen. We all looked at each other, smiling through tears of thankfulness, amazed by the Presence and power of Jesus to heal the brokenhearted with the fire of His love. (♫ Worship songs about God's fire and holiness include "Fire Fall Down," by Hillsong United; "You Won't Relent," by Misty Edwards; "In the Presence of Angels," by Roy Fields, etc. I always ask Jesus to ignite a fire in my heart that will burn with passion for Him and fill me with the power of His Spirit as I pray the lyrics to songs such as these.)

Stefania and I left that day, rejoicing, for our appointment in another city, but this couple called us every day while we were monastery hunting. They insisted that we stay with them on our return trip to Rome. We did. (The husband and wife gave us their bedroom, and they stayed at a friend's house.) Flowers decorated our room, as did the delicacies on our breakfast table. We met with some of their family over lunch and more family for coffee after lunch. When we prayed together, Jesus again powerfully revealed the amazing depths of His love. This husband and wife fell in love with Jesus the day His fire healed and empowered their hearts. And they fell in love with each other again. Words cannot describe how thankful we all were for the healing of their marriage, the protection of their children's hearts, and for this testimony to their family, their community, and me.

***

Now that you have embarked on your journey inside the garden and refuge of His Presence, you will find tools in Part 2 that bring to light the incomparable treasures and unsearchable riches of His glory. Part 2 also contains practical how-to information about many of the things that have been discussed thus far in this book, such as prayer and worship, how to always stay in the Lord's Presence, and how to make sure the voice you are hearing is His voice. It also contains pearls of great price. These are lessons I learned from the Lord's school of brokenness, and His graduate course in the mission field, that have affected my relationship with Jesus and others dramatically. God bless you as you continue your journey down the garden path, on the Kingdom way.

PART 2

The Garden Path— The Kingdom Way

I will lead the blind by ways they have not known,
along unfamiliar paths I will guide them;
I will turn the darkness into light before them
and make the rough places smooth.
These are the things I will do; I will not forsake them.

—Isaiah 42:16 NIV

Living In His Light

Send out your light and your truth; let them guide me.
Let them lead me to your holy mountain, to the place where you live.

— Psalm 43:3 NLT

It is my prayer that you have begun to discover the blessedness of brokenness in your healing journey. I never thought or even dreamed that one day I would see immeasurable value in the pain I had experienced. Every hardship took me into an even deeper place within my Father's heart, because hidden within every hardship was the pathway to my destiny. Now, I am so thankful for how my heart and my life have completely changed and for what I have now become—the adoring and confident child of my Father. The pain broke me and emptied me of myself—my pride and my selfishness—so that I could live in His Presence. It seems that we are not able to see our sinfulness, or God's amazing goodness and glory, until we are broken and humbled. As Job stated after his heart breaking trials, *"My ears have head of you but now my eyes have seen you* (Job 42:4 NIV)." It is then we are able to live a life of forgiveness, which is the foundation of His peace. *For I consider that the sufferings of this present time are not worthy to be compared with the glory which shall be revealed in us* (Romans 8:18). ♫ A wonderful song about the blessedness of brokenness is "God Bless the Broken Road," by Geoff Moore.

Now that you too have walked through the small gate, onto the narrow way that leads to the secret place and refuge of God's Presence, I want to share with you ways to guard that priceless freedom as you journey even deeper into the heart of Jesus.It is where life becomes radiant with the incomparable riches of His glory.

Jesus made everything so simple. He told us to live in His light (John 8:12). There is no life without light. God's first recorded words are *"Let there be light"* (Genesis 1:3). That light was the radiance of God's glory. It is the creating and sustaining force of all life, and it emanates from His spoken word. Jesus, the manifestation of the glory of God (2 Corinthians 4:6), is called the Word of God (John 1:1, 14). When we follow Jesus, listening to His words of truth and love, we will live within the light of life—God's glory. Jesus said, *"I am the light of the world. He who follows Me shall not walk in darkness, but have the light of life"* (John 8:12).

Living in the attraction to His light—in the radiant and manifested glory of His Presence—is the key to life. So the question becomes, how do we stay there? How do we avoid living in reaction to darkness? The answer is, we never stop communicating with Jesus, we never stop worshiping Him. We were created to be like our Father, to have an intimate relationship with Him, and the end result of our intimacy with Him is to worship Him.

What is worship? Worship is the adoration of God in every aspect of life. It is the response of the heart that truly *knows* Jesus—overflowing with His love into the lives of others. When worship of God becomes our greatest desire, when the light of His love is the one thing we desire above anything else, we discover our true identity and purpose in life. God created us in His image (or in the likeness of His spiritual, relational, moral, creative, and triune nature) so that we could commune with Him and thereby experience His love. The practical effect of worshiping God is this: God reigns on the throne of my life, and absolutely nothing else can usurp or dominate that place. There is simply no room for doubt or fear or other darkness to harm or discourage me. His peace rules supremely, His healing love flows continuously, and my life is radiant with the riches of His Presence.

All forms or expressions of worship keep us listening to His voice above every other voice, looking at His character above every circumstance, and thereby safeguarding His place on the throne of our lives. Below are some of the most important expressions of worship that will help us worship the Lord not as an activity or duty, but as an impassioned lifestyle that guarantees we will stay in the light of His love:

I. Meditate on the light of God's written Word.
II. Pray without ceasing in the light of thankfulness.
III. Look into the light of His face with songs.
IV. Seek His light for direction in life.
V. Seek the light of His fire.
VI. Share the light of His love with others.

For You have rescued me from death; You have kept my feet from slipping. So now I can walk in Your Presence, O God, in Your life-giving light.

(Psalm 56:13 NLT)

I. Meditate on the Light of God's Written Word

The statutes of the Lord are right, rejoicing the heart;
The commandment of the Lord is pure, enlightening the eyes;

—Psalm 19:8

Jesus said the most important thing we can *be* in life is His child, a lover of God, heart and mind and soul. And He said that the most important thing we can *do* in life is to sit at His feet and listen to Him. Why? *"The words that I speak to you are spirit, and they are life"* (John 6:63b). Because Jesus is the Word of God (John :1:14), His words, empowered by His Holy Spirit, heal and deliver us from the lies of the enemy. His words keep us in the peace of His Presence. Therefore, God's Word is the most essential sustenance of our lives. That is why Jesus is called our Bread of Life. Without daily feeding on His words in the Bible, we simply cannot survive spiritually and physically. Jesus said, *"It is written, 'Man shall not live by bread alone, but by every word that proceeds* (present tense - is proceeding) *from the mouth of God'"* (Matthew 4:4; Deuteronomy 8:3). *Joyful are those who listen to me, watching for me daily at my gates, waiting for me outside my home* (Proverbs 8:34 NLT).

We need to feed on the light of His Word until we are so full that there is no space for darkness. Jesus explains, *"Your eye is a lamp that provides light for your body. When your eye is good, your whole body is filled with light. But when it is bad, your body is filled with darkness.* (Remember, what we behold we will become.) *Make sure that the light you think you have is not actually darkness. If you are filled with light, with no dark corners, then your whole life will be radiant, as though a floodlight were filling you with light"* (Luke 11:33–36 NLT).

How do our souls become so flooded with the light of truth that there will not be even one corner for darkness to hide in? We must meditate on His word and hide, or fill, our hearts with it. *The entrance of Your words gives light; It gives understanding to the simple* (Psalm 119:30).

Meditate on God's Word Day and Night

This Book of the Law shall not depart from your mouth, but you shall meditate in it day and night, that you may observe to do according to all that is written in it. For then you will make your way prosperous, and then you will have good success. (Joshua 1:8)

When you meditate upon God's written Word, please remember two things. Firstly, you *can* understand it. Jesus died so that He could talk personally and intimately with you. He said He would send the Spirit of truth to teach us all things, to guide us into all truth (John 14:17; 16:13). Therefore, the best teacher you will ever have is the Holy Spirit. The truth—that you are able to understand God's Word—is so vital to living in His light that I have compiled for you many Scripture verses that communicate this promise and this enabling gift and power. (Please see appendix A.) Hearing God speak to us through His written Word and His "spoken" words (i.e., thoughts, pictures, songs, and other Scriptures that His Spirit brings to mind) is the key not only to revealing the lies hidden in our hearts but also to unlocking the mysteries and wonders of His glory. We will learn to hear the Lord most clearly in the Bible and in our lives when we meditate on the very words God spoke in the Bible. God's words are the light of His love.

Secondly, God's Word contains supernatural power to accomplish every promise He gave us (Isaiah 55:11, Jeremiah 23:29, Romans 1:16, 2 Corinthians 1:20, 1 Peter 1:23, John 6:51). Hebrews 4:12 states, *For the word of God is alive and powerful. It is sharper than the sharpest two-edged sword, cutting between soul and spirit, between joint and marrow. It exposes our innermost thoughts and desires* (NLT). God's Word is alive and so very powerful in our lives because it is a two-edged sword. One edge is *logos* or the written word (Hebrews 4:12) and the other edge is *rhēma,* the spoken or revealed word (Ephesians 6:14, 17). The Holy Spirit takes that sword and pierces our soul to reveal lies and excise them with God's truth to heal us. That same sword is the victorious armor we use in life's battles to protect us. Whatever our need in life, we must search the Scriptures for specific promises about that need and personalize, memorize, and speak aloud those verses that the Holy Spirit spoke most clearly and personally. *Those spoken verses will be the most powerful and effective of all for our victory and direction.*

Knowing how Jesus thinks and understanding His heart are so important to our healing (to the revelation of lies) and to our intimacy with Him that I highly recommend the Bible study below, which focuses on His words. Remember, before you read the Bible, always ask the Holy Spirit to open your eyes and your heart to the truth He wants to reveal to you that day. I always ask the Lord to show me things about His heart and my heart that I need to know to help me love Him more. Always remember to journal everything Jesus says to you.

1) First read the Gospels (Matthew, Mark, Luke, and John). A chronological Bible would be a great help here. The Gospels contain the very words of Jesus.

(Some Bible publishers print His words in red ink.) God tells us three times in the Gospels to listen to His Son—in Matthew 17:5, Mark 9:7, and Luke 9:35:

"This is my beloved Son ... listen to Him."

Life has no point, no purpose, or plan until we enter into that relationship for which we were created—deep intimacy with God our Father. His love is deeper than any human love. The only way to enter into that intimate relationship is by listening to His Son. *Jesus said to him, "I am the way, the truth, and the life. No one comes to the Father except through Me"* (John 14:6).

Jesus is the *logos* word, the written Word of God, as recorded in the Bible. *In the beginning was the Word, and the Word was with God, and the Word was God. He was in the beginning with God.* (John 1:1, 2) *And the Word became flesh and dwelt among us and we beheld His glory, the glory as of the only begotten of the Father, full of grace and truth* (John 1:14).

Because Jesus is the *logos* word, He is also the *rhēma* word. *The words* (rhēma) *that I speak to you are spirit, and they are life"* (John 6:63). Hence the *rhēma* words Jesus speaks into our minds through the Holy Spirit *must* agree with the *logos* word. *Rhēma* words are Scriptures, pictures, and inspired thoughts that come alive with revelation of personal significance and application. They are the words that transform and empower us to live a new life in God's Kingdom. Hence we cannot survive without the words that Jesus speaks to us (Matthew 4:4). They are our bread and water—our life source. Just as the manna (bread) from heaven and water flowing from the rock saved Israel in the desert, so Jesus, the bread of life (John 6:36) and the living water (John 7:38), saves us by giving us the most important food of all—His very words. We must listen to the voice of Jesus above any other voice in our life and compare *everything* we read, hear, and think to His words. "*Come to Me with your ears wide open. Listen, for the life of your soul is at stake*" (Isaiah 55:3 NLT). As Charles Stanley said, "Not to meditate daily on God's Word is like committing suicide."

2) Read I, II, and III John. John is the disciple whom Jesus loved. He was the one who leaned on Jesus' chest at the disciples' last dinner with Jesus. He adored Jesus, and his writings show it. John, unlike any other disciple, understood the heart of Jesus. And because of that intimacy with Jesus, John was given amazing and remarkable revelations and visions of Jesus in all His glory, some of which are recorded in the book of Revelation. Steps 1 and 2 will help you know Jesus' heart intimately so that you can hear His spoken words and think His thoughts. This is the important foundation you will need as you read the rest of the Bible, looking for the heart of Jesus in every book. (Google "Jesus in every book of the

Bible" and you will find several sites listing how Jesus is pictured in every one of the sixty-six books.)

3) The book of Acts takes Jesus' words in the Gospels and His heart in I, II, III John and puts them into action.

4) Finally, read the first five books of the Old Testament, sometimes called the Torah or the Pentateuch. Then go to the book of Hebrews in the New Testament. It will help you understand and appreciate much more all that Jesus accomplished for you on Calvary and what He is living to do in and through you.

Please know that there is a big difference between meditating upon the Bible and studying the Bible. To meditate means to contemplate and reflect; to think deeply or ponder in silence. When we meditate on God's words, we listen to His Spirit; we let Him bring His thoughts to our mind. This is the intimate conversation and wonderful revelation of *rhēma* words. Only the words of Jesus can restore—heal and deliver—our souls. To study means "to devote time and attention to acquire knowledge on a subject, especially by books." When we only study or examine God's Word intellectually by reading someone's opinions, our hearts are rarely engaged, and God's Presence is rarely felt. But the one who *meditates* day and night upon God's Word finds true wisdom and becomes rich with an understanding of God's character and love. *The fear* (holy respect) *of the Lord is the beginning of wisdom, and knowledge of* (intimacy with) *the Holy One is understanding* (Proverbs 9:10).

As you meditate upon the Bible, you will notice verses "jumping off the page" at you—*rhēma* Scriptures. Your interest in these verses is the Holy Spirit alerting you to something Jesus wants to say or reveal to you. By cross-referencing the verses that impress your spirit, you can have a conversation with Jesus. Only Jesus knows what is hidden in our hearts that keeps us from understanding His Word and experiencing the depth of intimacy He desires with us. *He reveals deep and hidden things; He knows what lies in darkness, and light dwells with Him* (Daniel 2:22 NIV). Ask Jesus questions about the verses and the passages you are reading. *Search the Scriptures: A Three-Year Daily Devotional Guide to the Whole Bible* provides questions for each daily Scripture reading; it can help you start the listening/meditation process. However, your own questions about the Scripture passage are most important. It was Jesus who put those questions in your mind so that He could show you things that are important to your individual heart and life.

An important and helpful research tool is a good reference Bible. One of the best is *The Thompson Chain Reference Bible*. With this Bible, you can search by subject, topic, word, or verse. The *New Spirit-Filled Life Bible,* edited by Dr. Jack Hayford (author of over 40 books), gives a very informative view of the very important work of the Holy Spirit. *The Treasury of Scripture Knowledge,* edited by R. A. Torrey (also authored over 40 books), is a wonderful five-thousand-verse cross-reference tool. It is sometimes referenced as TSK or TK and found on blueletterbible.org, and biblehub.com, biblestudytools.com, etc. A good free Bible software program is called WORDsearch Basic (Bible Explorer).

Be sure to note the names of God and Jesus as you read the Bible. How can we say we know someone if we don't know his or her name? How we perceive or know God is how we will hear Him. Each biblical name of God reveals an important aspect of His character and glory that directs our paths and comforts our hearts. The Lord never changes, and He remains faithful to His promises. This is revealed through His names. He has a name for your every need. You can research them topically in the above suggested resources, in Bible study books (e.g., by Kay Arthur and Ann Spangler) and in Bibles such as *The Complete Jewish Bible, The Orthodox Jewish Bible,* etc., on biblegateway.com. *"I will reveal My name to my people, and they will come to know its power. Then at last they will recognize that it is I who speaks to them"* (Isaiah 52:6 NLT).

Meditate on the way Jesus mirrors and fulfills God's names in the New Testament. Just one example: *"I am the Lord* (Jehovah-Rapha) *who heals you"* (Exodus 15:26). Jesus is revealed as Jehovah-Rapha in Matthew 8:16–17: *When evening had come, they brought to Him many who were demon-possessed. And He cast out the spirits with a word and healed all who were sick, that it might be fulfilled which was spoken by Isaiah the prophet saying: "He Himself took our infirmities and bore our sicknesses."* Isaiah 53 prophesies the death Jesus would die to heal us physically, emotionally and spiritually. Jesus spoke of Himself as Jehovah-Rapha when He stood up in the synagogue (Luke 4:18) and read from the book of Isaiah (61:1–3) and said that the Spirit of the Lord was upon Him to heal the brokenhearted. Jesus is the embodiment of *all* the names of God. *Therefore God also has highly exalted Him and given Him the name which is above every name, that at the name of Jesus every knee should bow, of those in heaven, and of those on earth, and of those under the earth, and that every tongue should confess that Jesus Christ is Lord, to the glory of God the Father* (Philippians 2:9–11).

In difficult times, it is so important to focus on God's names and His character, not on our circumstances. *The name of the Lord is a strong tower, the righteous run to it and are safe* (Proverbs 18:10). Whenever our heart is troubled, we can run to the specific name of the Lord that addresses our particular need. In that name, we will always find safety, rest, and hope, because in that name we will be assured of the Lord's love for us, of His faithfulness, and of the power that enables us to live the life for which Jesus died. Also be sure during times of trouble, and in times of joy, to make a list of everything the name of Jesus means to you.

♫ Some wonderful songs that will help you worship the Lord's name include: "What a Beautiful Name," by Hillsong Worship; "Your Great Name," by Natalie Grant; "Ana Adonai," by Marty Goetz; "Shema" and "Your Name is Holy," by Paul Wilbur; "We Cry Out" and "When I Speak Your Name," by Gateway Music; "No Other Name," by Hillsong Worship; "Your Name is Glorious," by Jesus Culture; and "No Sweeter Name," by Kari Jobe. *But for you who fear my name, the Sun of Righteousness will rise with healing in His wings. And you will go free, leaping with joy like calves let out to pasture* (Malachi 4:2 NLT). *Celebrate His wonderful name with music* (Psalm 135:3 NLT).

Hide God's Word in Your Heart and Mind

"Fix these words of mine in your hearts and minds; tie them as symbols on your hands and bind them on your foreheads." (Deuteronomy 11:18 NIV)

Finally, in regard to meditating night and day on God's Word, I would like to talk to you about hiding, or sealing, God's Word in your heart and mind.

When I was in India, I loved to sit with Alice and ask her questions about the Bible. Her knowledge of the Scriptures was amazing. For every question I asked her, she responded with three or four verses from memory! If I had a question about one of the verses she gave me, she would give me another verse to ponder, to take to Jesus. She gave no opinions, no doctrines, no explanation of church traditions—just Scripture. Alice exuded a peace that was so remarkable that I can only conclude it was because of her knowledge of and confidence in God's Word, and her love for Jesus. Even in the face of demonic situations we encountered in India almost daily, Alice was always calm, always confident in Jesus' authority and power.

The spiritual battle we all face every day is real. *Stay alert! Watch out for your great enemy, the devil. He prowls around like a roaring lion, looking for someone to devour* (1 Peter 5:8 NLT). Our most powerful and victorious weapons are weapons of prayer and praise; 1) the sword of the Spirit–the verses in God's word that Jesus spoke into our heart for the need at hand is what we must proclaim in our prayers, and 2) songs of praise and worship (Section III). If that verse and song are not in our arsenal, we are defenseless. *Your word have I hidden in my heart, that I might not sin against You* (Psalm 119:11). Jesus is always our model. He resisted satanic attack with Scripture sealed in His heart (see Matthew 4, Mark 1, Luke 4). This is how we win the war that is waged in our minds. Satan hurls his lies at us, but we are shielded by and victorious with God's words of truth that we have committed to memory. For *every* challenge in life, find at least one verse that has been clearly spoken to you by the Holy Spirit regarding the challenge, memorize it, and speak it out loud continuously until the problem is resolved.

Satan's desire, or mission, is for us to worship him. To accomplish this he must separate us from God, and he does that by attacking (lying about) our identity as a child of God. Note that when Satan attacked Jesus in the wilderness, he tried to get Jesus to doubt His identity. Jesus did not even engage in that discussion with Satan because He had heard His Father's words of love saying, *"This is My beloved Son, in whom I am well pleased,"* (Matthew 3:17; 17:5; 2 Peter 1:17). Jesus said that His sheep hear His voice and follow Him and no one shall ever be able to snatch those sheep out of His hand (John 10:27–30). When we hear His voice, we know Jesus intimately, and then we are absolutely certain of our wondrous, life-giving identity in Him. We are His child and His characteristics are within us, forming us into His image. We are defined by what our Father thinks of us, not how others have labeled us. It can be daily battle to fight the world's way of thinking, and respond instead with the Kingdom way of thinking. (I *highly* encourage you to listen to "The Language of Heaven," by Graham Cooke on YouTube.)

Finally, a valuable aid that helps me seal God's words in my heart is a Bible promise book (e.g., *God's Promises for Your Every Need*). This little book lists many of God's promises according to various topics. I tape notebook paper into the book and add my own favorite verses to topics that the publication may not have included. For every topic that is relevant to my life, I highlight two or three verses that speak to me most profoundly and commit to memory at least two verses in each topic. (I keep this personalized list on my cell phone along with topical Scripture apps such as "RhemaVoice," "Shut Up, Devil," etc.) I also stick verses on mirrors or on pictures around my home to renew my mind and attitude. Be sure to never forget the importance of speaking God's Word aloud. The tongue has the power of life and death (Proverbs 18:21).

II. Pray Without Ceasing in the Light of Thankfulness

Then Jesus spoke a parable to them,
men always ought to pray and not lose heart.

—Luke 18:1

To many, prayer is a means to change one's circumstances in life. But to God, prayer is a means to make us more like Him, to commune more deeply with Him. Prayer is not a religious duty but a way of life—a lifestyle of intimate and continuous, two-way conversations with God. Because prayer is all about and entirely dependent upon our relationship with our Father, we need to be praying with Him, not simply to Him. When we see prayer as a means of deepening our relationship with the Lover of our soul, the end result of prayer will always be joy, overflowing and transforming. Books have been written about the importance and methods of prayer, but in this short section I would like to emphasize just two simple and profound points.

Pray Without Ceasing (1 Thessalonians 5:17)

Jesus said that we must abide, or remain, in Him and in His love, because apart from Him we can do nothing (John 15:5, 9). If we are abiding, or living in His Presence, we will be continuously communicating with Him. Talking with God requires our listening to God. And because it's a spiritual conversation, the Bible says we need to always pray in the Spirit (Ephesians 6:18, John 4:24, Jude 20, Romans 8:26).

Romans 8:26 states, *Likewise the Spirit also helps in our weaknesses. For we do not know what we should pray for as we ought, but the Spirit Himself makes intercession for us with groanings which cannot be uttered.* Roman 8:34 and Hebrews 7:25 state that Jesus also is interceding for us. Have you ever thought about those intercessions, or wondered what was discussed after you put your request before the Lord? I believe that the essence of their intercession would be for us to be able to discern our Father's heart and what He desires concerning our prayer request. We were created in His image to be like Him, to think like Him. This is His will for our life and His will for our every prayer. When this is achieved as we pray, all our prayers will be answered. Jesus said if we ask anything according to His will, He will do what we ask (1 John 5:14,15). When our heart becomes one with the Lord during prayer, our intimacy with Him will deepen and joy will overflow. This is the relationship with us that Jesus prayed for and for which He died. Jesus' prayers were answered and His joy was full because He always sought His Father's will—He only did what His Father was doing or said what His Father was saying (John 5:19-20, John 12:49). The essential, ceaseless question is always, Father, what is your heart in this matter?

Because the Holy Spirit abiding within us is continuously interceding for us, He always knows the mind and thoughts of our Father, at each moment of the day. So throughout the day I can be in constant communication with my Father, listening to His heart. Each morning I ask for a sensitivity to His Spirit and then all day long, in whatever I see and think, I include Him. Before I make a phone call, write a letter, or have coffee with a friend, I ask the Lord to give me His words. Before I make a decision, no matter how small, I ask for His help. When I see beauty in nature, I thank Him. Whenever I hear a beautiful love song, I think of His love for me. Whenever I hug friends or hold my children or grandchildren, I pray they are blessed with the tangible love of the One who died for them. So to me, "praying without ceasing" means reflecting with my Father all day long, upon everything I see, hear, think, and feel. Prayer is a continuous communion with His heart.

The book *Practicing His Presence* (The Library of Spiritual Classics, Volume 1, published by Seedsowers) provides valuable insight about staying in the Presence of God. It is a collection of writings by Brother Lawrence and Frank Laubach. Brother Lawrence was a French monk who lived in the seventeenth century and believed "there is not in the world a kind of life more sweet and delightful than that of a continual conversation with God. Those only can comprehend it who practice and experience it." Mr. Laubach says the same thing as Brother Lawrence, but in twentieth-century language. Many know Mr. Laubach as the Apostle to the Illiterates. *Time* magazine called Mr. Laubach "Mr. Literacy," and the US Postal Service honored his burden for literacy in children by putting his picture on the Great Americans stamps.

But an even greater passion than literacy was Mr. Laubach's passion for experiencing the Presence of God. Mr. Laubach did his undergraduate and master's work at Princeton University, his doctoral work at Columbia University, and he received his doctor of divinity degree from Union Theological Seminary. But all that head knowledge left him with a "profound dissatisfaction" with his Christian life. So he determined to go deeper into the heart of God. I was interested to read that Mr. Laubach communicated his heart and passion with songs. The influence of the song "Moment by Moment" upon Mr. Laubach was included in his book *Letters by a Modern Mystic*.

We used to sing a song in the church in Benton which I liked, but which I never really practiced until now. It runs:

"Moment by moment, I'm kept in His love
Moment by moment I've life from above;
Looking to Jesus till glory doth shine
Moment by moment, O Lord, I am Thine."

It is exactly that "moment by moment," every waking moment, surrender, responsiveness, obedience, sensitiveness, pliability, "lost in His love," that I now have the mind bent to explore with all my might. It means two burning passions: First, to be like Jesus. Second, to respond to God as a violin responds to the bow of the master. Open your soul and entertain the glory of God and after a while that glory will be reflected in the world about you and in the very clouds above your head (from Letters by a Modern Mystic).

To stay in continuous communication with God, Mr. Laubach determined not to let an hour go by, no matter what he was doing, without asking, "What, Father, do you desire said? What, Father, do you desire done this minute?" He found his determination became a natural habit, and no longer a conscious effort. I would call it a lifestyle.

Mr. Laubach's life showed me that intimacy with God does not depend on academic degrees but upon a deep desire and a reliance upon God's Spirit. As a matter of fact, I have found that all my education caused me to look more to what man was saying than to what God was saying; to think the rational way man thinks rather than the spiritual way God thinks. The Christian life is a life that flows out of intimacy with God, not information about God. It is a life lived in, and controlled by, His Spirit.

Talk to your Father without ceasing. Always ask Him what *He* wants you to say and do. If you don't soon hear an answer to your questions, wait until He does respond, resting on His promise that His sheep hear His voice. This approach protects us from regrets and disappointments and safeguards the Lord's peace in our hearts. And if you have the slightest doubt about what He wants you to say or do, don't do anything until you are certain. Because the Lord repeats Himself to make sure we have heard Him clearly, the maxim "When in doubt, don't" is a valuable safety net. Confusion is not of the Lord; when He speaks, everything becomes crystal clear.

Give Thanks to Him, No Matter What

To pray without ceasing also means giving thanks to the Lord continuously. Thanksgiving is important to experiencing God's joy our lives.When we give thanks for who He is, for His terrible sufferings and death on Calvary to set us free, for His peace and His love for us, and for His gifts and answers to our prayers, our joy becomes *full!* "*These things I have spoken to you, that My joy may remain in you, and that your joy may be full*" (John 15:11). "*Until now you have asked nothing in My name. Ask, and you will receive, that your joy may be full*" (John 16:24).

Thankfulness radically changes our attitude because we are compelled to stop and listen to our Father as we list in our minds the things for which we are grateful. It causes us to remember God's goodness and guards the awareness of His Presence in our lives. The following verses contain powerful directives that will aid our listening to God's voice:

Rejoice always. In everything give thanks; for this is the will of God in Christ Jesus for you. (1 Thessalonians 5:16, 18)

Be anxious for nothing, but in everything by prayer and supplication, with thanksgiving, let your requests be made known to God; and the peace of God, which surpasses all understanding, will guard your hearts and minds through Christ Jesus. (Philippians 4:6–7)

And whatever you do in word or deed, do all in the name of the Lord Jesus, giving thanks to God the Father through Him. (Colossians 3:17)

If you try applying these verses for one day, consciously *thanking God* all day long for every situation, for His gifts to you, and *especially for His love for you*, you will find negative and condemning words disappearing from your vocabulary. Do this day after day until thankfulness becomes not just a habit but a lifestyle. You will experience a new type of living that overcomes challenging circumstances and negative feelings. How do I know? God's Word promises it. Thankfulness to God is a form of praise, and God Himself inhabits the praises of His people.

I have one last important encouragement concerning the powerful subject of thankfulness. Please write a memoir (book, booklet, essay, journal, etc.) for your family. What greater legacy and inheritance could you leave your loved ones than a written testimony of the Lord's faithfulness in your life? No monetary or material bequest could ever compare to this powerful gift of thankful remembrance and unshakeable assurance. Revelation 12:11 states that the enemy is defeated by the blood of the Lamb and by the word of our testimony. (♫ "Overcome," by Jeremy Camp is a powerful song on this subject.) Also, Psalm 78:4–8 encourages us not to hide God's faithfulness from our children, but to tell them about the Lord's glorious deeds, His power, and His wonders. Why? Communicating testimonies of the wondrous miracles and faithfulness of Jesus in your life and in the lives of others will gift to your children a powerful spiritual and "legal" perspective to claim those miracles for themselves! *For the testimony of Jesus is the spirit of prophecy* (Revelation 19:10). Finally please know of a surety that your taking time to listen and write a memoir with Jesus will cause you to fall even deeper in love with the passionate Pursuer of broken hearts, the faithful and true Lover of your soul. I was simply amazed, as I was writing this book, to learn of mysteries in His Word that I had never before entertained, and mysteries of His compassion in my life that I had never before understood. Truly, the writing of your memoir will be another wonder-filled experience found only within the quietest moments of His Presence!

III. Look into the Light of His Face with Songs

Come before His Presence with singing ...
Enter into His gates with thanksgiving and into His courts with praise.

—Psalm 100:2b, 4a

In every manner of worship (intimate communication) we have with the Lord, we are brought closer into His Presence. This is especially true with artistic praise. Because we are all fearfully and wonderfully made (Psalm 139:14), we sense the Lord's Presence as we worship Him in different and creative ways. We are all made in God's image, but we are all individuals with unique personalities and talents. I believe that our giftedness—our particular talent or ability—was designed and given to us by our Creator as a special means to uniquely and intimately communicate with Him. Through artistic gifts, such as dance, painting, music, and writing, many people are able to sense and enter the Lord's Presence and experience all they were created to be. That is why I encouraged my children to explore all their interests, find their passion, and I prayed that the talents they discovered would not only bring them much joy, but also bring them closer to the Lord, the giver of all good gifts.

The most powerful form of artistic praise, hence the one that is commanded, is singing and making music to the Lord. So very important is singing and making music to the Lord in the Bible that more than 1,150 verses mention musical instruments and more than 600 verses deal with praising the Lord, both with and without musical instruments. Why? Because God inhabits the praises of His people (Psalm 22:3). He planned our lives to be filled with His joy. God created music for our enjoyment of Him and His enjoyment of us, for God Himself sings to us! The following verse is one of my very favorites: *The Lord your God is in your midst, the Mighty One, will save; He will rejoice over you with gladness, He will quiet you with His love, He will rejoice over you with singing* (Zephaniah 3:17).

Music is the most powerful form of communication. Hence, Ephesians 5:19 tells us to speak to each other with songs (written songs), hymns (Scripture songs), and spiritual songs (spontaneous songs). And in Colossians 3:16, it says we are to teach and admonish each other with songs and hymns and spiritual songs. Could these Scriptures mean that we should be spending more time singing to the Lord and to each other, and listening to Him sing to us, than we spend preaching to one another?

When we sing about God, His indwelling Spirit is raised up to new heights of brightness in our hearts and lives. Our minds are transformed when God is put back upon the throne of our lives through our songs of praise and thanksgiving. Therefore, songs of God's holiness and His glory are especially powerful. (♫ "You Reign," by Anna Blanc, is a very powerful song of God's glory. Please listen to this important song on YouTube.com.) When I sing of God's holiness, I most powerfully sense the refuge and safety of His Presence. Hence, it is during the most difficult and despairing times that I sing songs magnifying His majesty and songs of His love for me. I understand well that the last thing we want to do during times of despair is to sing praises to God. So when I am unable to sing, or even read and pray, I lie down in the Presence of the Lord and let the Holy Spirit sing to me as I listen to worship songs. *"You shall surround me with songs of deliverance"* (Psalm 32:7). (Note also Psalm 18:19: *He delivered me because He delighted in me.*) The enemy of our souls makes it his priority to prevent us from singing and giving thanks to the Lord in the midst of darkness. But that is precisely why we must sing. It is a most important weapon in our war against lies.

The best example of all that I can think of from the Bible regarding the importance of worship during difficult times is seen in Jesus' last evening with His disciples. He knew the horrible death that He would suffer the next day. Yet, as He and His disciples left to pray in Gethsemane, they sang their way into the night (Mark 14:26).

In the Old Testament battles, whenever Israel called on the name of the Lord, the Lord Himself fought Israel's battles and gave His children supernatural victories against overwhelming odds. Most of the time, all Israel had to do was to go into the battle singing! Isaiah 42:12—13 states that when we sing praises to God, *The Lord shall go forth like a mighty man; He shall stir up His zeal like a man of war. He shall cry out, yes, shout aloud; He shall prevail against His enemies.* Meditate on the very powerful story of King Jehoshaphat's supernatural victory in 2 Chronicles 20. Note especially verse 22: when they began to sing and to praise, the Lord set ambushes against Israel's enemies, and they were defeated! Israel's strongest and most experienced soldiers did not lead the advance. No, the Levites led the way. The Levites were priests who had consecrated themselves to the Lord, and they dedicated their lives to worshiping Him. In the New Testament, everyone who loves the Lord and worships Him is a saint and a priest—one who is called to enter life's battle with songs of worship. Singing emphasizes the great need to vocalize—to speak forth—truth. ♫ An important and powerful song regarding the battle and the victory that has already been won is "Victor's Crown," by Darlene Zschech.

Worshiping God in song is a supernatural process and a wonderful experience that transforms our lives with God's love and hope. Below are a few thoughts to help you make worship a lifestyle:

♫ **Pray for an awareness of the Lord's Presence before you do anything,** including singing to Him. Ask the Lord to open your eyes to see Him, your ears to hear Him, and your spirit to feel His Spirit communicating to you in whatever way He chooses. "We become what we behold," John Piper. We cannot become what we have not seen or heard. Asking God for a hunger for His Presence will certainly ensure that we will behold His beauty (Psalm 27:4).

♫ **Personalize your songs of worship.** We can make worship songs the prayers of our hearts by personalizing them with "I," "me," and "my" in the place of "we" and "our." Especially during corporate worship, it is very helpful to close our eyes to avoid distractions and to picture what the song is communicating. Many times during worship, as I make the words of the song a personal prayer, I see wonderful pictures in my mind about that prayer. Once, as I was praying the worship song "Open the Eyes of My Heart," I saw myself standing on the front porch of my home in Cleveland, and the Lord rode up to me on a beautiful white horse. He reached down, and as I took hold of His hand, He lifted me up behind Him onto the back of the horse. Then we rode off together into the distance, toward the East, until we disappeared. I was living in Columbus, Ohio, at that time, having run away from the heartache of my shattered marriage and having sought shelter in my hometown. However, just a few months later, my Father took me away, eastward, on my first mission trip to Italy. Then we continued eastward on other missions trips to Israel and India!

Another time I was worshiping in song and a picture of Jesus walking through enormous waves came to mind. I did a topical research on the word "waves" and Jesus gave me a verse that dealt with a problem I had been struggling with for several days. When I read God's truth about the problem, it was finally settled in my heart. His truth sets us free.

♫ **Sing worshipful songs daily. Never leave the Lord's Presence until you have heard Him speak to you (with a Scripture, picture or thought) or sensed His glory touch your spirit and surround you.** I listed in Chapter 10 many places to find worship music. Be sure to give Jesus time to speak to you during the song or after the lyrics have ended or while just instrumental music plays on. A beautiful example is Anna Blanc's most powerful version of Psalm 73:25, "Whom Have I but You" (on YouTube). Also listen to very meditative music, sometimes called "soaking music," by artists like Julie True. When Jesus brings to your mind a picture or thought, look it up in a biblical topical index, as noted above. Cross-reference the verse you found in the index and have a conversation with Jesus using *The Treasury of Scripture Knowledge*.

The tangible "manifest weight," or touch, of God's glory during your worship will be an intimate experience for the one who loves God. For me it is a time of confession and adoration and a time when I most fervently pray for those I love. Then it becomes a time of rest and quiet reassurance. I just sit and listen to His words of love for me and feel His love surround me. When the Lord reveals His glorious Presence to me in this way I never cease to be amazed, and I always think, "Oh my goodness, this is real. My faith is real! The Healer and the Lover of my soul lives and breathes within me and envelops me with His love." When I spend time like this in the Lord's Presence, His peace goes with me the best of the day. If ever something terribly difficult happens and attempts to shatter my confidence in the Lord's love for me, I run to my place of refuge with the Lord and sing or listen to songs of worship until I experience the cleft of the Rock embracing me once again.

Finally, I set aside one day each week as the Sabbath, and I worship the entire day. Did you know that God said the Sabbath was to be a day of rest *and* a day to remember that we are called to be holy (Exodus 31:13; Ezekiel 20:11–12, 19–20)? Many people call the Sabbath an observance of one of the ten commandments, but I call it a celebration. Isaiah 58:13–14 calls it a delight. On that day I listen to Jesus all day long, along with worship songs and Scriptures. As I listen, thoughts and pictures come to mind that I search for in the Bible. Many of the Scripture verses lead to another worship song. It is the most enjoyable and relaxing day of my week, a day of continuous communication with Jesus, a day of falling even deeper in love.

♫ **Worship regularly with a small group of friends.** One of the most precious and powerful times that you will ever have with your friends is when hungry and thirsty hearts gather together to cry out to the Lord for His intimate Presence. It is the desperate cry that opens the heart of God to us and our hearts to Him. In those gatherings, tears of desire bring flames of God's passionate and purifying love. This is church. Encourage your friends to be free to share the Scriptures and pictures that the Lord brings to mind during a worship song. This helps and encourages the one who is leading worship. Provide time to listen to Jesus after each song.

The best place to find these friends is in a church (and parachurch ministries) that communicates Jesus' Kingdom ministry: the First and Second commandments and the power of His Presence. (*Basileia* is the Greek word for Kingdom and it means the power of the King's domain.) Listening to the Lord's voice as we worship Him in song is as important as listening to His voice throughout the sermon and the time of prayer ministry during or after the service. We will love the Lord our God with our all heart, mind, soul, and strength when we listen to His voice. Spending time in the Presence of Jesus is what heals and empowers us to go out into the world and share His hope with others. Whenever you attend a true Kingdom gathering, you will always come away knowing that you have been with Jesus, and burdened to share His love with others.

A powerful way to share the Lord's love with the world and to make an impact upon your community is through worship gatherings. Hopefully, your small group of friends will blossom into many worship groups. Wouldn't it would be wonderful if every city and community had a place where Christians of all denominations could gather together once a month, lay down their divisive differences, and just worship Jesus in song? Wouldn't it be wonderful if every home had a room that was dedicated to worshiping the Lord—a safe haven and refuge where family and friends could go to feel the Lord's peace and love? I have seen so many miraculous healings take place where there was much time spent in worship. I saw people healed who just came to listen to the worship music. God's glory was so powerfully present that they simply walked into the room and were healed.

Truly, worshiping in song can lead to many healing experiences with Jesus. Words to a song can bring to mind a memory. Then the Holy Spirit opens the heart with that memory, and out bursts a buried heartache and its debilitating lie. One day I was worshiping and dancing to the Newsboys song "Something Beautiful" when the Lord revealed a pain I had unknowingly buried a few years earlier. The song is such a happy, joyful song about the amazing new life Jesus gives us, and it sings of many wonderful examples of the beauty of this life. I love the chorus, which says, "It's a Voice that whispers my name; it's a Kiss without any shame, something Beautiful!" But when it sang of the beauty of a child on her wedding day and the father who gives her away, down on my knees I went with a memory of my elder daughter's wedding. My former husband brought his new wife to the wedding and saddened for me our family celebration, which should have been filled with so many happy family memories. As I cried out for Jesus to take the pain of that memory away, all of a sudden I saw Jesus walk up to me and take me out onto the ballroom floor at my daughter's wedding and dance with me, twirling me in a circle of His love. Then He spoke Isaiah 54:5–10, about His being my Husband, into my mind and heart. The wonderful memory of the song "Dance with Me" filled me with His peace. I rested there in His Presence for quite some time. Then I got up and danced to another Newsboys song, "I Am Free." *You turned my wailing into dancing; You removed my sackcloth and clothed me with joy, that my heart might sing praises to You and not be silent. O Lord my God, I will give You thanks forever* (Psalm 30:11, 12 NIV).

♫ **Enjoy "secular" songs of love.** Whenever I listen to beautiful love songs, my spirit instantly thinks of the love of Jesus. "You are Loved," "When You Say You Love Me," "To Where You Are," by Josh Groan and Celine Dion's song "I Know What Love Is," could be beautiful communications of the Lord's love for us. Sometimes I sing to Jesus "I Surrender All," by Celine Dion. Often I will change a few words to a song as I sing along to make it speak even more powerfully of our need for God's love. Try it with Sarah Brightman's "Wishing You Were Here Again" from *Phantom of the Opera*, and "No One Like You," from her *Time to Say Goodbye* CD, and also with Haley Westenra's "Dark Waltz," and "The Prayer." So many songs can have spiritual meaning when the message is interpreted in the ear of the listener who is seeking God. As I think back on songs I liked as a young girl I can see that the Lord was trying to communicate to me through secular songs that had themes concerning broken hearts and the battle for our hearts, such as "Listen to Your Heart," by Roxette, "Shadows in the Night," by Pat Benatar, and many other songs that expressed the heart's pain, the heart's need. *O God, You have taught me from my youth: and to this day I declare Your wondrous works* (Psalm 71:17).

God wants to redeem everything for His glory, including all the arts. It is good to discipline our minds and teach our children to look for God's Kingdom message (or lack thereof) in everything we see and hear: paintings, poems, novels, speeches, movies, musicals, etc. When I watch heroes fight against all odds in movies, such as *Cinderella Man* and *Gladiator*, I am thankful that the Lord loved me so much that He fought to rescue me from the darkness that would harm me. Secular movies and even musicals portray the battle for light in a world of darkness, but most never seem to find the definitive, unfailing hope or the answer to that battle. Think of *Dr. Jekyll and Mr. Hyde, Phantom of the Opera, Les Miserables*, etc. Point out to your children the fallacy and implications of the line, "No right, no wrong, no rules for me, I'm free!" in the otherwise powerful song "Let It Go," from Disney's animated movie, *Frozen*. It is so very important to interpret everything in our lives in the light of God's liberating truth.

IV. Seek His Light for Direction in Life

Your word is a lamp to my feet and a light to my path.

—Psalm 119:105

♫ A wonderful and encouraging song to begin this chapter about guidance is "Thy Word," written by Michael Card and recorded by Amy Grant. It is the beautiful, musical rendition of Psalm 119:105.

Sometimes Christians become confused over what they should do in life. They agonize, wondering what God's will is for their lives and how they should make important decisions. I have found that when I live a life of worship—loving God first and then overflowing with that love to others—God Himself will step into the middle of the question, clarify it and answer it. Life simply, and beautifully, flows out of intimacy with Jesus. There are so many needs in this world, so many lives to touch with His love, that we can become overwhelmed and overextended if we try to address too many. Hence it is critical that we do only what He wants us to do. Jesus did only what He saw His Father doing. Hence He had to watch Him and wait for His direction. We need to trust Jesus to make our opportunities clear. This is why Elisabeth Elliot's advice about discerning God's will—"just do the next thing"—was so valuable. Also, did you ever notice in the Bible that all those whom God called to do something for Him were just doing the next thing in their life—that day's challenge or responsibility? They weren't out looking to do something great for themselves or for God. And when God called, He enabled.

Asking Jesus questions is the first and most exciting step in learning to hear His voice, as previously discussed, as well as an important step to receiving directions. Other things that help us hear Him direct us include: listening to His heart, applying the test of three infallible witnesses, being aware of His repetitions, and obeying Him.

Listen to the Heart of Jesus

Jesus made everything so simple. He summarized about six hundred religious laws into only two: the first and second commandments. The first commandment, also known as the Great Commandment, states that we are to love the Lord our God with all our heart, soul, and mind (Matthew 22:37). This enables us to obey the second commandment—to love others as ourselves (v. 39), or to treat others as we would want them to treat us. His instruction was so elementary that even children could understand Him. This was just one reason the religious leaders hated Him. If the people listened to Jesus, they would be set free from onerous religious rules and traditions and the legalistic or law-based control of their leaders. To me, the "spirit of religion" is one of the most deceitful and destructive of all demonic spirits. Jesus said that religious laws (traditions and institutional rules) were burdens too heavy for the people to bear. An intimate relationship with Jesus is what is needed to order our lives. When we truly love Him, we *want* to obey Him (John 14:23).

As I meditated on this one day, I realized that everything could be viewed, understood, and resolved in relation to His heart. As I applied this to my life and to controversies among families and churches in the mission field, I saw that inquiring of the heart of Jesus in every matter answers questions powerfully and ends most doubts and disputes. It also ensures a totality perspective of the Bible. When disputing parties lay down their verses, theologies, opinions of others, and desires to control and be right, and instead get down on their knees and ask Jesus what is His heart in the matter, a powerful event occurs. The parties always hear (that is, if they want to) Jesus respond to their dilemma in accordance to the reason He died: to bring healing and reconciliation to relationships, first in our relationship with our Father and then with others. And that resolves the controversy. I have never seen this solution fail when the parties have wanted help.

Also, I can spread the heart of Jesus to others. Because Jesus lives in me, I am able to powerfully affect the lives of others (including my "enemies") when I bless them with the Presence of Jesus. That is why the Bible says the power of life (and death) is in the tongue (Proverbs 18:21). The floodgates of blessing from heaven will open upon you and upon those to whom you bless. In my opinion, there is no more powerful prayer than blessing others with the Presence of Jesus (asking Jesus to make them aware of His Spirit) and the knowledge of His heart for them. Another way of speaking a powerful blessing upon people is to pray with them that Jesus will manifest Himself to them. This is how we won Muslims to Jesus in Jericho, which I describe in greater detail in Part 6, "Sharing the light of His love with others." Conversely, I believe there are no more destructive words that can be spoken to another than words of condemnation and judgment; those words throw open the gates of hell and give "legal entry" for the enemy to come and destroy both the person spoken to and the speaker. Jesus said, "Judge not, and you shall not be judged. Condemn not, and you shall not be condemned. Forgive, and you will be forgiven" (Luke 6:37). The tongue of the wise will only speak words of blessing, words of healing (Proverbs 12:18).

To illustrate, I share with you the most powerful story of blessing I have ever heard, as told to me by missionary Karen Dunham, with whom I worked in Jericho, Palestine. Her twenty-year-old son Blake was tragically hit by a bus in London. His injuries were massive—four brain lesions, a fractured spine, a broken neck, severe brain damage—resulting in the deepest level of coma. When Karen arrived in London, the doctor told her that Blake either would not survive or would not have any "quality of life." Karen politely responded, "With all due respect, doctor, I will not receive those words of sickness and death. My God raises the dead." Karen spoke blessings out loud over her son—truths from the Bible, words of hope, healing, and love—continuously, day after day, week after week. People around the world prayed for Blake. Incredibly and miraculously, Blake walked out of that hospital with his mother. I met Blake in Rome two summers later. His body was completely healed—gifted with a most precious and compassionate heart!

Finally, in regard to listening to the heart of Jesus, follow the simple and most powerful principle of *The Love Exchange*. This little book by Margaret Therkelsen presents the essence of an intimate relationship with Jesus. Each day, take six minutes to do the following: First, spend three or so minutes telling Jesus how much you love Him—how good He is, how thankful you are for Him, etc. You can share a song, (♫ e.g., "The More I Seek You," and "My Everything," by Kari Jobe; "Sinking Deep," by Hillsong Young & Free; "How I Love You," by Christy Nockles; "Whom Have I but You," by Anna Blanc; "My Desire" and "I Love You, Lord," by Kelly Willard; "Jesus Lover of My Soul," by Shelly Jennings, "This Heart of Mine," by Sheri Carr; "Lord I Want You," by Misty Edwards and David Brymer; "What Am I Without You," by Twila Paris; "I'm a Lover of Your Presence," by Brain and Katie Torwalt; "All I Want" and "Deep In Love With You," by Michael W. Smith, "Looking Forward," by Michele Wagner; "One Thing I Ask," by Ruth Fazal; "When You Say You Love Me," by Josh Groban, etc.), a Scripture verse, a poem you have written for Him, or a picture you have drawn, etc.

Secondly, spend three or so minutes listening to Jesus tell you how much He loves you; this is very important. Let His Spirit bring to your mind anything that describes to you how much He loves you—e.g., thoughts, pictures, songs, such as ♫ "My Beloved," by Kari Jobe; "Truly the Rose of His Heart" and "You Have Ravished My Heart," by Carolyn Billing; "Do You Know The Way You Move Me," by Misty Edwards; "I am the Bread of Life," By John Michael Talbot; "Come to Me," by Bethel Music, etc., and the following Scriptures:

Psalm 139:17-18; Proverbs 8:17, Song of Songs 1:15; 2:10, 14; 4:7; Isaiah 30:18; 38:17; 41:9; 41:18; 43:1–2, 4, 25; 44:3–4; 45:2–3; 46:4; 49:15–16; 51:3, 11–12a; 54:5, 10, 17; 61:3, 10; 63:9; 66:12–13; Jeremiah 31:3; Hosea 2:19; Zephaniah

3:17; John 3:16; 14:21, 23; 15:9; 16:27; 17:23; Romans 5:8; 8:37; 1 Corinthians 8:3; Galatians 2:20; Ephesians 1:5–6; 2:4–7; Colossians 1:27; 2 Peter 1:3–4; 1 John 3:1, 2; 4:16, 19; Revelation 1:5–6.

During this exchange, Jesus will not only talk to you about the depths of His love for you, but because of that love, He at times will also talk to you about things that are hiding in your heart that hinder His love from touching your life. What safer place is there, and what more intimate place is there to hear of such things, than the place where love is exchanged?

Apply the Test of Three Infallible Witnesses

J. C. Hedgecock cried out to God to show him how he could know for sure that what he was hearing in his life was truly from the Lord. He wanted to be certain he was hearing God's voice and not his own voice or the voice of the enemy. The Lord answered the cry of his heart with the three infallible witnesses test. Jesus the Son, who is called the Word of God (John 1:1), is the first witness. God the Father manifesting His peace is the second. And the perceptible movement of the Holy Spirit is the third.

Hedgecock's little booklet *The Three Infallible Witnesses* is a concise and profound instruction in discerning God's voice and direction in our lives. In Italy, this booklet is available from perciballieditore.com. In the USA, you can order it from Mr. Hedgecock's ministry at ptr.of.solm@cox.net (solm.org). The booklet showed me that I had been using the tests incorrectly, or backward, for most of my life!

When the Lord directs us in a matter, we can know we are hearing His voice:

1) **When the direction or counsel is consistent with all Scripture in God's Word, the Bible.** To me, this means it reveals the heart of Jesus. Exegesis, or biblical interpretation, made simple is this: any one verse or passage in the Bible needs to be interpreted in light of the whole Bible, and any unclear verse must be interpreted in light of all the clear verses on a subject. I used to go to the Bible and look for a verse that was consistent with or supported what I thought the Lord was saying to me. The problem with this is that we can always find a Scripture that supports what we want to hear. Therefore, the real test is to ask the Lord to show you if there is anything in His Word that would be *contrary* to what you think He is saying. Just ask the Lord to show you this, and He will.

2) **When the direction or counsel preserves the peace of God.** I used to conclude that I had heard God's voice on a matter when I experienced peace

after I prayed about it. I had this wrong too. The Christian is supposed to be abiding or living in the peace of His Presence continuously. Hence, the real test is this: if we have truly heard the voice of God on a matter, His peace will *remain*. Accordingly, if I become anxious regarding a step I want to take, I know that this direction or decision is not of Him. What makes this so profound is that I can see that the Lord allowed that anxiety so that I will ask Him *why* His peace is not ruling in my heart and, thus, regain it. The peace of Jesus is a peace that surpasses understanding; meaning, it just doesn't make sense that we could have peace in the most difficult and trying of circumstances. But we can. It will remain no matter what we are going through. *And the peace of God, which surpasses all comprehension, will guard your hearts and minds in Christ Jesus* (Philippians 4:7 NASB). It is a peace that is supernaturally, miraculously, and amazingly powerful because it is His peace living inside of me. I believe that the peace of Jesus is the Christian's litmus test—the most obvious indication of a life lived in the Presence of Jesus, the evidence of a heart in love with Jesus. Hence, I would add one other indication to test number 2: the counsel we hear from others preserves the peace of God *and* produces fruit that honors Him in our relationships with others.

I experienced a life-and-death situation in Africa that taught me the truth and importance of test 2. Stefania and I were sitting on a high bank of a river, taking pictures of several dozen absolutely enormous hippopotamuses interacting in their den with their babies. (I am convinced American zoos house only pygmy wild animals.) It was an amazing sight. We were certain that our pictures would shame National Geographic. All of a sudden, I had a panic attack. My heart beat uncontrollably. I told Stefania we needed to leave. She assured me those fat animals (who kill more tourists than any other animal in Africa and can run thirty miles an hour) could never get up our steep bank. My heart continued to race. So I got up and took a walk along the bank. Much to my horror, I came to a section of the bank that had washed out and was like a ramp to our level of the river! I ran back to my friend, and we ran to our car. Just as I started the car, a hippo bolted out of the same path after us! The Lord's removal of His peace in my heart truly saved our lives.

Finally, the "why" questions are important to our intimate relationship with Jesus and are always answered in His Presence, at His perfect time. I used to shrug my shoulders at a problem or something that did not go my way and just say, "It wasn't God's will." Now, however, I ask the Lord: "Please, Lord, show me what it is about Your heart and my heart that I need to learn from this problem." Maturity and intimacy, resulting in more freedom in our lives, will always be the outcome.

3) **When the direction or counsel is confirmed by the movement of His Spirit upon me.** In the next section, Section V, "Seek the Light of His Fire," I will

discuss the great need in our lives to be perceptibly touched by the manifested glory of God.

There is one other test that I would personally add: independent confirmation by godly counsel. God's Word states we are to examine or carefully prove all things, and always test what we hear (1 Thessalonians 5:21, I John 4:1). Because the Lord repeats Himself to confirm what He is saying (see below), when we believe we have heard a word of direction from the Lord, others who love Jesus and are praying for us will also hear the same thing. Be sure *not* to tell them what the Lord has said to you when you ask them what they believe the Lord is saying in this matter! The test is only profitable when everyone is listening individually to the Lord and without influence from the one who is seeking God's direction. Thereafter we will see the Lord bringing circumstances and events into our lives that confirm we have heard His voice correctly and that will guide us along His intended path.

Be Aware of God's Repetitions in His Word and in Our Life

I will instruct you and teach you in the way you should go; I will guide you with My eye. (Psalm 32:8)

Because God loves us and wants us to live in His Presence, He will always repeat Himself when He talks with us. God is not a God of confusion, but a God of peace (1 Corinthians 14:33). Sometimes I miss His voice the first or second time He speaks, but for sure I get it by the third time! The first time I encounter a difficulty or closed door, I usually regard the problem as just "life." The second time the same thing happens, I wonder whether it is the enemy trying to influence me or if it is the Lord's direction to stop or go another way. So I pray before I attempt a third and final try at the problem and ask the Lord for His will to be done, knowing nothing can thwart His perfect plan for me. If I am stopped a third time, I completely halt all my plans and wait upon the Lord for further directions. *The steps of a good man are ordered by the Lord, and He delights in his way* (Psalm 37:23).

After my alimony ended in the winter of 2009, seven years after my divorce, I entered a life of complete dependence upon the Lord. Jesus had taken me to many countries around the world to work with "independent" missionaries who did not have a mission organization or council of churches to be a fundraising or networking vehicle for them. Every single one of them told me that the most important thing I needed before I left for the mission field was not all my financial support, but an absolute knowledge that I was called to the work.

Then I could be assured that my Father would provide everything I needed. Jesus promised in Matthew 6:33, if we *"seek first the Kingdom of God and His righteousness,"* our every need will be provided. Jesus told us to go. Waiting until I had all the financial security I thought I needed did not look like going out in faith, as He commanded. Again, listening to His voice is key.

Also, on the flight out to Colorado, my plane had to make an emergency landing for an engine check. We were delayed fifteen minutes on the ground, and because of that, I was given a $250 coupon for my next flight. Then, when I took that flight the next year, the airline asked if anyone would give up her seat because of overbooking. I did and received a $400 coupon for another flight! That's three free flights to Colorado to visit my daughter!

One night in Rome, I had three dreams in the same night about a very heart breaking event that had happened to a member of my family. I had not known anything about this event. When I woke up the next morning, I remembered the dreams and called my mother in the States. She informed me the tragic dreams were true.

The Lord does speak to us in dreams. I never act upon dreams to make them reality; I only talk to Jesus about them, except when they come in threes, or after I have already received many Scriptural directives. I always pray against or refuse dark or negative dreams. And I always bless the Lord and the situation in a dream He gives me when it is consistent with His heart. One dream, however, I talked about with everyone! It was the most amazing dream I ever had in my life. It was in vivid, spectacular color, and it was about Jesus and His second coming!

After these experiences, I was delighted to find many places in the Bible where God spoke in threes or man listened after the occurrence of three similar events (e.g., God calling young Samuel, God commanding that the fire on the altar never be put out, Gideon's verification of God's calling, Daniel being touched three times by God, David inquiring of the Lord after three years of famine, Paul entreating the Lord three times to take away his "thorn in the flesh," God saying Jesus is His beloved Son and that we are to listen to Him, Jesus questioning Peter about Peter's love for Him, etc.). *God does all these things to a person—twice, even three times—to turn them back from the pit, that the light of life may shine on them.* (Job 33:29–30 NIV)

Obey God's Word / Obey God's Voice

He who has My commandments and keeps them, it is he who loves Me. And he who loves Me will be loved by My Father, and I will love him and manifest Myself to him. (John 14:21)

Now therefore, if you will indeed obey My voice and keep My covenant, then you shall be a special treasure to Me above all people; for all the earth is Mine. (Exodus 19:5; see also Deuteronomy 28:1-2; Jeremiah 7:23)

To know God is to love God, and to love God is to obey Him. Obedience is not only not hard for the one who has been touched with His healing love, but it also becomes the heart's desire. Why? His commands protect us, provide for us, and direct us along a garden path that leads to the *bountiful* blessings of His intimate Presence—a life filled with His light and love. When we disobey Him, the light of His love is obscured and the enemy is able to plague our lives with darkness. *Unless your law had been my delight, I would have perished in my affliction* (Psalm 119:92).

A mark of true followers of Jesus is that they listen to His voice above a denominational label. *"and the sheep follow him, for they know his voice"* (John 10:4b). Religious rules and traditions demand obedience from people to control them. True Kingdom ministry seeks to empower people rather than control them. Hence, God tells people to obey Him so that He can set them free to experience the love for which they were created. When Jesus came to set us free from religious rules (and from ourselves), He reduced about six hundred Jewish laws down to only two—the First and Second Commandments: Love God. Love others. This is the key to contentment and success and why He tells us to obey Him. The best definition of the word "love" is found in 1 Corinthians 13. My favorite musical description of love is "Arms Wide Open," by Misty Edwards (See Part 1, Chapter 4).

In short, the life that loves and obeys God is a life that wills to sacrifice. Love that will not sacrifice is simply selfish. Jesus says, *"If anyone desires to come after Me, let him deny himself, and take up his cross daily, and follow Me. For whosoever desires to save his life shall lose it; but whosoever shall lose his life for My sake will save it. For what profit is it to a man if he gains the whole world and is himself destroyed or lost?"* (Luke 9:23–25). When we have taken up our cross, we have crucified everything in ourselves and in our lives that is not of Him. Then He is able to bountifully fill us and bless us with the incomparable riches of His Presence. And that is when we truly become a blessing to others. Obedience, then, is the radiance of the attributes of Jesus—His love for His Father, His unconditional and sacrificial love for others, His compassion, forgiveness, mercy, long-suffering, etc. These traits are always evident in the life of one who loves and worships God.

Notice that whenever people in the Old Testament encountered God, they worshiped Him. They built an altar, sacrificed an offering, and bowed down before Him. God's covenant of love requires the same obedience of us. *Give to the Lord the glory due His name; Bring an offering, and come before Him. Oh, worship the Lord in the beauty of holiness!* (1 Chronicles 16:29).

What offerings can we bring in obedience to Him? First of all, a heart full of love for Him. Another sacrifice would be one of continuous thanksgiving. *I will offer to You the sacrifice of thanksgiving and will call upon the name of the Lord* (Psalm 116:17). A very powerful sacrifice of thanksgiving is to sacrifice what I am struggling with by proclaiming or singing thankfulness for God's future provision in the matter. In the process of thanksgiving, we give up or surrender every thought that is not consistent with the heart of Jesus and guards His Presence in our lives. This becomes not only a sweet offering to Him but also the salvation of our souls. *But giving thanks is a sacrifice that truly honors Me. If you keep to My path, I will reveal to you the salvation of God* (Psalm 50:23 NLT).

We are to give God our physical bodies also. Paul writes, *So, dear brothers and sisters, I plead with you to give your bodies to God because of all He has done for you. Let them be a living and holy sacrifice—the kind He will find acceptable. This is truly the way to worship Him* (Romans 12:1 NLT). When Jesus lives in us, our bodies become the temple of the Holy Spirit. *Do you not know that you are the temple of God and that the Spirit of God dwells in you?"* (1 Corinthians 3:16). His amazing glory resides and moves and breathes purity, passion and power in this temple so that more of Him is revealed in us. The more we become like Jesus the more we will see and hear Him. *"Be holy for I am holy"* (1 Peter 1:16, Leviticus 11:45). When our body is a temple for God, God's holiness always protects us. *"I have consecrated this temple ... by putting my Name there forever. My eyes and my heart will always be there"* (1 Kings 9:3 NIV). Defilement of God's temple brings darkness and separation from Him; it brings death into our lives.

We are to offer our material possessions to Jesus. When Jesus called His disciples to follow Him, He told them to sell their possessions and give to charity so that they would have eternal treasures. (Jesus' favorite charities benefit the poor.) When Zacchaeus told Jesus he would give half of his goods to the poor and restore fourfold anything he had wrongfully taken, Jesus took note of Zacchaeus' heart and said that salvation has come to his house. Jesus knows our hearts; *"For where your treasure is, there your heart will be also"* (Luke 12:33–34). Because He made us, He knows that material things will never bring us contentment or fulfillment. When I finally understood that everything I have is a gift to me from God, I no longer struggled with giving back to God a portion of what He has given me (including my time). And when I finally entered into the garden and refuge of His Presence and fell in love with Him, I knew He would always provide for my every need. Then I desired to give to Him not just a portion, but everything.

Did you ever notice Jesus never talked in terms of "portions" or "parts"? He always talked in terms of "everything." He said in the first commandment to love the Lord our God with *all* our heart, soul, mind, and strength—with our *entire* being. His Word says that we are to take *every thought captive to make it obedient to Christ* (2 Corinthians 10:5 NIV). How do we do that? We simply ask Jesus if the thought is true. The battle is waged in our minds, and victory is sure when every thought is of truth. One lie can become a stronghold and totally defeat us. That is why Jesus commanded us to be transformed *by the renewing of our minds* (Romans 12:2). This is absolutely critical. Renewal is a daily process that begins with repentance. This opens our ears to hear truth and our minds to think and speak truth. A renewed mind seeks to think like Jesus.

Hence, before we offer any gift to the Lord, we need to come before Him with no unforgiveness in our hearts and with a heart that has attempted to reconcile with those who have something against us. So often we think of the need to seek forgiveness only for the wrong things we have said or done to or thought about another. But remember, it also includes the other way around. We are to seek forgiveness from those who are upset with us even when we think we are innocent (Journey 5). "*Therefore, if you bring your gift to the altar, and there remember that your brother has something against you, leave your gift there before the altar, and go your way. First be reconciled to your brother, and then come and offer your gift*" (Matthew 5:23-24). This is the ministry of Jesus—the reconciliation of broken hearts, living in right relationship with God and others. And it is the ministry He has entrusted to us with His life (2 Corinthians 5:18-19).

Finally, if we struggle with obeying God, we need to ask Him why we struggle. I believe that obedience, faith, trust, etc., are not our real problems. Our real underlying problem is always a love problem. Hence, when I struggle to obey, I ask the Lord to reveal what lie is hiding inside my heart that is hindering my love for Him. And whenever He reveals what is not of Him in the hidden places of my heart, I simply repent, and I am set free to love Him, to obey Him. We also need to seek Jesus if ever we find ourselves obeying Him not out of love for Him, but out of fear of punishment from Him. Usually this is because an earthly parent or trusted individual punished us severely and we now fear the same of God, our heavenly parent. When God saves us and then heals us, He sets us free to live in a brand-new home with a brand new Father, where obedience is always motivated by love. "Jesus answered and said to him, "*If anyone loves Me, he will keep My word; and My Father will love him, and We will come to him and make Our home with him*" (John 14:23). And in this new home is brand-new family—brothers and sisters who love Jesus and, accordingly, who will love the way Jesus loves us (Psalm 68:6; John14:18).

Seek the Totality Perspective of the Bible; Read the Bible from Cover to Cover

Oh, send out Your light and Your truth! Let them lead me. (Psalm 43:3)

For so much of my life, I only studied the Bible. I did not meditate upon it, as directed by God's Word. And I also studied only parts of the Bible—various topics and particular books. The problem with this is that I never gained a totality perspective of the Bible. This posed difficulties in both interpretation and direction. As stated, in respect to biblical interpretation, it is very important to see and understand each part of the Bible in light of the whole Bible. Furthermore, it is impossible to understand and appreciate the New Testament without a foundation in the Old Testament. The Bible is a book of progressive revelation. I never saw the fire of God nor truly understood His glory in the New Testament until I meditated upon those things in the Old Testament. *"Jesus Christ is the same yesterday, today, and forever"* (Hebrews 13:8). And in regards to direction for my life, I did not have a thorough knowledge of the Bible to know if the direction I was going was *inconsistent* with God's Word (the first "infallible witness" test). Accurately hearing God's voice and walking with Him in the direction He wants us to go requires that we gain an understanding of the entire Bible—the total picture.[11]

There are many Bible reading plans available to help you read several chapters of the Bible each day so that you can finish the entire book in a year. Each reading enumerates the month and day and provides the Scripture passage for each day of the year. Using such a plan helps keep me accountable to read every day. I especially enjoy reading *The One Year Chronological Bible,* which has the daily readings arranged in the order in which events actually occurred. That way I can read all the passages in the Bible about a particular event or subject at one sitting, and I am able to get a more complete picture. The New Living Translation (NLT) and the New International Version (NIV) are easier to read, but when memorizing or meditating upon specific verses, I always compare them with the New King James Version (NKJV) or the New American Standard Bible (NASB). The NKJV and NASB are said to be the most accurate translations from the original Hebrew language of the Old Testament and the Greek language of the New Testament. I find all these translations on Bible websites (e.g.; blueletterbible.org; biblehub.com; biblegateway.com). Let me give you three examples of how words can vary from one version to another:

11 Regarding the direction of this book: It is interesting to note that I started reading through the entire Bible every year shortly after I began writing the book in 2002. After reading though the Bible eight times, *When Jesus Answers* was birthed in 2010 to communicate what I believe is the most important subject of all—one's ability to hear and obey God's voice. It is the key to intimacy with our Father, healing and deliverance, and power.

1) Isaiah 61:1: The NKJV states that the Lord "heals" the brokenhearted. The NLT uses instead the word "comfort." Friends can comfort us. Only Jesus can heal us. It is also interesting to note that in Luke 4:18 (where Jesus quotes His mission from Isaiah 61:1), the statement that He was sent to "heal the brokenhearted" appears in the NKJV and in *Young's Literal Translation* but not in the other versions.

2) Deuteronomy 13:4: The NKJV states that we are to keep God's commands and obey His voice. The NIV states that we are to keep God's commands and obey Him. The NIV is not only redundant but also misses the most important part of obedience—listening to God speak to us.

3) Psalm 34:18: The NKJV states, *The Lord is near to those who have a broken heart, and saves such as have a contrite spirit.* The NLT and NIV state a "crushed" spirit. There is a big difference in our being crushed or devastated by an experience in life and our being contrite or convicted and repentant in the way we responded to the experience. And that difference is crucial to our healing.

No matter what is going on in your life, no matter what book of the Bible you are reading, the Lord will speak to you through His Word. It is amazing and wonderful to see something new and different in the Bible every time you read it. When you see something new in God's Word, that is Jesus speaking to you. Always journal whatever Jesus speaks to you. It's wonderful to know we have a God who wants so much to talk with us! You will reach a point on your garden journey when you wake up in the morning with a desire so deep for His Presence that you can hardly wait to get into His Word to see what He has to say to you that day. This hunger and thirst for His words of truth and love will deepen and deepen, and so will your love for Him. It is one of those incomparable riches of His Presence. *O send out Your light and Your truth, let them lead me; Let them bring me to Your holy hill and to Your dwelling places* (Psalm 43:3 NASB).

Read Biographies about People Who Loved God's Presence

Jesus said the two most powerful communications to defeat the enemy are the blood of the Lamb, and the words of our testimony (Revelation 12:11). The autobiographies and biographies of Corrie Ten Boom, *The Hiding Place;* Amy Carmichael, *A Chance to Die,* by Elisabeth Ellliot; Brother Yun, *The Heavenly Man;* Smith Wigglesworth, John G. Lake, Reinhard Bonnke, William Booth, St. Augustine, George Mueller, Catherine Marshall, Jim Elliott, *Through Gates of Splendor,* by Elisabeth Elliot; and Heidi Baker, *Always Enough,* just to list a few, are good examples of influential testimonies. (Remember, be sure to write for your family your own memoir about the faithfulness of Jesus.)

Most of the above books were recommend to me by other people. However, Jesus Himself told me to read about the life of St. Teresa of Avila. How did He tell me this? One day I was walking down XX Via Septembre in Rome. I just "happened" to walk by a church that caught my eye because my daughter's name was on it. Well, sort of; it was called Santa Maria della Vittoria. It was a rather humble-looking church on the outside, but when I walked inside, mamma mia! (as the Italians say). It was incredibly beautiful! There were Bernini marble angels flying everywhere. As I walked to the front of the church, I saw why Jesus had brought me there. Bernini's famous life-size sculpture of "The Ecstasy of St Teresa" was to the left of the altar, framed by marble columns. Before that day, I had never heard about this Bernini sculpture or its story, so I stood there, overcome by its beauty and, especially, its subject. This powerful sculpture depicts Teresa's vision of an angel piercing her heart with an arrow; when the arrow was drawn out, it left her on fire with the love of Jesus. Theresa of Avila, who lived in the 1500s, said that her "devotions of silence" and "devotions of ecstasy" brought her to a "perfect union" with God, wherein she frequently experienced a rich "blessing of tears."

V. Seek the Light of His Fire

...and the fire of the altar shall be kept burning on it ...
And the fire on the altar shall be kept burning on it; it shall not be put out ...
A fire shall always be burning on the altar; it shall never go out.

—Leviticus 6:9, 12–13

Ask for God's Fire to Empower Your Life

The fire of God's Presence is just that—a fire. It burns flames of purification, passion, and empowerment. The fire emanates from His glory. When it descends upon us, we are consumed with His love, and we are purified, empowered, and impassioned until we glow with His beauty and likeness. A fire burns hot, and it will always be seen and felt. There is no such thing as a lukewarm fire. It either burns hot or it goes out. That's why God's Word tells us never to let His fire go out. When it does, the smoke of darkness rises and suffocates our spirit. We either love God with all our heart, mind, soul, and strength, or we really don't love Him at all. Love is a consuming fire, and it always falls upon a sacrifice. It was in the mission field that I came to the conclusion that the Kingdom life doesn't really work in my life unless I give it 100 percent. If I give God 90 percent of my life, the enemy sprinkles his yeast of deception in that remaining 10 percent, and before I know it, I become a lump of doubt or fear. Now I understand why Jesus used the word "all" in the first commandment.

I love the story of Elijah and his contest with the worshipers of Baal (1 Kings 18). Really, it was no contest at all, just a wonderful display of the majesty of our God and the tragedy of those who worship what their hands have made. Elijah said words that day that became an ember in my heart: *"How long are you going to waver between two opinions? If the Lord is God, follow Him! But if Baal is God, then follow him!"* (1 Kings 18:21 NLT). But that ember did not grow into fire until the walls around my heart came down, allowing the breath of God to fan those flames. As Elijah had said to the people that day, *"The God who answers by fire, He is God"* (1 Kings 18:24). How true!

From Genesis to Revelation, the fire of God came down to ignite hearts so that lives could return to live in the garden and refuge of His Presence, to be clothed in His love and to be enflamed to radiate the riches of that love to others.

God's fire is a wonderful topic to study, and most important, it helps us realize that God intends for our lives to be exciting, passionate, and overflowing with the wonder and "incomparable riches" of His manifested glory. As I look back on my journey, I see that my earlier life as a Christian was very ineffective and boring in comparison to life now lived with His Presence burning in my heart. Below are just a few points on this immense subject I would like to share with you that I discovered as I studied about God's glory in the Bible. I hope you will find a few embers that can help light the path to the fire of His amazing Presence *continually* burning in your life.

The Fire of God's Glory is Found in Both the Old and New Testaments

Whenever the glory of God appeared, it was communicated or manifested in a tangible or visible manner. In other words, whenever God's glory suddenly appeared, the people saw it, felt it, or heard it. God's manifested glory is unmistakable. It is miraculous. Here are just some of the ways people experienced it: in a cloud (Exodus 40:34, 35; Matthew 17:5), through God's fire (Exodus 24:17; 2 Chronicles 7:3; Acts 2:3), in the appearance of angels (Luke 2:13, 14), in the sound of a rushing mighty wind (Acts 2:2), in the quake of a mountain (Exodus 19:18), in the winning of battles supernaturally (Exodus 14:24-26; Joshua 10:10-12), in prophecies and languages (1 Corinthians 12:10), in the quake of a building (Acts 4:31), at the descent of a dove (Matthew 3:16; John 1:32), in the radiance of faces (Exodus 34:29, Matthew 17:2; Acts 6:5), in God's audible voice (Deuteronomy 4:12, 36; 5:4, 24, 26; 1 Kings 19:12; Isaiah 6:8; Daniel 10; Matthew 3:16; 17:5; Acts 9:3–4; Revelation 1:17), in dreams and visions, and in many physical and emotional healings and other miracles.

Take time to meditate on the verses where God's voice is heard in the midst of His glory. I love especially Deuteronomy 4:12: *"And the Lord spoke to you out of the midst of the fire."* His Presence is His voice, and when He speaks, we feel His love, we encounter His glory.

When God's glory descends upon us, we can sense the movement of His spirit—His Spirit touching our spirit. Two Old Testament examples are Daniel and Isaiah. Meditate on Daniel chapter 10, noting the circumstances surrounding Daniel's amazing experience of being touched three times by the Lord. In Isaiah chapter 6, Isaiah sees the Lord in all His glory. When Isaiah hears God's voice, he feels the doors of the temple shake. And then, in the midst of that glorious Presence, he feels his lips touched by a burning coal.

Isaiah's body and speech were purified by the touch of God. Look now in the New Testament. In two accounts of the glory of God coming upon Jesus, we see in one the Holy Spirit descending upon Jesus at His baptism in the form of a dove and in the other, at His transfiguration, the brilliant radiance of light emanating from Him. In Acts 2 and 4 the heads of the new believers were touched by God's fire and notice that, like Isaiah, when they were touched they were empowered to speak to others about God. It is a touch that cannot be denied and a love that cannot be contained. Meditate upon the touch and life of Jesus in the New Testament. His healing touch and words changed lives forever. Reflect every day upon the truth and power of His Spirit being alive in us. *Christ in you, the hope of glory* (Colossians 1:27b). When this truth has taken hold, when we finally come to grasp the amazing effect upon our lives brought about by Jesus Himself, His Spirit, residing within us, there will be nothing that we cannot do for Him and for our loved ones.

The Fire of God's Glory Comes upon Us during Worship

One of my favorite passages in the Bible regarding the power of worship and the manifestation of God's glory is found in 2 Chronicles 5. This is a wonderful chapter! During the dedication of the temple in Jerusalem, the sanctified (purified) priests carried the ark of the covenant (signifying God's Presence) into the Most Holy Place of the temple and sang with the priests who were singers and trumpeters to make one sound of united praise and thanksgiving to the Lord. They sang, "For He is good, for His mercy endures forever" (verse 13). Then the temple was filled with a cloud ... *so that the priests could not continue ministering because of the cloud; for the glory of the Lord filled the house of God* (verse14). When I read that, I began to dream. Oh, how wonderful it would be if one day church services became times when believers gathered together to invite the Lord's Presence, and worshiped God in song until the manifest weight of His glory came down to fill their hearts and the place where they gathered. Oh, how very wonderful!

The Lord said to Solomon after the glorious temple dedication, *"For now I have chosen and sanctified this house, that My name may be there forever; and My eyes and My heart will be there perpetually"* (2 Chronicles 7:16). God told Moses and His children that He would always meet with them and speak with them in the Tabernacle, and that the Tabernacle would be made holy by His glory (Exodus 29:42–43).

The Fire of God's Glory Descends upon the New Testament Temple

The above is not just an old Old Testament story. The Old Testament was the foundation upon which Jesus fulfilled and revolutionized our relationship with God. In the Old testament the fire of God came down upon the sacrifice and His glory filled the temple (2 Chronicles 7). The Tabernacle and temple buildings and altar sacrifices are gone, but God's Presence remains. When the Holy Spirit lives in us, our bodies become God's temple. We are made holy and clothed with the fire of His Presence when we cry out for God's glory to come upon us. His heart is in us and His eyes are upon us. We are the priests who have been sanctified by the blood of the Lamb. Because we carry the Presence of Jesus inside us, we can always go directly and boldly into the Most Holy place with Him and there hear Him speak to us and be empowered by His Holy Spirit. Please listen to "Shekinah Glory," by Jaye Thomas and Cory Asbury.

The Fire of God's Glory Will Radiate from Our Faces

As you can see, there will always be a noticeable and obvious realization in our heart and spirit that the fire of God's glory has descended upon and moved within us. It is a time of purification and inexpressible intimacy with Jesus and will be evidenced in our changed lives—and even in our faces. Throughout the Bible, there were people who saw the Lord and heard Him speak, then became radiant with His glory (Moses in Exodus 34:29; Jesus in Matthew 17:2; and Stephen in Acts 6:15). I have been in the presence of people who loved the Lord so much that they exuded a peace I could feel and a radiance of Jesus in their faces I could see. This is what happens when we go *from glory to glory* (2 Corinthians 3:18)—each day being touched with the intimacy and transforming power of His glorious Presence.

The Fire of God's Glory Moves Personally and Individually

There is no limit how God's Spirit may choose to manifest Himself physically to each individual. (See Exodus 34:29; 2 Chronicles 5:13–14; 7:1–3; Matthew 3:16–17; Luke 3:16; 8:46; Acts 2:1–3; 4:31; 6:15.) The movement of the Holy Spirit upon us can take the form of an emanating warmth, a whispering wind, an all-consuming peace, a gentle weight encouraging us to bow down, or it can bring tears, exuberant joy, tingling sensations, or a radiant, even glittering glow, etc.

Because we are "fearfully and wonderfully made" (Psalm 139:14), we will respond to the moving of the Holy Spirit in different ways. The usual response of my spirit is that tears suddenly come to my eyes. These are not tears of sorrow, but tears of His Presence. Other times, I sense His nearness when a peace comes upon me that is so weighty I can hardly move, so I just rest upon His chest, listening to His heart beat with mine and listening to His words of love for me. The key to experiencing the manifest Presence of Jesus is a daily desire, a deep hunger to be with Him and never to stop crying out, as Moses did, "Please show me Your glory!" And it will come; I promise you this, as does He who died for you. "Show Me Your Glory," by Jesus Culture is a powerful song. My favorite stanza is, "I long to look on the face of the One that I love; Long to stay in Your Presence, it's where I belong!" I hope the song blesses you.

In Chapter 9 I shared that I was told the Christian life was not about feelings but only about faith. This instruction caused me to miss the greatest joy and most amazing experience of life—feeling the nearness and love of Jesus. Oh, how I wished I had listened to His Word instead of man's words. His Word states that His Kingdom and the fruit of His Spirit are love, joy, and peace (Galatians 5:22; Romans 14:17). His peace is not an emotion; it is a state of being—that peace being the Prince of Peace living inside us! We can and do feel the incredible and wonderful movement of His Spirit as His glory falls upon us and clothes us. Truly, there is nothing on earth more precious to the child of God than the tangible awareness of the Lord's manifest Presence when He speaks His words of love or when His Spirit moves to manifest Himself and the peace of His unmistakable nearness. To me, the manifestation of God's glory moving upon one's spirit is one of the greatest evidences of the existence of God, one of the greatest "riches" of His glory. The other great evidence is the radically, powerfully, and miraculously transformed life of the individual who knows Jesus as his Savior and Healer. Evidences of the descent of the glory of God upon us us will be seen in the manifestation of a supernatural gift or gifts of the Spirit such as wisdom, languages (known and spiritual), healings, prophecy, etc., (I Corinthians 12:4-11). The ultimate evidence will be seen in the life that reveals the heart of Jesus—what good is my gift to heal deaf ears if I do not have compassion upon the poor, or if I am unforgiving?

If that awareness or sensitivity to the movement of His Spirit upon us is missing in our lives, we need to ask the Lord for it and seek it with all our heart. (See "Prayer to be Clothed with God's Glory" in Chapter 12.) It may require long hours and may require many days spent alone with the Lord. And most certainly, we need a deep hunger that cries out from our heart for His manifest Presence. So deep is this hunger that fasting, praying, worshiping in song, reading, and listening to Him becomes the deepest desire of our hearts as we seek His royal robes. His Presence will be the one thing (Psalm 27:4) we desire and seek more than anything else. *"I love those who love me, and those who seek me diligently will find me"* (Proverbs 8:17). ♫ This truth is expressed in a most beautiful and *wonderful* song "The More I Seek You," by Kari Jobe. Please listen to this song on YouTube and be very blessed.

O God, we meditate on Your unfailing love as we worship in Your Temple.
(Psalm 48:9 NLT)

VI. Share the Light of His Love with Others

Come and hear, all you who fear God, and I will declare what He has done for my soul.

—*Psalm 66:16*

[Jesus said] Heal the sick, cleanse the lepers, raise the dead, cast out demons.

—*Matthew 10:8*

I believe there are two reasons Jesus told us to go into all the world and preach the gospel to every creature. (Jesus loves His animal creation too! See Proverbs 12:10; Psalms 36:6, 50:10–11; Jonah 4:11, etc.)[12] He sends us out to share His love in order to lift us outside of ourselves as a means to heal us (Isaiah 58:10). And He sends us out to complete His perfect plan for us—when we fall in love with Him we will overflow with that love to others. Our lives are made whole and joyous through intimate relationship—first with God, and then with others. Note this fact of creation in nature: when something receives, it then gives back. For example, when the mountains are blessed with rain, the water runs off to the valleys downstream, and the plants receive much-needed moisture. When the light of the sun shines on green plants, the plants give off, or breathe, oxygen. This is a wonderful analogy to the life-giving radiance and glory of God. As the sun spreads its rays on the ground, plants grow, and the farmer reaps seeds for the future crops of vegetables that he sells to the grocer, who then provides food for the city dwellers. Accordingly, we who have received the incomparable riches of God's grace will want to give to others from the bounty of physical and spiritual blessings that God has freely bestowed on us.

Only fear the Lord, and serve Him in truth with all your heart; for consider what great things He has done for you. (1Samuel 12:24)

Furthermore, a lake that receives rainwater but doesn't give away that water becomes stagnant and salty. It loses the freshness of the pure water pouring into it. This is what has happened to the Dead Sea. It is so saline that nothing can exist

12 Did you ever notice that after God created Adam, and said that Adam needed a helper and companion, the very next thing God did was not to create Eve, but to bring the animals to Adam? This is why healing prayer ministry using relational animals such as horses (Faith Based EAP) and dogs is so powerful—they exude God's unconditional love and they respond to what we cannot see inside ourselves.

in its waters. And it will happen to us too if we don't become a conduit for God's grace and love. When we store up God's blessings just for ourselves, our lives will become stale and dissatisfying. But the more we share His love and grace with others, the fresher and more exciting will be our own faith. Our lives will be content. It is simply how our Father created us—it is a fact of creation, it is our spiritual DNA—that we come into God's light and then we radiate it. Our lives were not planned to come into a church building and stay there.

I believe that churches should be places that minister healing to the broken. One church I attended has this wonderful phrase written on the front of its sanctuary: "Where broken vessels are made new." The testimony of the healed and delivered heart is more powerful than any sermon. If we are not walking in the miraculous, then we need to ask Jesus why. Jesus said we are to go into all the world and preach the gospel (Mark16:15). "*And as you go, preach, saying, 'The Kingdom of heaven is at hand.' Heal the sick, cleanse the lepers, raise the dead, cast out demons. Freely you have received, freely give*" (Matthew 10:8; see also Mark 6:13, 16:17–19; Luke 9:2, 10:9). This is God's plan and prayer: that His Kingdom comes and His will is done on earth, *just as it is in heaven* (Matthew 6:9). ♫ Two powerful songs about this plan and prayer are "Heaven On Earth," by Micah Stampley and "Our Father," by Bethel Music with Jenn Johnson.

In this section, I take you to the foreign mission field and share in the context of mission stories, hands-on subjects such as prophecy, living by faith, spiritual warfare, and healing miracles, which I hope will embolden you to pursue the truly miraculous Kingdom life.

But before we do that, here are three points you can implement right now in your most important mission field of all—your family and friends. They concern prayer partners, prayer evangelism, and communion.

A. Family and Friends Missions

Prayer Partners are Indispensable

Two are better than one, because they have a good reward for their labor... For if they fall, one will lift up his companion. But woe to him who is alone when he falls, for he has no one to help him up ... Though one may be overpowered by another, two can withstand him, and a threefold cord is not quickly broken. (Ecclesiastes 4:9–10, 12)

A tremendous encouragement and necessary support to me in my Christian journey has been a small group of prayer partners. (Even Jesus Himself had prayer partners—Peter, James, and John.) Prayer partners provide much-needed accountability and support in our lives and can be the arms of Jesus to hold and encourage us in each stage of our life's journey. As my children were going through school, I would meet almost every week with a Moms in Touch group to pray for our children, their schools, and our families. I mentioned in Chapter 3 how Natalie's prayer partnership helped me through a most difficult time in my life. That partnership with Natalie grew with the addition of three other women in our neighborhood—Mary, Jane, and Janie. Together, we prayed for our families and hosted coffees and luncheons to share the love of Jesus with our friends. Pray for a prayer partner as your first step in reaching out to others. That prayer partnership will hopefully blossom into a small worship and prayer group—a most blessed and powerful community.

Whenever you gather for prayer or Bible study, be sure to invite or welcome the Presence of Jesus. Then encourage everyone to listen to Jesus during the prayer and Bible study time and share freely the verses and thoughts of truth and love that the Holy Spirit brings to mind. Do not confine gatherings merely to the opinions of the author of the study book or the leader of the group. It's wonderful to see how often different people hear Jesus say the same thing! He does repeat Himself.

Prayer Evangelism is Compassionate and Beautiful

One of the easiest and most precious ways to share the Lord with your friends who do not know Jesus intimately is to simply pray with them. Praying with friends blesses them with the Lord's Presence and love. One way you can help open the door to ministering to your friends is to ask them what is the deepest burden they are carrying. Many times when I have had only one opportunity to pray with someone, that question has helped identify and scale the biggest mountain in the person's life and help start the listening journey with Jesus. The Lord will use this information to bring a verse of Scripture or a song (the universal language) or a book to your mind to share with your friends so they can see your concern for them and the relevancy of God's Word in their life. Be sure to personalize the Scripture and tell them to always speak it aloud. When they see answers to these prayers, they will certainly want to know more about the One who cares so much about their sufferings and worries that He would listen to their prayers and answer them.

One other evangelistic tool: As I was traveling from country to country and meeting so many people everyday, I asked Jesus what was the most important thought I could leave with them. He told me to tell them, "Did anyone ever tell you Jesus loved you so much that He died on a cross so that He could talk with you?" What a profound seed.

Daily Communion Keeps Us Focused and Thankful

A Malaysian missionary talking to a women's group in Rome had just returned from a revival in Florida, and she was ablaze with the radiance of Jesus! Her love for Jesus and her confidence in His power to radically change lives was also quite evident. She talked about a subject that was so simple yet so profound—the importance of taking communion (thanking the Lord for His death and resurrection with bread and wine) in our lives daily.

When I was a young girl, my church observed communion once a month. Later I attended a church that observed it every Sunday. However, looking back, I saw that in contrast to the intimate experience it was when this missionary shared communion with us, my Sunday communions at church had become just a rote experience. Occasionally we had time to discuss the problem of our sin. Less time was available for us to get on our knees and tell Jesus how sorry we were for our sins. And very rarely was there any time for us to invite the Lord's Presence to reveal the things hiding in our hearts that grieved Him.

After spending time with this missionary, our church community in Rome started sharing communion together almost daily. It had a profound effect upon me to pause daily to reflect upon all the Lord had gone through to set me free so I could hear Him tell me about the love that sent Him to Calvary. I could only wonder what a powerful impact sharing communion together in homes could have on marriages and families! I am very sorry to say that my family and I never once shared communion together in our home. We simply practiced church tradition and never practiced the Presence of Jesus in this manner. I encourage you to make communion an unceasing prayer of thankfulness and consistent part of your life without turning it into a legalistic rite that loses its intimacy and joy. Powerful songs you might want to worship with when you observe communion include "I am the Bread of Life," by John Michael Talbot; "Remember Me," by Steve Camp; and "Communion Song," by Laura Kaczor (Chapter 7).

B. Foreign Missions work - The College of the Kingdom

And if you extend your soul in behalf of the hungry and satisfy the needs of the oppressed, then your light will rise in the darkness, and your night will become like the noonday. (Isaiah 58:10)

To me, one of the most powerful ministry experiences one could ever experience is foreign missions work. I found the mission field to be a place of healing and a world of wonder. While working in the States, I thought I knew what the Kingdom life was all about. So much of my ministry in America was experienced through a church organization, group Bible study, or other organized event, and usually only with people in my church. Missions work opened my eyes and heart to a radically different life. Meeting and listening to the hearts of Christians from other cultures was fascinating and inspiring. I loved to listen how Jesus had captured their hearts and how He was moving in the hearts of their families and in their country. The mission field showed me the Kingdom world in simple events and in the simple lives. I saw in the mission field why the poor were so close to the heart of Jesus. And that new awareness helped set me free from the prison of materialism and man's opinions of Jesus in America. Missions gave me a new understanding of my Father's heart, my heart, and my need to share His love every day with whomever I met. Working in missions put life into perspective for me at last.

My vistas expanded greatly when I participated in miraculous Kingdom life experiences, such as healings, deliverances, transformations of hearts and homes and villages, and many other ways I saw the love of Jesus manifested in the mission field. All this produced in me a faith and a fire that I had never possessed before in my life. It became a flame in my heart that I could not contain; I had to share it. No one had to tell me about the Great Commission, which is Jesus' instructions for believers to share their faith with the world (Matthew 28:18–20). I was able to experience how dynamic and transforming the Great Commission was in every place I traveled.

I would have to write another book to share all the amazing experiences I encountered in the mission field. The following are just a few that communicate some helpful insights I learned in ministering to the hearts of others. It was in the mission field that I received the most important and priceless education of all. Truth-for-life lessons abound in missions work. There were so many things in the Bible I either did not see or did not understand until I experienced these things in obedience to Jesus' command to go. Truly the mission field was where I discovered the answer to the many ponderings of my heart as I experienced the heart of Jesus in every situation in life.

What Is "The Gift of Knowledge," What Does It Look Like?

In 2003, at the age of fifty-three, I took my first mission trip, an experience that opened a new world to me. I learned for the first time that I could hear Jesus speak to me about the pain in another's heart without even talking to that person. I had previously experienced, in healing prayer ministry, the Lord graciously and mercifully reveal to me the cause of an individual's problems, either through conversation or during prayer with the individual. But one night after a service in Sicily, I was waiting at the front of the church with Pearl Foti to pray with whomever came forward for prayer. (Pearl is the wife of Franco, the leader of our Harvest International Ministries team, to whom I will forever be grateful for opening for me the door to a brand-new and fascinating world.) A woman approached us. But before the woman even spoke, Pearl told her the precise reason she had come forward for prayer. The woman nodded and cried. I was amazed. Our prayer together was precious for this broken woman. Later that evening, I asked Pearl if she had asked the Lord for this gift of discernment. She said no, adding that she had only asked Jesus to give her His eyes to be able to see people as He did. And she did. I carry that advice close to my heart and that prayer on my lips for whomever I meet.

"The Righteous Shall Live by Faith." What Does a Life Lived by Faith Look Like?

Before the team left for the States, leaving me alone to tour Italy, Franco introduced me to a young widow in Rome. (My Father knew I could not travel alone in a country whose language I could not speak.) Stefania is an editor and publisher of Christian books in Italy: Perciballi Editore at perciballieditore.com. Like most Italians I met, she graciously offered me hospitality while I was in Rome for the week. However, that week turned into three months, and then her home became my home mission base for eight years. The Lord is so amazing; Italy was the one country in the world I had always wanted to visit, and He took me there to live, providing for my every need in Italy and in countries beyond. Stefania and I became dear friends and ministry partners. We traveled together to many countries to serve with various missionaries, some of whom Stefania had met during her travels to more than thirty countries. As she went to churches and conferences throughout Italy, distributing her books, she took me to meet and minister with the wonderful people of Italy. I fell in love with the Italian people, their country—a land of hugs and kisses—and the most delicious food I had ever eaten. For the first time in my life, I understood what Psalm 103:5 means when it says, [He] *satisfies your mouth with good things.*

Stefania was the first person I had ever met who lived 100 percent by faith—not 99 percent, but 100 percent. She lives the red-letter words of Jesus, literally, and faithfully ministers to the poor. I think the best way to describe her heart of faith is in her stated conviction: "Everything that Jesus accomplished on Calvary and in His resurrection two thousand years ago is completely sufficient for every need I will ever have in my life." And absolutely everything is miraculously provided for her. I am so grateful for her living testimony and challenge to me to scale to heights that I did not even know existed in the Kingdom world.

One of Stefania's ministries is to Afghan refugee boys. For many years, Stefania and Walter, a dear friend, a precious lover of God, and former banker in Italy, have faithfully ministered every Wednesday night to these young men (16 to 30 year olds) at the Ostiense train station in Rome. These boys were really a ministry to me. Many times they told us amazing and heartbreaking stories of their escape from the Taliban. Some boys had witnessed the Taliban murder their family or friends. When one of these young Muslim boys comes to know Jesus as his Savior, his baptism is like witnessing a party in heaven. One night, Walter, Stefania, and I slept outside all night on the hard, cold concrete ground of the train station on pieces of cardboard boxes with the boys to show them just how much we cared for them. Many of them gathered around us in a squatting position and just stared at us. When I finally fell asleep around three or so in the morning, I remember seeing a few of them still squatting near us and looking at us with incredulous eyes.

Stefania's and Walter's examples impressed upon me my own need to reach out to the poor and the broken—a ministry so close to the heart of Jesus, and a ministry that touched my own heart with healing. I never realized just how many times the Bible mentioned our need to help the poor until I witnessed and experienced that burden in Walter's and Stefania's hearts. Their example gave me a burden for the poor that resulted in wonderful opportunities to build an orphanage, a women's shelter, and a water well in third-world countries. Well-building is a most powerful way to analogize to the people that they will never thirst again and to exemplify the love that we should pour out for each other.

Does the Lord Work through Visions?

Ministry in so many diverse countries yielded the same strong confirmations from the Lord that the path I was on was certainly the ministry that He intended for me. As the Bible says, the Lord repeats Himself. He will not leave us guessing or floundering.

On one of my mission trips to France, I met a young Christian woman, and as I do with all new friends, I asked her to share her story with me. She told me about her conversion experience but then shared with me how terribly she suffered from depression. So severe was this depression that her family had her admitted to a mental hospital. Counseling and shock treatments had not helped. The cause of her depression had never been discovered; therefore, she remained in a horrible emotional prison. I asked her if anyone had ever told her how the Lord heals the broken heart. "Has anyone ever prayed with you that the Holy Spirit would go into the depths of your heart to reveal the cause of your depression?"

She said no. She had never heard of the Lord's ministry to the brokenhearted from any friend or from any church that she had attended. So I asked if she wanted to pray and ask Jesus to reveal what was buried in her heart. She said yes.

We invited the Presence of Jesus and asked the Holy Spirit to reveal that broken, hidden place in her heart. We waited for Jesus to speak to us. We waited and waited. Nothing. She did not hear one word. We prayed again. And we waited an even longer time. Nothing. Because Jesus died to heal the broken heart, I knew He would speak to her heart, but when and how I did not know. I assured this young woman of this truth; however, it did not console her. I felt terrible, absolutely horrible. She seemed even more despondent than when we first started talking together, and I felt responsible. I cried out to Jesus in my heart and told Him there was no way I was able to help this woman. "Only You can help this woman. Would You please, please have mercy upon her and speak to her."

I sat next to her as she looked helplessly and hopelessly into the empty distance, listening to an unwanted silence. We were seated by a pond in a beautiful garden in Paris. I sat there watching baby ducks swim aimlessly and blindly by me as I pondered the deafness of my ears to the voice of Jesus. All of a sudden, a picture of a red-and-white tricycle came into my mind. I had learned through ministering to others that I could test a picture that came into my mind by consciously thinking of something else for a moment. Then, if the picture returned, I knew it was a communication from Jesus. (The Lord always graciously repeats Himself.) So I thought about my daughters, pictured them in college, and thanked the Lord for their lives. Then the picture immediately returned. Hence, I turned to this woman and asked her if a red-and-white tricycle meant anything to her. She pondered only for a short while, and then tears poured from her eyes. I held her in my arms until her sobbing completely exhausted her ability to cry any longer.

She told me the story that had been hidden in her heart. The Lord used this picture to bring to her mind a trauma so painful that neither any person nor any procedure could uncover it. Only Jesus could reveal the depth and the extent of the pain she had suffered when she was a young girl. The tricycle had belonged to her little brother who had died, and she had not been allowed to attend the funeral. Her mother had gone into a terrible depression and emotionally abandoned her daughter. The pain had pierced her soul, and it had been buried there for twenty years, never to be uncovered by anyone until that day when Jesus opened the eyes of her heart. Words could never describe the light that surrounded us that day as we listened to Jesus speak His words of truth and love into her heart (Isaiah 58:10).

The Lord speaks to us in so many ways. He speaks through His Spirit in Scripture *and* He speaks His words of truth and love to us in visions, in dreams, through thoughts of truth and love, through others, creation, movies, music, the arts, our senses, our circumstances (good and bad), through pain, through miraculous healing, and through His peace, etc. What we hear the Lord say in our dreams, visions, movies, music, circumstances, etc., must be consistent with Scripture, and it must be tested. *"Every matter must be established by the testimony of two or three witnesses"* (2 Corinthians 13:1 NIV; also see Section IV, "The Three Infallible Witnesses"). "I Can See," by David Meece would be a wonderful song to listen to here as it describes so well the intimate communication we all can have with Jesus.

Should We Pray for Jesus to Manifest Himself?

When I went to the garden of Gethsemane in March 2005, I attended an Easter service where American missionary Karen Dunham was the speaker. Karen had become very burdened about the terrible suicide bombings in Israel. As she cried out to Jesus about this situation, Jesus told her the only way to stop the killings was to share His love with the Muslims. After much prayer, she sensed the Lord's call to Jericho, a terrorist refugee camp in Palestine. And so, without any organizational support, she obeyed and went to Jericho, right after 9/11. That Easter morning, Karen spoke of things the Lord was doing in Jericho that were remarkable and, to be honest, sounded rather unbelievable. So I asked Karen if I could volunteer at her mission base when I returned to Israel in October for the Feast of Tabernacles (Festival of Shelters). She graciously consented.

Muslims believe that Jesus was only a prophet and that He was neither crucified nor resurrected. They believe Allah merely took Jesus to heaven. Furthermore, they believe that our Bible is not trustworthy because it has been translated too many times. They believe the Quran is the only original, authentic holy book. Hence, Karen shared the Lord with the Muslims in the most unique way I had ever witnessed.

Because of God's grace and calling upon Karen, she was given permission to place gospel tracts inside rice bags that we prepared as gifts for the people of Jericho, a very impoverished area. When we gave these bags to the people, we would tell them Jesus had sent us to feed them, and we would tell them how much He loved them. Then we prayed for the people that Jesus Himself would reveal to them who He is (that He would manifest His love to them). The next day, without fail, there would always be a knock at our mission base door.

Standing there would be two or three Muslims, mostly women, who came to tell us what happened after we prayed for them. The very first testimony I heard was from a woman who told us that Jesus had come to her in a dream, showed her the scars on His hands and feet, and told her that He loved her so much He died for her. She saw the glory of God. All the people who came to the base after having a dream or vision of Jesus were very open and willing to read the Bible verses regarding salvation and pray to receive Christ as their Savior.

When I returned to Jerusalem from Jericho, I attended a gathering that Christine Darg of CBN-TV was also attending, and I found out about her book *Miracles Among Muslims: The Jesus Visions.* It references Karen's work in Jericho and describes how Christ Himself is appearing to Muslims in dreams and visions all over the Middle East. It is a fascinating book and is available on Amazon.

Should We Pray for Healing Miracles?

The Lord gave us many wonderful experiences in Jericho, such as riding donkeys around the desert to share the Lord with Bedouins, singing worship songs one evening to an entire Muslim family who had prayed with Stefania and me to receive Christ as their Savior, escaping a fire at our mission base after it was torched with Molotov cocktails, and spending the night on the top of the Mount of Temptation to pray for Jericho. That evening we experienced loud blasts from Stefania's shofar echoing with astonishing effect from hill to hill around the mount. The echo sent a terrified Israeli military troop running out of their tent with rifles on the hill next to us. We stood there motionless, as they lowered their guns looking at us incredulously. But the most amazing, most miraculous event I have ever witnessed in my life occurred inside our little mission base in Jericho.

One day, several Muslim women came to the base with a little boy. He was around five years old and seemed a little agitated. They had come because of our communication in the street the previous day about the love of Jesus for them. The mother of the boy asked if Jesus would heal her son, who had been born deaf and mute. She said he had become increasingly angry over his inability to communicate. Without blinking an eye, Karen said, "Yes, Jesus will heal your son." I looked at Karen, amazed and fascinated by her unabashed and unshakable confidence in Jesus. She invited them inside for prayer. Before Karen began praying, she explained very clearly to the women that neither she nor I was going to heal the boy, but that Jesus alone was going to heal him. They nodded. Karen put her hands on the little boy's ears and very simply asked the Lord to open the boy's ears so that he could hear how much Jesus loved him. Of all the physical healings I have ever witnessed, I wish I had a video of this one. The

Lord's Spirit descended as vividly as a sunset and as precisely as the movement of a thermometer. First, furrowed creases on the boy's forehead relaxed, and then his angry eyes softened and became peaceful. Next, the tenseness around his mouth relaxed, and then his clenched jaw dropped, and as his entire body relaxed, he slumped back into his mother's arms. While he rested there, we all watched him and waited. Well, really, I watched and waited; Karen just sat there and smiled. Then the child turned his head to the right to look up at his mother.

At that moment, Karen snapped her fingers to the left of the boy so that he could not see her. Incredibly, the child jumped as he quickly turned in the direction of the sound. Can you imagine the heart of that mother and the wonder of that little child? Can you imagine my heart? There are just no words to describe the joy in that room. Karen, still not acting as though this was anything out of the ordinary but rather just a typical day down on the desert (which it was), took his little chin into her hands and taught him how to say his very first word, "Jesus," in Arabic.

What was the secret to the amazing work that was and is being done on those "typical" days at the mission base in Jericho, and now also at their new base in Jerusalem? First of all, obedience to Jesus' words of ministry: *Heal the sick, cleanse lepers, raise the dead, cast out demons* (Matthew 10:8). Secondly, obedience to Jesus words of worship. Every day we all gathered corporately at 7:00 a.m. to worship, pray, and listen to Jesus until 9:00 a.m.. Then we would disperse and individually spend from 9:00 a.m. until 11:00 a.m. in God's Word, praying and listening to Jesus. No other base where I worked spent so much time worshiping the Lord before the day's work, seeking the power of His glorious Presence. And on no other base had I experienced as many miracles and blessings as that base in Jericho. To follow the amazing work that is being done in Israel through this ministry, or to volunteer at one of the bases, go to livingbreadchurch.com.

I came away from Jericho absolutely convinced that no circumstance or situation in life is too difficult—truly "nothing is impossible with God" (Luke 1:37, Matthew 19:26). My confidence in the Lord's sovereignty and power increased one hundredfold, and my desire to understand the mysteries and wonders of His Kingdom grew even deeper.

What is Prophecy?

Prophecy is the act of speaking forth the words of God to encourage another. The words came from the Holy Spirit and will always be consistent with the Bible and accordingly, with the heart of Jesus. The gift of prophecy comes from our deep desire for the gift and by asking the Holy Spirit for it. *Pursue love, and desire spiritual gifts, but especially that you may prophesy* (1 Corinthians 14:1; 12:11). Also we need to spend much time reading the Bible and listening to Jesus. The more truth we read in God's Word, the more truth we will hear Him speak into our hearts about His heart for others. The end result of true prophecy is evidenced in the Christlike fruit it produces, especially in a deeper love for Jesus and others. *For the testimony of Jesus is the spirit of prophecy* (Revelation 19:10).

First Corinthians 14:3 lists three purposes of prophecy: *to edify* or enlighten and strengthen our faith; *to exhort* us to lead holy lives filled with love, worship, giving, and evangelism; and *to give comfort,* encouragement, and hope. Therefore, we can speak forth Scriptures, and we can speak forth words from our Father's heart for a person. The greatest encourager in my life to pray the Lord's heart over people was Lyn, a prayer partner of mine in Columbus, Ohio. No matter what the person with whom we are praying has done or not done, Lyn will bless that individual with everything they are and will be in Jesus. I believe Lyn interprets the above three purposes of prophecy as meaning to instill in people their identity in Christ in the most beautiful and powerful way possible—the way Jesus sees them.

"Prophetic" prayers and words that speak forth Scripture verses are the most powerful prayers and words we can pray and speak because Scriptures are infallible, powerfully enabling words. In your devotions every day, pray out loud one of the verses the Lord impressed upon your heart. For example, I was reading in Jeremiah 24 one day when my heart was stirred by verse 7: *"I will give them hearts that will recognize me as the Lord. They will be my people and I will be their God, for they will return to me wholeheartedly"* (NLT). So I prayed, "Thank you, Lord, for giving to me and my children and grandchildren (I said their names) hearts that will recognize You as the Lord. I proclaim that we are Your people, that You are our God, and that we will follow You with all our heart and mind and soul and strength, for You have promised to put Your laws in our minds and write them on our hearts." Jesus brought the First Commandment and Hebrews 8:10 to my mind as I meditated on Jeremiah 24:7, so I also included them in the prayer. Hence, when someone shortly thereafter tells me that the Holy Spirit told them to gift me with a particular Scripture concerning my children, I am *most* encouraged in my faith and in my wonder of the intimacy of the love of Jesus.

To me, there is nothing more wonderful, when telling others of Jesus' love, than to communicate to people about a burden they are carrying in their heart that only Jesus would know, and to assure them that He will lift it from them. This communication is a word of knowledge that only God can give us, and speaking forth His desire to heal that particular wound or problem is prophetic and powerful. The same is true when we speak words of life to people that contain words of specific and personal encouragement that only Jesus would know, as Lyn taught me to pray. We are speaking forth the treasure that God sees in them and celebrating it with them.

Prophecy is also a wonderful way to hear the Lord repeat Himself as He speaks to us through another about something He has already spoken to us. It's really wonderful when what we have heard the Lord speak to us is repeated from the lips of a total stranger. This is a tremendous encouragement to us as we desire to hear clearly the Lord's voice, the most important, and most intimate, word-giving voice of all.

Because of my love for the life-giving words found in prophecy, I become saddened when I observe the following events in a prophet and in the church. When I went to the mission field, I observed Christians at church standing in long lines and waiting a very long time to receive a word from a prophet, as if the direction for their lives depended upon it. I noticed that the line next them, for healing prayer, was always much shorter. When I talked with some of the people in the lines waiting for a prophetic word, I discovered that many did not know how to hear Jesus speak to them. I pondered, what would they do with their need for help and direction when the prophet left? How will they ever find the intimacy they were created for if they listen to the words of a prophet above the words of Jesus? That inquiry turned my thoughts to the real issue, related to the prophet and the church. Why weren't they also teaching the people (edifying them) how to they can personally hear from the Lord and instructing people how to discern whether or not words of prophecy were truly from God and not man? Remembering that supernatural, sacrificial love is always the greatest miracle, the gift of prophecy is to be desired and encouraged above all gifts (1 Corinthians 14:1). However this gift seems to be one of the least discussed subjects in churches today. No wonder people are unaware they were created to hear God's voice.

The fear in some churches, that people will not be speaking authentic words from the Holy Spirit, is unfounded. The Bible is very clear that all prophetic words must be tested. Prophets are not infallible. Hence, the prophetic words spoken by an individual must be tested and found to be consistent with Scripture and confirmed within the spirit of several mature Christians who love the Lord. (See Philippians 1:9-10; 1 Thessalonians 5:19-21; 2 Corinthians 13:1; Colossians 1:9, 3:15.) Also as stated above the important end result of authentic prophecy will be evidenced in the Christlike fruit it produces—love, humility, peace, joy, unity, healing, kindness, strength, compassion, etc.,—a hunger for more of God and His Presence, and a desire to speak life-giving prophetic words over others. *Your words were found, and I ate* [devoured] *them, And Your word became for me a joy and the delight of my heart; For I have been called by Your name, O Lord God of hosts* (Jeremiah 15:16 NASB).

Just one other concern I have in this area is that the prophetic is not exalted above the words of Jesus spoken in His Word, nor above His words spoken directly to us. I have observed that when people spend more time seeking prophetic words than they spend time listening to Jesus, spiritual warfare engages the battle over supremacy, bringing about confusion, discord, and sometimes sickness and, most tragic of all, loss of our precious intimacy with Jesus

One evening I was in the home of some Christian friends I loved very much. Throughout our dinner together, one friend continuously talked about this prophet's and that prophet's prophecies concerning guidance for her family. At times, it seemed to me that the prophecies spoke conflicting directions. Confused by all these "words," I turned to this friend, thanked her for sharing this, and then asked her what Jesus Himself had spoken to her about this situation. Anger that I had never seen before came into my friend's eyes, and words were angrily spoken that I know were not my friend's. Our God is a jealous God; He values our intimate relationship with Him—our sitting at His feet listening to His words that are spirit and life to our souls, and our worshiping Him above anyone or anything else.

In the beginning was the Word, and the Word was with God, and the Word was God. He was in the beginning with God. (John 1:1–2, 14)

In the past God spoke to our forefathers through the prophets at many times and in various ways, but in these last days he has spoken to us by his Son, whom He appointed heir of all things, and through whom He made the universe. The Son is the radiance of God's glory and the exact representation of His being, sustaining all things by His powerful word. (Hebrews 1:1–3 NIV)

What about Spiritual Warfare As We Go?

A. Should we ever engage in a battle with Satan?

Stefania and I had been invited to Wales to visit a missionary we had met in Jerusalem and to minister in her church. Her pastor was a precious man; he was kind and humble, and sensitive to the Lord's Spirit. His prayers for us were most encouraging and very poignant. This dear pastor was greatly burdened for his church. Many months before, much sickness, physical and mental, spread throughout his congregation. Even his own wife was suffering emotionally. These events left only a handful of people attending his church. The afternoon after ministering in his church, we were asked to attend a prayer meeting. While en route to the meeting, much to my dismay, I was told we were going to pray at a place that had formerly been a site of satanic ritual. I asked him why we were going there.

"To pray against Satan and what he has done to this church and community," he responded.

Now it all made sense to me, and I didn't want to go to that site. But what could I do? We were already on our way, and I was a guest. I could only ask the Lord to get me out of this situation.

Many years ago, before I went to the mission field, I had observed devastation to ministries that emphasized intercessory (prayer) warfare specifically against Satan. When I talked with Jesus about my sorrow and perplexity over the demise of those once seemingly powerful ministries, He led me to a book by John Paul Jackson entitled *Needless Causalities of War*. It warned to never to engage Satan directly through treats and accusations. Because Satan is not omnipresent (all present) or omniscient (all knowing), when we engage him with our accusations and conversations, he will stop his roaming around the earth, seeking whom he may devour, and come like a flood upon us in attempts to destroy us. Even Michael the archangel dared not slander or accuse Satan but asked the Lord to rebuke him (Jude 9). I thought this was a very interesting perspective on spiritual warfare and pondered, why would I want to engage Satan himself when I didn't have to?

Hebrews 2:14 states that on Calvary, Christ rendered *powerless him who had the power of death, that is, the devil.* Through His resurrection and ascension to His Father, Jesus lives to reign in glorious power and beauty. When He sends the power of the Holy Spirit upon us and clothes us with His glory, there is never a need to engage Satan in a battle. Our focus in upon the victory that has been won as we *stand* (Ephesians 6:11) armed with God's Word of truth in our hearts and His songs of praise and adoration upon our lips. After my experience in Jerusalem, I saw so clearly the power, peace, and joy that are present when our focus is upon the light of God's glory, and never upon the darkness of the enemy. There is simply no space or place for the enemy when the heart and the worshipful home are consumed with God's glorious Presence. *My enemies retreated; they staggered and died when You appeared* [at Your Presence NKJV] (Psalm 9:3 NLT).

So when we arrived near the ritual site, there was no way I wanted to go to that demonic place. I prayed once more for the Lord to please get me out of this situation. I did not want to go with that group and engage Satan and I did not want to offend the pastor in front of his church. Do you know what my Father did? He rescued me from that difficult situation by having me meet a family who "happened" to be camping near the location. As I walked by them, I started talking to the mother of the family. I spent the whole time talking with her about how much Jesus loved her, and she prayed with me to receive Jesus as her personal Savior. The next day, absolutely everyone else in our group who went to that ritual site was terribly sick. However, I spent the day rejoicing for the love that young mother had found in Jesus.

B. What about Evil Spirits?

Ephesians 6:12-13 states: For we do not wrestle against flesh and blood, but against principalities, against powers, against the rulers of the darkness of this age, against spiritual hosts of wickedness in the heavenly places. Therefore take up the whole armor of God, that you may be able to withstand in the evil day, and having done all, to stand.

As previously stated, unlike our heavenly Father, Satan is not omnipresent (all present) or omniscient (all knowing). So he has an army of demonic spirits whose every evil thought, like their commander's, is to harm, kill, and destroy us. Hence, we are fighting against evil spirits, not against people and events.

When Jesus was resurrected and ascended to His Father, He made available to us, through the power of the Holy Spirit, *all* authority—His victorious authority and power—to defeat the rulers of darkness. *Behold, I give you the authority to trample on serpents and scorpions, and over all the power of the enemy, and <u>nothing shall by any means hurt you</u>* (Luke 10:19; see also Luke 10:1,17; Matthew 10:7-8; 28:18-20; Mark 16:15-18). *You are of God, little children, and have overcome them, because He who is in you is greater than he who is in the world* (1 John 4:4). Not only would this power protect us, but also, the authority in that power would set people free from demons and command the sick to be made well. *And these signs will follow those who believe: In My name they will cast out demons ... they will lay hands on the sick, and they will recover"* (Mark 16:17a, 18b; see also Matthew 12:28). This power came from the Holy Spirit who anointed believers as they cried out for this manifestation of God's glory with their passionate prayers and songs of praise. When we understand that our Father rules and reigns in glorious and victorious beauty, evil spirits simply become an ugly nuisance to be swept away by the blood and the authority of Jesus, and by our chorus of praise to Him who sits upon the throne.

Ephesians 6:14-17, which lists the six pieces of the believe's armor, states that the truth of God's Word is the greatest weapon on earth to combat the lies of the enemy. As this entire book has presented, the only battle we have in life is against lies, and it is fought in our minds with the victorious weapon of God's truth (2 Corinthians 10:4). An often neglected weapon, which should always be our companion weapon, is the fruit (singular) of the Spirit—*love, joy, peace, patience, kindness, goodness, faithfulness, gentleness, self-control; against such things there is no law* (Galatians 5:22, 23). If we fight life's battles without the fruit of Spirit flowing from our hearts and touching the hearts of others, what have really we gained? We have won the battle but lost the war.

The first experience I had with the evil spirits occurred just shortly after I had arrived in Italy on my very first mission trip. I was asked to pray for a woman who suffered from depression. She told me she was too depressed to read her Bible or worship and that she had been praying and going to church faithfully but could not get rid of her terrible despair. This woman was completely unable to focus on one subject or to look at me with her glazed eyes, and her speech was erratic, making it impossible to communicate with her. It seemed to me to be evidence of demonic oppression and that I needed to pray for her to be set free from the evil spirit that tormented her so that I could talk with her.

This was the first time that I, personally, had ever prayed such a prayer with anyone. I remember being told once in the States that I was never to attempt deliverance prayers "alone" and to make sure that I was praying for the individual along with someone who had much experience in this area. But there was no one else to help me that day. So I asked the woman to excuse me for a few minutes. I went into a bedroom of the home where we were meeting and got down on my knees and confessed to Jesus my fear and ignorance of how to pray for her deliverance. I asked Him to have mercy upon her, and upon me, and to *please* help me. God mercifully revealed His glory. I went back out to where this woman was seated and told her I needed to pray a short prayer for her before we could proceed, as I sensed a spirit was oppressing her. All I did was command the evil spirit to be gone in the name of Jesus and by the power of His blood. I didn't know what spirit it was, what its name was, how it had gotten there, or where it was going. I just said that simple prayer.

Instantly she started to cough so hard that she became sick to her stomach. And then an amazing peace came upon her and a wonderful relief came over me. Jesus set her instantly free from that oppressive spirit. We prayed for the Holy Spirit to fill the place the evil spirit had left. This is very important according to Matthew 12:43–45. It is also critical that the delivered individual is discipled, gets a prayer partner, and is surrounded with a community of believers. (Really, we all need this.) Then we were able to continue our time together seeking the Lord's guidance as to what had given the enemy an open door or "legal entry," into her heart to oppress her. This revelation will most times reveal a cause, if not the root cause, of the heart's pain and the lies of which the individual needs to confess and repent.

I would like to include here an observation about what sometimes happens after Jesus has spiritually or physically healed someone. The enemy will often attempt to steal the Lord's healing miracle by attacking the individual again with false and deceiving symptoms of the illness that Jesus had healed. When he does this, it is very important to refuse those symptoms and to proclaim out loud, in the name of Jesus, the words Jesus spoke to us in His Word about our sickness which we had claimed for our healing.We must also proclaim the truth that we have been healed by His stripes (Isaiah 53:5 and Matthew 8:16–17). Remember Isaiah 54:17; *No weapon formed against you shall prosper, And every tongue which rises against you in judgment you shall condemn. This is the heritage of the servants of the Lord, And their righteousness is from Me," Says the Lord.* Our faith is evidenced and greatly fortified when we step out and take actions that show we truly believe that God has healed us. Remember the lepers Jesus healed? Jesus told them to go and show the priest that they had been healed. However, they were not healed while standing in front of Jesus. They were healed on their way to the priest. It is very important to step out, to take acts of faith, for our healing.

Jesus will also rescue us from oppression of which we are unaware . During my eight years traveling from country to country and from mission base to mission base, I would return to my home base in Rome to rest for a while, to minister to the wonderful people of Italy and, most gratefully, to be ministered to by others. Because so many international ministries come to Rome, I gained valuable insights from missionaries from other cultures who have sacrificed greatly for their faith. And I saw vividly how the Lord mightily rewarded their humility and selfless dedication with His Presence and power, including the power to deliver people from hidden oppression.

One evening, after about five years in the mission field, I was listening to a missionary who was burdened about the church understanding its authority to cast out demonic spirits. During his message, this missionary paused and said there was a heavy "spirit of oppression" in the room because people were listening to lies. I nodded, knowing that this would certainly be a problem for many in the room. When he prayed at the end of his talk, he said there was a missionary in the room who was heavily oppressed by words spoken to her that she should not be in the mission field. She had been told she was wasting her time and talents. Then he left the podium, and in front of the entire congregation, he walked to the back of the church where I was sitting and put his hands on my head. He prayed in the name of Jesus and by the power of the Holy Spirit that the Lord would set me free. I had never seen or heard of this man before in my life.

Tears poured from my eyes. And with those tears, I heard the condemning words that I had unknowingly buried for years: "Why are you doing missions work when you have a law degree?" I also felt the pain of returning from the mission field to the States so many times and not having people care about the work that was being done overseas, but instead hearing them tell me other work would be more profitable. (Speaking condemnatory/judgmental words, also called curses, opens the door to the enemy to send in his evil, lying spirits to harm both the speaker, and also the one spoken against if that person "receives" or believes those words (Matthew 7:1).) I had thought those negative words spoken to me didn't bother me because I was working for the Lord, not for them. However, I was unknowingly listening to the lies that my work was not valuable, hence my life was not significant, and I had buried the unrecognized pain. I wasn't listening to what Jesus was saying about my identity in Him. This opened the door to my heart to an oppressive spirit. But when this man placed his hands upon my head and prayed, Jesus instantly lifted that burden from me. The freedom was indescribable and the result wonderful—I fell even deeper in love with Jesus. He is so faithful to deliver and heal us of things hidden in the depths of our hearts. A few days later, Jesus repeated Himself when He led me to Misty Edwards' song, "I Will Waste My Life." The song was so on point that I believed Jesus had Misty write it just for me! He does things like that, you know. Another very powerful song about laying one's life down for the love of Jesus is "Waste It All," by Kim Walker-Smith. If your heart cries out to live in the Presence of Jesus, regardless of the opinions of others, you will love these songs. Both songs are on YouTube.

In regards to the above, it is important to know that evil spirits cannot *possess* a believer who has the Spirit of Christ living inside, but they can *oppress* a believer if that Christian is living in disobedience to God's Word. Disbelief, unconfessed sin, unforgiveness, occult activities and associations and possessions, breaking vows, condemnation, compromise, idol worship in our life and in family generations, etc., make us easy prey to defeat and torment—to a life of living the lie. (Idol worship is anyone or anything, including religion, in our life that takes supremacy or priority over the place and position of Jesus and His words.) Hence, it is absolutely critical that we have a solid and thorough foundation in God's Word, that Jesus is Lord of our life, that we are clothed in God's glory, and that we live in community: worshiping with people who love Jesus, surrounded and grounded with accountability and support.

In light of Scriptures, my personal experience, and conviction regarding the influence of the demonic in healing ministry, I would like to summarize the above as follows: I do not believe that we have to spend time figuring out what demons are where, what is their job, or what they are named. As stated, that focus can actually bring darkness into our lives. We must never live life in reaction to darkness. Our pursuit, our passion must be the attraction of Light. I have observed much harm, confusion, and diversion from the individual's responsibility to repent of wrongdoing, or wrong thinking when one's approach to healing ministry begins first with an inquiry into demonic oppression. (The exception to this is illustrated in the first story above and in obviously demonically oppressed areas such as villages controlled by witchdoctors and communities besieged by satanic worship.) Instead, I believe the first inquiry in healing ministry should always be about the person's salvation experience—was there real, sorrowful repentance, did the individual make Jesus the Lord of his or her life, and what evidence is there that individual has been clothed with the glory of God? Then I ask the Holy Spirit to uncover any hidden lies and unforgiveness by asking probing yet caring questions, especially questions that will uproot feelings. One of my favorites is, "Please tell me about the deepest burden you are presently carrying." When healing ministry is approached in this way, darkness will at some point be exposed without having given it the attention it desires.[13]

We must always remember to look to the most important teacher and greatest authority of all, Jesus: Wherever He went He healed and delivered people from evil spirits: Luke 4:40-41; Mark 1:23-27, 32-34, 39; Luke 13:11-16, 32, and please also listen to a most powerful song about Jesus' deliverance ministry ♫ "Man of the Tombs," by Bob Bennett. Many times physical illnesses are caused by the demonic, either directly, or indirectly by our believing lies. Please note that in Jesus' healing ministry, Jesus did not go out looking for evil spirits but whenever they manifested, He immediately cast them out "with a word." Jesus never focused on the existence of spiritual warfare but upon His mission to bring people into the light of the Kingdom of His glorious Presence to live—a place where darkness cannot hide or thrive. We too cast out demons with a word - the name of Jesus. Hence our prayers for deliverance must always acknowledge who Jesus is and what His death and resurrection accomplished, confession of any sins (including unforgiveness, etc., and any occult involvement), sincere repentance, <u>proclamation of Jesus as Lord in every aspect of one's life</u>, and praying for empowerment—that the individual is clothed by the Holy Spirit with

13 Francis MacNutt, PhD., christianhealingmin.org, and John & Paula Sanford, elijahhouse.org, write about deliverance within the context of healing; see also *The Broken Image* (healing & homosexuality) by Leanne Payne & authors such as Beth Moore, *Praying God's Word, Breaking Free From Spiritual Strongholds*; Kenneth E. Hagin, *The Believer's Authority*, etc. (ASIDE: re ministry of Dr. MacNutt; The Southern Medical Association Journal actually reported the success of "direct contact intercessory prayer" upon heumatoid arthritis patients in a study done with Dr. MacNutt, (sma.org Archives, Vol. 93, Dec. 2000)).

the power of God's glory. A good video that provides a summary of this subject, and includes a prayer for deliverance at the end is "Basics of Deliverance," by Derek Prince (derekprince.org). Once an individual is delivered of evil spirits it is critical that the individual receives healing ministry and is embraced and discipled in a small group fellowship. The gospel message is sozo - salvation and healing and deliverance. Each of the three ministries need to operate in the context of the other two.

Finally, never forget that worship is absolutely essential in every battle we face. The enemy has nowhere to stand in the Presence of the Lord; there is simply no place for any of his deceitful attacks and lies. During worship we are empowered by God's glory, strengthened with truth and with the love and joy of His Presence. His Presence comforts, His glory conquers. ♫ Powerful worship songs regarding the battle are; "Victor's Crown" by Darlene Zschech; Chris Tomlin's "Whom Shall I Fear/God of Angel Armies;" "Still Believe," by Kim Walker-Smith; and "You Reign," by Anna Blanc, etc., (Section III).

Is The Outpouring of the Fire and Glory of God All We Need?

This question is answered in Chapter 11 about Moses, but I wanted to give you a real-life application. In so many places where I traveled, I saw not only an amazing outpouring of prophecy among young and old alike (prophesied in Joel 2:28–29), but also a wonderful communication of the glory and fire of God. That fire is becoming a flame igniting hearts across the nations of this world. So much can be done so quickly by the fire of God's Presence burning up the chaff in our lives and empowering us to be witnesses of His love. It is utterly amazing to worship with hundreds, sometimes thousands, of people and have the manifest Presence of God's glory descend to heal the people of ailments and diseases simply as they stand there, worshiping and crying out to Him. But if I have learned anything in the mission field at all, I have learned this—let God be God.

I was at a mission base in 2011 that was absolutely on fire for the Lord. The people were worshiping 24/7, and all the discussion and teaching at the base was upon the fire of God's Presence, His all-consuming glory, and how to minister to others through the gifts of the Spirit. His Spirit was moving so powerfully, and everything the Lord was doing in the lives of the people there was simply amazing. Habakkuk 2:14 states, *The earth will be filled with the knowledge of the glory of the Lord, as the waters cover the sea.* It was all so remarkable that I started asking the Lord whether this book's discussion about the importance of the healing journey would become unnecessary.

Jesus brought me His answer a week later through His Word and through an experience. I was meditating one day on one of my favorite passages concerning the events surrounding the dedication of the temple in 2 Chronicles 5. King Solomon was given the privilege and great honor to build this first and absolutely magnificent temple. He witnessed the amazing glory of God descend and fill the temple. Sadly, Solomon chose the intimacy of women over intimacy with God. He chose to disobey God's command not to marry foreign women, whose gods would lead Israel into idolatry (1 Kings 11:2). That idol worship led to the ruin of the wisest and greatest king on earth, and the devastation and division of his kingdom, Israel. I saw that the pursuit of God's glory apart from the healing of the soul and a lifestyle of holy intimacy with Him can become a spiritual high or merely an emotional experience that neither transforms lives nor transmits God's love to others. Also remember the stories of Moses and Elijah. Moses' life revealed the very important need of pursuing and experiencing God's intimate glory—not solely His majestic glory (miracles, signs, and wonders). Elijah too saw wind and fire but found assurance and power in God's still, small, intimate voice (1 Kings 19:11–12).

Then the Lord repeated Himself through a personal experience. A young woman came to me at this mission base and asked if we could pray together. Before this day, we had had lunch many times together and discussed the wonderful things that were happening on the base. I had shared with her my testimony and my love to communicate Christ's ministry to the brokenhearted. That day she confided in me that she felt she was the only one in her group who was unable to receive the gifts of the Spirit, though she had poured out her heart to the Lord requesting them. I was very surprised, as God's glory was so powerfully present in so many meetings on the base. As we talked together, I realized that her salvation experience was real and that she greatly desired to minister in the gifts to touch the hearts of others. So we decided to go to the Lord and ask Him to reveal any hindrance hiding in her heart. She told Jesus about her discouragement in not responding to His Presence as others had at the base, and the feelings associated with that discouragement, and then she started to tell Jesus of other discouragements in her life.

It was then that the Lord's Spirit brought out an anger hidden inside her heart. It was very deep and intense, and my heart broke for her. But as she continued to talk with Jesus, her heart softened, and then the tears came—tears of repentance and healing. These tears opened the doors of her heart to hear Jesus' words of truth, which broke through the lies that had bound her. It was then that she was finally able to experience everything Jesus wanted her to experience about Him, His love for her, and life in the Kingdom.

Sometimes Jesus heals and empowers instantaneously as His glorious Presence comes upon us in a worship or prayer gathering. Most times it is a process, a journey. Sometimes He touches us with His healing while we pray with a friend. Many times He touches us when we are all alone with Him. Sometimes people have faith to be healed; sometimes they don't and yet they are healed. He can touch us in so many ways and always at the perfect time and in His perfect way. There is no formula. We must let God be God.

I remember Elisabeth Elliot telling me, in response to one of my "great" thoughts concerning God's ways, "Loren, whenever you think you have figured out God, think again." How true. His ways are so much higher than our ways; His thoughts are so much higher than our thoughts (Isaiah 55:9), and *our God is in heaven; He does whatever He pleases* (Psalm 115:3). What pleases Him most is to reveal the majesty and the intimacy of His glory—His love for us—and to see us respond in adoring worship, talking with Him, listening to Him, falling in love with Him, and sharing His love with others.

♫ Two really wonderful songs that are prayers to close this chapter are called "For the Sake of the World" and " For the One," by Bethel Music / Brian and Jenn Johnson. "For the sake of the world burn like a fire in me, light a fire in my soul for every eye to see!" And when we sing the words to "For the One," may the prayer of our hearts be to love others just like Jesus does, and may that love be so powerful that when people look into our eyes, they see Him, and when they see us smile at them, they will actually feel the Father's love!

God Bless You All for Journeying with Me!

Who is this, coming up from the wilderness, leaning upon her beloved?

—Song of Songs 8:5

I pray with all my heart that your journey in this book has opened the gate into the garden and refuge of His Presence, where you have fallen in love with Jesus. It is where you were created to live—listening to His words of truth and love, clothed in His radiant beauty, walking, talking, singing, and dancing together in His world of wonder. May you forever go from glory to glory, deeper and deeper into the heart of Jesus, and overflow with that love to others. I dearly hope that overflow brings about for your family and friends your own written testimonial of the faithfulness and power of the Lord's love in your life!

Thank you so much for sharing via email (additions@LorenLoving.com) or on the book's web site (LorenLoving.com) your own personal favorite songs and Scripture verses that came to your mind as you read this book. Your contributions will bring about a wonderful second edition! Also don't forget to read about the amazingly powerful equine-assisted revelation and healing opportunities on the book's web site. God bless you and your family!

Because of His great love,
Loren

For this reason I bow my knees to the Father of our Lord Jesus Christ, from whom the whole family in heaven and earth is named, that He would grant you, according to the riches of His glory, to be strengthened with might through His Spirit in the inner man, that Christ may dwell in your hearts through faith; That you, being rooted and grounded in love, may be able to comprehend with all the saints what is the width and length and depth and height—to know the love of Christ which passes knowledge; that you may be filled with all the fullness of God.

—Ephesians 3:14-19

If you, too, are burdened to communicate the message of this book,
Please send your tax-deductible contributions to:
In His Steps Foundation, P.O. Box 11, Twinsburg OH, 44087
Please note on your check's subject line: The First Commandment Fund/WJA Book

APPENDIX A

60 Scriptures: You Are Created to Hear the Lord's Voice and Understand the Bible

My heart has heard You say, "Come and talk with Me."
And my heart responds, "Lord, I am coming."

— Psalm 27:8 NLT

Three times in the gospels, God says of His Son Jesus, "*This is my beloved Son, listen to Him*" (Matthew 17:5; Mark 9:7; Luke 9:35). The voice of Jesus is the most important voice of all.

We were designed in our Father's image to be like Him so that we could communicate with Him and thereby possess the most intimate relationship of all, adorned with all the attributes of our Father. Hence, when the resurrection Spirt of Jesus, the Holy Spirit, comes to live in our hearts, our spirit is made new (reborn) with the attributes of our Father. Hence, our ability to hear Jesus speak to us is inherent to our new nature—it's in our spiritual DNA. "*... put on the new man who is renewed in knowledge according to the image of Him who created him* (Colossians 3:10). This truth, that we were designed to hear, and therefore can hear, the voice of God is repeated throughout Scripture:

Out of heaven He let you hear His voice, that He might instruct you; on earth He showed you His great fire, and you heard His words out of the midst of the fire. (Deuteronomy 4:36)

Today you have proclaimed the Lord to be your God, and that you will walk in His ways and keep His statutes, His commandments, and His judgments, and that you will obey His voice. (Deuteronomy 26:17)

The Lord confides in those who fear Him; He makes His covenant known to them. (Psalm 25:14 NIV)

Whether you turn to the right or to the left, your ears will hear a voice behind you, saying, "This is the way; walk in it." (Isaiah 30:11 NIV)

But He answered and said, "It is written, 'Man shall not live by bread alone, but by every word [rhēma] *that proceeds from the mouth of God.'* " (Matthew 4:4; Deuteronomy 8:3)

[Jesus said to them] ... "He who is of God hears God's words [rhēma]."(John 8:47)

"*He calls his own sheep by name and leads them out. After he has gathered his own flock, he walks ahead of them, and they follow him because they know his voice.*" (John 10:3–4 NLT)

"*My sheep hear My voice, and I know them, and they follow Me.*" (John 10:27)

Then he said, "The God of our fathers has chosen you that you should know His will, and see the Just One, and hear the voice of His mouth." (Acts 22:14)

Meditate on the following verses to help you understand God's promise that not only can you hear His voice but you also <u>can understand His word</u>:

New Testament Scriptures:

Then Jesus prayed this prayer: "O Father, Lord of heaven and earth, thank you for hiding these things from those who think themselves so wise and clever, and for revealing it to the childlike." (Matthew 11:25 NLT)

Then Jesus said, "Come to Me, all of you who are weary and carry heavy burdens, and I will give you rest. Take My yoke upon you. Let Me teach you, because I am humble and gentle at heart, and you will find rest for your souls." (Matthew 11:28–29 NLT)

"*To those who listen to My teaching, more understanding will be given, and they will have an abundance of knowledge.*" (Matthew 13:12 NLT)

"*For truly I tell you, many prophets and righteous people longed to see what you see, but did not see it, and to hear what you hear, but did not hear it.*" (Matthew 13:17 NIV)

Then He asked them, "But who do you say I am?" Simon Peter answered, "You are the Messiah, the Son of the living God." Jesus replied, "You are blessed, Simon son of John, because my Father in heaven has revealed this to you. You did not learn this from any human being."
(Matthew 16:15–17 NLT)

"*Anyone with ears to hear should listen and understand." Then he added, "Pay close attention to what you hear. The closer you listen, the more understanding you will be given—and you will receive even more. To those who listen to my teaching, more understanding will be given. But for those who are not listening, even what little understanding they have will be taken away from them.*" (Mark 4:23–24 NLT)

... Jesus was filled with the joy of the Holy Spirit, and He said, "O Father, Lord of heaven and earth, thank you for hiding these things from those who think themselves wise and clever, and for revealing them to the childlike. Yes, Father, it pleased You to do it this way." (Luke 10:21 NLT)

"And when you are brought to trial in the synagogues and before rulers and authorities, don't worry about how to defend yourself or what to say, for the Holy Spirit will teach you at that time what needs to be said." (Luke 12:11–12 NLT)

They said to each other, "Didn't our hearts burn within us as He talked with us on the road and explained the Scriptures to us?" (Luke 24:32 NLT)

He opened their understanding, that they might comprehend the Scriptures. (Luke 24:45)

The woman said to Him, "I know that Messiah is coming" (who is called Christ). "When He comes, He will tell us all things." (John 4:25)

"As it is written in the Scriptures, 'They will all be taught by God.' Everyone who listens to the Father and learns from Him comes to Me." (John 6:45 NLT)

"But when the Father sends the Advocate as my representative—that is, the Holy Spirit—He will teach you everything and will remind you of everything I have told you." (John 14:26 NLT)

"When the Helper (Advocate, Comforter) *comes, whom I will send to you from the Father, that is the Spirit of truth who proceeds from the Father, He will testify about Me."* (John 15:26 NASB)

"When the Spirit of truth comes, He will guide you into all truth. He will not speak on His own but will tell you what He has heard. He will tell you about the future. He will bring Me glory by telling you whatever He receives from Me." (John 16:13–14 NLT)

Pilate therefore said to Him, "Are You a king then? Jesus answered, "You say rightly that I am a king. For this cause I was born, and for this cause I have come into the world, that I should bear witness to the truth. Everyone who is of the truth hears My voice." (John 18:37 NKJV)

Now when they saw the boldness of Peter and John, and perceived that they were uneducated and untrained men, they marveled. And they realized that they had been with Jesus. (Acts 4:13)

Forty years later, in the desert near Mount Sinai, an angel appeared to Moses in the flame of a burning bush. When Moses saw it he was amazed at the sight. As he went to take a closer look, the voice of the Lord called out to him, "I am the God of your ancestors—the God of Abraham, Isaac, and Jacob." Moses shook with terror and did not dare to look. Then the Lord said to him, "Take off your sandals, for you are standing on holy ground. I have certainly seen the oppression of my people in Egypt. I have heard their groans and have come down to rescue them. Now go, for I am sending you back to Egypt." (Acts 7:30–34 NLT)

One day as these men were worshiping the Lord and fasting, the Holy Spirit said, "Dedicate Barnabas and Saul for the special work to which I have called them." (Acts 13:2 NLT)

For as many as are led by the Spirit of God, these are sons of God. (The children of God will be led by the Spirit.) (Romans 8:14)

And the Holy Spirit helps us in our weakness. For example, we don't know what God wants us to pray for. But the Holy Spirit prays for us with groanings that cannot be expressed in words. And the Father who knows all hearts knows what the Spirit is saying, for the Spirit pleads for us believers in harmony with God's own will. (Romans 8:26–27 NLT)

But it was to us that God revealed these things ["what God has prepared for those who love Him"] *by His Spirit. For His Spirit searches out everything and shows us God's deep secrets. No one can know a person's thoughts except that person's own spirit, and no one can know God's thoughts except God's own Spirit. And we have received God's Spirit (not the world's spirit), so we can know the wonderful things God has freely given us. When we tell you these things, we do not use words that come from human wisdom. Instead, we speak words given to us by the Spirit, using the Spirit's words to explain spiritual truths. But people who aren't spiritual can't receive these truths from God's Spirit. It all sounds foolish to them and they can't understand it, for only those who are spiritual can understand what the Spirit means. Those who are spiritual can evaluate all things, but they themselves cannot be evaluated by others. For, "Who can know the Lord's thoughts? Who knows enough to teach Him?" But we understand these things, for we have the mind of Christ.* (1 Corinthians 2:10–16 NLT)

I pray that the eyes of your heart may be enlightened, so that you will know what is the hope of His calling, what are the riches of the glory of His inheritance in the saints, and what is the surpassing greatness of His power toward us who believe. (Ephesians 1:18, 19a)

God, who at various times and in various ways spoke in time past to the fathers by the prophets, has in these last days spoken to us by His Son, whom He has appointed heir of all things, through whom also He made the worlds. (Hebrews 1:1–2)

"This is the new covenant I will make with my people on that day," says the Lord: "I will put my laws in their hearts so they will understand them, and I will write them on their minds so they will obey them." (Hebrews 10:16 NLT; see also Jeremiah 31:33)

If you need wisdom, ask our generous God, and He will give it to you. He will not rebuke you for asking. But when you ask Him, be sure that your faith is in God alone. Do not waver, for a person with divided loyalty is as unsettled as a wave of the sea that is blown and tossed by the wind. Such people should not expect to receive anything from the Lord. Their loyalty is divided between God and the world, and they are unstable in everything they do.
(James 1:5–8 NLT)

But you have an anointing from the Holy One, and all of you know the truth.
(1 John 2:20 NIV)

But you have received the Holy Spirit, and He lives within you, so you don't need anyone to teach you what is true. For the Spirit teaches you everything you need to know, and what He teaches is true—it is not a lie. So just as He has taught you, remain in fellowship with Christ.
(1 John 2:27 NLT)

"*Anyone with ears to hear must listen to the Spirit and understand what He is saying to the churches.*" (Revelation 3:6 NLT)

I was in the Spirit on the Lord's Day, and I heard behind me a loud voice, as of a trumpet saying, "I am the Alpha and the Omega, the First and the Last" ... Then I turned to see the voice that spoke with me ... His head and hair were white like wool, as white as snow, and His eyes like a flame of fire; His feet were like fine brass, as if refined in a furnace, and His voice as the sound of many waters. (Revelation 1:10–12, 14–15)

Old Testament Scriptures:

Out of heaven He let you hear His voice, that He might instruct you; on earth He showed you His great fire, and you heard His words out of the midst of the fire. (Deuteronomy 4:36)

The Lord spoke to Joshua ... "This Book of the Law shall not depart from your mouth, but you shall meditate in it day and night, that you may observe to do according to all that is written in it. For then you will make your way prosperous, and then you will have good success. Have I not commanded you? Be strong and of good courage; do not be afraid, nor be dismayed, for the Lord your God is with you wherever you go." (Joshua 1:1, 8, 9)

I will bless the Lord who has given me counsel; My heart also instructs me in the night seasons ... You will show me the path of life; in Your Presence is fullness of joy; at Your right hand are pleasures forevermore. (Psalm 16:7, 11)

He guides the humble in what is right and teaches them his way. (Psalm 25:9 NIV)

The Lord says, "I will guide you along the best pathway for your life. I will advise you and watch over you." (Psalm 32:8 NLT)

The Lord directs the steps of the godly. He delights in every detail of their lives. (Psalm 37:23)

Behold, You desire truth in the inward parts, and in the hidden part You will make me to know wisdom. (Psalm 51:6)

My soul waits in silence for God alone. (Psalm 62:1)

O God, You have taught me from my youth; And to this day I declare Your wondrous works. (Psalm 71:17)

Then I realized that my heart was bitter, and I was all torn up inside ... Yet I still belong to you; you hold my right hand. You guide me with your counsel, leading me to a glorious destiny. (Psalm 73:21, 23-24 NLT)

I listen carefully to what God the Lord is saying, for He speaks peace to His faithful people. (Psalm 85:8 NLT)

Blessed is the man whom You instruct, O Lord, and teach out of Your law. (Psalm 94:12)

Your testimonies [statutes] *also are my delight and my counselors.*
Oh, how I love Your law! It is my meditation all the day.
You, through Your commandments, make me wiser than my enemies; for they are ever with me.
I have more understanding than all my teachers, for Your testimonies are my meditation.
I understand more than the ancients, because I keep Your precepts.
I have not departed from Your judgments, for You Yourself have taught me.
Through Your precepts I get understanding;
My lips shall utter praise, for You teach me Your statutes.
(Psalm 119:24, 97-100, 102, 104, 171)

The fear of the Lord is the beginning of knowledge … Turn at my rebuke; surely I will pour out my spirit on you; I will make my words known to you. (Proverbs 1:7, 23)

… If you receive my words, and treasure my commands within you … And lift up your voice for understanding, If you seek her as silver, and search for her as for hidden treasures; Then you will understand the fear of the Lord, and find the knowledge of God. For the Lord gives wisdom; from His mouth come knowledge and understanding … When wisdom enters your heart, and knowledge is pleasant to your soul, discretion will preserve you; understanding will keep you. (Proverbs 2:1, 3–6, 10)

Blessed is the man who listens to me, Watching daily at my gates, Waiting at the posts of my doors. (Proverbs 8:34)

Many people shall come and say, "Come, and let us go up to the mountain of the Lord, to the house of the God of Jacob; He will teach us His ways, and we shall walk in His paths." (Isaiah 2:3; see also Micah 4:2)

Though the Lord gave you adversity for food and suffering for drink, He will still be with you to teach you. You will see your teacher with your own eyes. Your own ears will hear Him. Right behind you a voice will say, "This is the way you should go," whether to the right or to the left. Then you will destroy all your silver idols and your precious gold images. (Isaiah 30:20–22a NLT)

And I will give you treasures hidden in the darkness—secret riches. I will do this so you may know that I am the Lord, the God of Israel, the One who calls you by name. (Isaiah 45:3 NLT)

This is what the Lord says—your Redeemer, the Holy One of Israel: "I am the Lord your God, who teaches you what is good for you and leads you along the paths you should follow. Oh, that you had listened to My commands! Then you would have had peace flowing like a gentle river and righteousness rolling over you like waves in the sea." (Isaiah 48:17–18 NLT)

He awakens Me morning *by morning, He wakens My ear to hear as the learned.* (Isaiah 50:4 NKJV)

But I will reveal My name to My people, and they will come to know its power. Then at last they will recognize that I am the one who speaks to them. (Isaiah 52:6 NLT)

All your children shall be taught by the Lord, And great shall be the peace of your children. (Isaiah 54:13)

"Come to Me with your ears wide open. Listen, for the life of your soul is at stake." (Isaiah 55:3a NLT)

Then you will call upon Me and go and pray to Me, and I will listen to you. And you will seek Me and find Me, when you search for Me with all your heart. (Jeremiah 29:12–13)

"This is the new covenant I will make with the people of Israel on that day," says the Lord. "I will put My instructions deep within them, and I will write them on their hearts. I will be their God, and they will be My people. And they will not need to teach their neighbors, nor will they need to teach their relatives, saying, 'You should know the Lord.' For everyone, from the least to the greatest, will know Me already," says the Lord. "And I will forgive their wickedness, and I will never again remember their sins." (Jeremiah 31:33–34 NLT; see also Hebrews 8:11)

"You know with all your heart and soul that not one of all the good promises the Lord your God gave concerning you has failed. Every promise has been fulfilled; not one has failed."

(Joshua 23:14 NIV; see also 2 Corinthians 1:20)

APPENDIX B

70 Scriptures on Healing: God's Miraculous Medicine

My heart has heard You say, "Come and talk with Me."
And my heart responds, "Lord, I am coming."

— Psalm 27:8 NLT

As presented in this book, whenever we are faced with a difficulty or trial, we need to claim a promise in God's Word that the Lord has spoken to us, and then personalize it, memorize it, and always speak it out loud.Because Jesus is the Word of God, the words He speaks to us will always be consistent with who He is and therefore possess the power to do what He has spoken.

The list below is not exhaustive. So be sure to search for other verses that may speak more personally and individually to you. Also, YouTube.com has many healing scripture videos with beautiful background music. One of the most beautiful videos I have seen is set in Israel and is titled, "Healing Scriptures by Revelation TV."

"Worship the Lord your God, and His blessing will be on your food and water. I will take away sickness from among you." (Exodus 23:25 NIV) Personalize and speak aloud, e.g.: "I will worship the Lord my God. His blessing will be on my food and water. He will take sickness away from me."

"You shall have no other gods before Me." (Exodus 20:3)

And He [the Lord] *said, "My Presence will go with you, and I will give you rest... I will make all My goodness pass before you, and I will proclaim the name of the Lord before you."* (Exodus 33:14, 19)

I call heaven and earth as witnesses today against you, that I have set before you life and death, blessing and cursing; therefore choose life, that both you and your descendants may live; that you may love the Lord your God, that you may obey His voice, and that you may cling to Him, for He is your life and the length of your days. (Deuteronomy 30:19, 20a)

How can I know all the sins lurking in my heart? Cleanse me from these hidden faults. (Psalm 19:12 NLT)

O Lord my God, I cried out to You, And You healed me. (Psalms 30:2)

I will be glad and rejoice in Your unfailing love, for You have seen my troubles, and You care about the anguish of my soul. (Psalm 31:7 NLT)

I sought the Lord, and He heard me, And delivered me from all my fears. (Psalm 34:4)

The Lord is near to those who have a broken heart, And saves such as have a contrite spirit. (Psalm 34:18)

Righteousness and justice are the foundation of Your throne; Mercy and truth go before Your face. (Psalm 89:14) *Do not take revenge, my dear friends, but leave room for God's wrath, for it is written: "It is mine to avenge; I will repay says the Lord."* (Romans 12:19; Deuteronomy 32:35) *Let my vindication come from Your Presence;* (Psalm 17:2a)

He who dwells in the secret place [Presence] *of the Most High Shall abide under the shadow of the Almighty ... "Because he has set his love upon Me, therefore I will deliver him; I will set him on high, because he has known My name. He shall call upon Me, and I will answer him; I will be with him in trouble; I will deliver him and honor him. With long life I will satisfy him, And show him My salvation."* (Psalm 91:1,14-16; please meditate on Psalm 91)

Bless the Lord, O my soul; And all that is within me, bless His holy name! Bless the Lord, O my soul, And forget not all His benefits: Who forgives all your iniquities, Who heals all your diseases, Who redeems your life from destruction, Who crowns you with lovingkindness and tender mercies. (Psalm 103:1-4)

Then they cried out to the Lord in their trouble, and He saved them from their distress. He sent forth His word and healed them, And delivered them from their destruction. Oh, that men would give thanks to the Lord for His goodness ... (Psalm 107:19-21a)

I will not die, but live, And declare the works of the Lord. (Psalm 118:17)

He heals the brokenhearted And binds up their wounds. (Psalms 147:3)

My son, give attention to my words; Incline your ear to my sayings. Do not let them depart from your eyes; Keep them in the midst of your heart; For they are life to those who find them, And health to all their flesh [whole body]. *Keep your heart with all diligence, For out of it spring the issues of life. Put away from you a deceitful mouth, And put perverse lips far from you* (Proverbs 4:20-24).

Death and life are in the power of the tongue. (Proverbs 18:21a)

Pleasant words are like a honeycomb, Sweetness to the soul and health to the bones. (Proverbs 16:24)

A merry heart does good, like medicine, But a broken spirit dries the bones. (Proverbs 17:22) *You will show me the path of life; In Your Presence is fullness of joy; At Your right hand are pleasures forevermore.* (Psalm 16:11)

Do not sorrow, for the joy of the Lord is your strength. (Nehemiah 8:10b)

You will keep him in perfect peace, Whose mind is stayed on You, Because he trusts in You. (Isaiah 26:3)

But those who wait on the Lord Shall renew their strength; They shall mount up with wings like eagles, They shall run and not be weary, They shall walk and not faint.
(Isaiah 40:31; see also Micah 7:7 below)

"So fear not, for I am with you; Be not be dismayed, for I am your God. I will strengthen you, Yes, I will help you, I will uphold you with my righteous right hand." (Isaiah 41:10)

Be still, and know that I am God; I will be exalted among the nations, I will be exalted in the earth! (Isaiah 46:10)

Surely He took up our pain and bore our suffering, yet we considered Him punished by God, stricken by Him, and afflicted. But He was pierced for our transgressions, He was crushed for our iniquities; the punishment that brought us peace was on Him, and by His wounds [stripes] we are healed. (Isaiah 53:4-5)

"The Spirit of the Lord GOD is upon Me, Because the Lord has anointed Me to preach good tidings to the poor; He has sent Me to heal the brokenhearted, To proclaim liberty to the captives, And the opening of the prison to those who are bound. (Isaiah 61:1)

"But I will restore health to you And heal you of your wounds," says the Lord.
(Jeremiah 30:17)

"Behold, I am the Lord, the God of all flesh. Is there anything too hard for Me?
(Jeremiah 32:27)

And I will give them singleness of heart and put a new spirit within them. I will take away their stony, stubborn heart and give them a tender, responsive heart. (Ezekiel 11:19 NLT)

"*Beat your plowshares into swords And your pruning hooks into spears; Let the weak say, 'I am strong* [a mighty warrior].'" (Joel 3:10)

But as for me, I watch in hope for the Lord, I wait for God my Savior; my God will hear me. (Micah 7:7 NIV)

"But for you who fear my name, the Sun of Righteousness will rise with healing in His wings. And you will go free, leaping with joy like calves let out to pasture. (Malachi 4:2 NLT)

Therefore if you bring your gift to the altar, and there remember that your brother has something against you, leave your gift there before the altar, and go your way. First be reconciled to your brother, and then come and offer your gift. (Matthew 5:23-24)

And behold, a leper came and worshiped Him, saying, "Lord, if You are willing, You can make me clean." Then Jesus put out His hand and touched him, saying, "I am willing; be cleansed." Immediately his leprosy was cleansed. (Matthew 8:2-3)

[Jesus said] *"Pray, then, in this way: 'Our Father who is in heaven, Hallowed be Your name. Your Kingdom come. Your will be done, On earth as it is in heaven.* (Matthew 6:9-10) "*And as you go, preach, saying, 'The Kingdom of heaven is at hand. Heal the sick, cleanse the lepers, raise the dead, cast out demons. Freely you have received, freely give.'"* (Matthew 10:8)

And when Jesus went out He saw a great multitude; and He was moved with compassion for them, and healed their sick. (Matthew 14:14)

When evening came, they brought to Him many who were demon-possessed; and He cast out the spirits with a word, and healed all who were ill. This was to fulfill what was spoken through Isaiah the prophet: "He Himself took our infirmities and carried away our diseases." (Matthew 18:16-17 NASB; Isaiah 53:4)

Then Jesus said to the centurion, "Go your way; and as you have believed, so let it be done for you." And his servant was healed that same hour. (Matthew 8:13)

"Again I say to you that if two of you agree on earth concerning anything that they ask, it will be done for them by My Father in heaven. For where two or three are gathered together in My name, I am there in the midst of them." (Matthew 18:19)

"Have faith in God," Jesus answered. "Truly I tell you, if anyone says to this mountain, Go, throw yourself into the sea,' and does not doubt in their heart but believes that what they say will happen, it will be done for them. Therefore I tell you, whatever you ask for in prayer, believe that you have received it, and it will be yours." (Mark 11:22-24 NIV)

"And whenever you stand praying, if you have anything against anyone, forgive him, that your Father in heaven may also forgive you your trespasses. But if you do not forgive, neither will your Father in heaven forgive your trespasses." (Mark 11:25)

And He said to them, "Go into all the world and preach the gospel to every creature. He who believes and is baptized will be saved; but he who does not believe will be condemned. And these signs will follow those who believe: In My name they will cast out demons; they will speak with new tongues ... they will lay hands on the sick, and they will recover." (Mark 16:14-18)

"He will baptize you with the Holy Spirit and fire." (Luke 3:16) *"And behold, I am sending forth the promise of My Father upon you; but you are to stay in the city until you have been clothed with power from on high."* (Luke 24:49 NASB)

"The Spirit of the Lord is upon Me, Because He has anointed Me To preach the gospel to the poor; He has sent Me to heal the brokenhearted, To proclaim liberty to the captives And recovery of sight to the blind, To set at liberty those who are oppressed."
(Luke 4:18; Isaiah 61:1-3)

And the whole multitude sought to touch Him, for power went out from Him and He healed them all. (Luke 6:19)

"Most assuredly, I say to you, he who believes in Me, the works that I do he will do also; and greater works than these he will do, because I go to My Father.
(John 14:12; see Luke 3:16 above)

Peace I leave with you, My peace I give to you; not as the world gives do I give to you. Let not your heart be troubled, neither let it be afraid. (John 14:27)

[Jesus said] But you will receive power when the Holy Spirit comes upon you. And you will be my witnesses, telling people about me everywhere ...(Acts 1:8a NLT) *And He said to them,"Go into all the world and preach the gospel to every creature...And these signs will follow those who believe: In My name they will cast out demons; they will speak with new tongues; ...they will lay hands on the sick, and they will recover."* (Mark 16:15, 17, 18b)

"Now, Lord, look on their threats, and grant to Your servants that with all boldness they may speak Your word, by stretching out Your hand to heal, and that signs and wonders may be done through the name of Your holy Servant Jesus." And when they had prayed, the place where they were assembled together was shaken; and they were all filled with the Holy Spirit, and they spoke the word of God with boldness. (Acts 4:29-31)

And you know that God anointed Jesus of Nazareth with the Holy Spirit and with power. Then Jesus went around doing good and healing all who were oppressed by the devil, for God was with Him. (Acts 10:38 NLT; see Luke 6:19 above) *"The thief does not come except to steal, and to kill, and to destroy. I have come that they may have life, and that they may have it more abundantly."* (John 10:10)

May the God of hope fill you with all joy and peace as you trust in Him, so that you may overflow with hope by the power of the Holy Spirit. (Romans 15:13 NIV) *Now hope does not disappoint, because the love of God has been poured out in our hearts by the Holy Spirit who was given to us.* (Romans 5:5)

For I consider that the sufferings of this present time are not worthy to be compared with the glory which shall be revealed in us. (Romans 8:18)

And we know that all things work together for good to those who love God, to those who are the called according to His purpose.... Who shall separate us from the love of Christ? Shall tribulation, or distress, or persecution, or famine, or nakedness, or peril, or sword?... For I am persuaded that neither death nor life, nor angels nor principalities nor powers, nor things present nor things to come, nor height nor depth, nor any other created thing, shall be able to separate us from the love of God which is in Christ Jesus our Lord. (Romans 8:28, 35, 39)

Gifts of the Spirit: *But the manifestation of the Spirit is given to each one for the profit of all: for to one is given the word of wisdom through the Spirit, to another the word of knowledge through the same Spirit, to another faith by the same Spirit, to another gifts of healings by the same Spirit, to another the working of miracles, to another prophecy, to another discerning of spirits, to another different kinds of tongues, to another the interpretation of tongues.* (1 Corinthians 12:7-10) *but if I didn't love others, I would have gained nothing*. (1 Corinthians 13:3b NLT; see Fruit of the Spirit: Galatians 5:22-23 below)

For we walk by faith, not by sight. (2 Corinthians 5:7)

For though we walk in the flesh, we do not war according to the flesh. For the weapons of our warfare are not carnal but mighty in God for pulling down strongholds, casting down arguments and every high thing that exalts itself against the knowledge of God, bringing every thought into captivity to the obedience of Christ. (2 Corinthians 10:3-5)

But the fruit of the Spirit is love, joy, peace, longsuffering, kindness, goodness, faithfulness, gentleness, self-control. (Galatians 5:22-23)

Finally, my brethren, be strong in the Lord and in the power of His might. Put on the whole armor of God, that you may be able to stand against the wiles of the devil. For we do not wrestle against flesh and blood, but against principalities, against powers, against the rulers of the darkness of this age, against spiritual hosts of wickedness in the heavenly places.Therefore take up the whole armor of God, that you may be able to withstand in the evil day, and having done all, to stand. Stand therefore, having girded your waist with truth, having put on the breastplate of righteousness, and having shod your feet with the preparation of the gospel of peace; above all, taking the shield of faith with which you will be able to quench all the fiery darts of the wicked one. And take the helmet of salvation, and the sword of the Spirit, which is the word of God. (Ephesians 6:10-17)

Be anxious for nothing, but in everything by prayer and supplication, with thanksgiving, let your requests be made known to God; and the peace of God, which surpasses all understanding, will guard your hearts and minds through Christ Jesus. (Philippians 4:6-7)

And my God will supply all your needs according to His riches in glory in Christ Jesus. (Philippians 4:19 NASB)

For the Spirit God gave us does not make us timid [fearful], but gives us power, love and self-discipline [sound judgment]. (2 Timothy 1:7 NIV)

Let us hold unswervingly to the hope we profess, for He who promised is faithful ... So do not throw away your confidence; it will be richly rewarded. You need to persevere so that when you have done the will of God, you will receive what He has promised. (Hebrews 10:23, 35, 36 NIV)

And by faith even Sarah, who was past childbearing age, was enabled to bear children because she considered Him faithful who had made the promise. (Hebrews 11:11)

Jesus Christ is the same yesterday, today, and forever. (Hebrews 13:8)

See to it that no one falls short of the grace of God and that no bitter root grows up to cause trouble and defile many. (Hebrews 12:15 NIV)

Is anyone among you sick? Then he must call for the elders of the church and they are to pray over him, anointing him with oil in the name of the Lord; and the prayer offered in faith will restore the one who is sick, and the Lord will raise him up, and if he has committed sins, they will be forgiven him. Therefore, confess your sins to one another, and pray for one another so that you may be healed. The effective prayer of a righteous man can accomplish much. (James 5:14-17 NASB)

Cast all your anxiety upon Him, because He cares for you. (1 Peter 5:7 NIV)

Beloved, if our heart does not condemn us, we have confidence toward God. And whatever we ask we receive from Him, because we keep His commandments and do those things that are pleasing in His sight. And this is His commandment: that we should believe on the name of His Son Jesus Christ and love one another, as He gave us commandment. (1 John 3:21-22 NASB)

Beloved, I pray that you may prosper in all things and be in health, just as your soul prospers. (1 John 1:2)

How can I know all the sins lurking in my heart? Cleanse me from these hidden faults. (Psalm 19:12 NLT)

The Son of God appeared for this purpose, to destroy the works of the devil. (1 John 3:8b) *You are of God, little children, and have overcome them, because He who is in you is greater than he who is in the world.* (1 John 4:4)

And they overcame him [Satan] by the blood of the Lamb and by the word of their testimony. (Revelation 12:11a)

Then they cried out to the Lord in their trouble,
and He saved them from their distress.
He sent forth His word and healed them,
And delivered them from their destruction.
Oh, that men would give thanks to the Lord for His goodness.

(Psalm 107:20, 21a)

CPSIA information can be obtained
at www.ICGtesting.com
Printed in the USA
FFOW02n0739160318
45625136-46437FF

9 781633 371910